TOM MUR

D1759878

Plays: 5

Too Late for Logic
The Wake
The House
Alice Trilogy

with an introduction by Nicholas Grene

Methuen Drama

METHUEN DRAMA CONTEMPORARY DRAMATISTS

Published by Methuen Drama 2006

1 3 5 7 9 10 8 6 4 2

Methuen Drama
A & C Black Publishers Limited
38 Soho Square
London W1D 3HB
www.acblack.com

Typeset by Deltatype Ltd, Birkenhead, Merseyside
Printed and bound in Great Britain by Bookmarque Ltd, Croydon, Surrey

Contents

Tom Murphy:
A Chronology

Introduction

'Looking at it rationally,' says Alice in the final part of the *Alice Trilogy*, 'the worst has happened.' In all four plays in this volume, the central characters contemplate the worst that has happened, and try to make sense of it, even if for all of them it is 'too late for logic'. Throughout his drama Tom Murphy has been concerned to represent emotional extremities, from the fratricidal violence of *A Whistle in the Dark* (1961) through the dystopic fairy tale *The Morning after Optimism* (1971) to the storytelling endgame of *Bailegangaire* (1985). Murphy's characters are forced to revisit their past, whether it be that of a community, a family or an individual. Confronting their own messed-up lives, they ask themselves questions: Where and when did it go wrong? Was there an earlier time when it was different, when things might have taken another turn? Or at least the more self-conscious and reflective among Murphy's people ask these questions. In the case of the inarticulate and unself-aware – and they make up the majority – the plays ask the questions on their behalf. In his most recent plays, Murphy returns to this central anguished interrogation but with new dramatic forms and new theatrical effects.

Too Late for Logic (1989) uses an operatic analogue like *The Gigli Concert* (1983). But where *The Gigli Concert* dramatised the yearning for a restorative, rejuvenatory magic of Faust, the theme music for *Too Late for Logic* comes from Gluck's failed resurrection myth *Orfeo ed Eurydice*. The dead woman whom Christopher must seek to recall to life in the play is not his (estranged) wife Patricia but his sister-in-law Cornelia who has just died of cancer. His real quest, however, which he undertakes most reluctantly, is for his brother Michael, who has gone missing and apparently threatened suicide in his grief over his wife's death. The urban underworld into which Christopher has to descend is the basement nightclub the Priory, so anticipatory of Celtic Tiger Ireland in its kitsch cultivation of the antique and would-be smart modernity. Michael is duly rescued, and it is Christopher who takes over his brother/double's drive towards suicide. The comic/satiric counterpoint to the play's quest motif is a television lecture that

Christopher is preparing on the philosophy of Schopenhauer. There is a poignant illustration of Schopenhauer's pessimistic conviction that the will to survive and reproduce is man's tragic delusion in Christopher's tangled and unhappy relationship with his son and daughter. In the play's Schopenhauerian view of things, suicide seems the truer, more authentic choice as against the illustion of restored family harmony in the party scene following Cornelia's funeral.

Cornelia does get a wake of sorts, if only after rather than before the burial. It is this social ritual, what Joyce in *Finnegans Wake* called a 'funferal', that was never accorded to Vera's grandmother in *The Wake* (1998), Murphy's dramatic reworking of his own novel *The Seduction of Morality* (1994). Vera, who has emigrated to America where she works as a call girl, cherishes memories of her childhood life with her grandmother. Learning of the death, she returns home to pay her respects only to discover that her grandmother died months before in a preventable accident which was at least partly the fault of her predatory family the O'Tooles, pillars of the community who own half the town and dominate the rest. There had been no wake but an inquest. By her scandalous flouting of town decorum and by her ownership of the family hotel that her brother and sisters desperately want to acquire, Vera forces them to participate in a sort of belated substitute wake in the climactic scene of the play. The hilarious range of party pieces performed, from American muscial numbers to sentiminal Irish kitsch – Murphy's musical tastes are nothing if not eclectic – sends up middle-class modern Ireland so remote from the community traditions enacted in the keen and the wake. Yet the recitation by Mary-Jane, fiercest of the acquisitive, materialist O'Tooles, has another degree of expressiveness. The poem she declaims, with choric support, is James Clarence Mangan's 'A Vision of Connught in the Thirteenth Century'. Written during the Famine, it bespeaks the desolating contrast with an imagined time of peace and plenty. As Ireland has been historically haunted by this vision of a pristine past, so Vera has depended on a childhood illusion of home and family. At the play's end, having given over the hotel to her siblings in a gesture of defiant indifference, she has exorcised the idea of home in a 'first acceptance of her isolation'.

Christy, protagonist of *The House* (2000), cannot give up on the notion of home, is in fact obsessed by it, the more so because it is a home he never had. Here Murphy is back on his own home ground, the provincial Tuam of his youth in the 1950s. It is in fact his richest and most evocative study of that culture of the small town, leeched of its life by emigration, dramatised earlier in *A Crucial Week in the Life of a Grocer's Assistant* (1969) and *Conversations on a Homecoming* (1985). We watch the extended carnival of the two weeks' holiday return of the emigrants from the first cash-flush carousings in Bunty's bar to the last hungover, penniless hours before departure. The desolation underlying the forced and frenetic bacchanalia is brilliantly caught in the monologue by Peter, one of the returnees, where he describes the vacancy of the early-morning town. Counterpointing the group drama of the returning emigrants is the individual case of Christy. He looks like one of them, comes back to the town at the same time as they do, but it emerges that he does not work on the buildings in England like the others. Greeted jocularly by his stay-at-home mate Jimmy as a 'whoremaster', it appears that he is in fact a pimp, who has earned enough to be able to pay cash for the house, the home of his beloved de Burcas, when it comes up for auction. Christy's story is like a reworking of the plot of *The Cherry Orchard* – Murphy did, in fact, subsequently do a version of Chekhov's play for the Abbey Theatre in 2004. Christy idolised the de Burcas in childhood as Lopakhin did the Ranevsky family for their kindness and their aristocratic glamour. But he is not, like Lopakhin, the representative of an emerging entrepreneurial middle class for whom the purchase of the cherry orchard is a marketplace opportunity. On the contrary, Christy wants to stop the sale of the house, even buy it himself, to freeze the past and the one bearable part of his childhood embodied in the house. This is a specifically Irish psychopathology. Christy is the last of a long line of characters in Murphy who work in the sex trade: Harry in *A Whistle in the Dark*, James and Rosie in *The Morning after Optimism*, Harry and Francisco in *The Sanctuary Lamp*, Vera in *The House*. The

psychological origins of this may come from religious repres-
sion, materialist need, a sort of wilful self-degradation. With
Christy it means that he cannot reciprocate the love for him
shown in various forms by all three daughters of Mrs de Burca.
His obsession is with the house and the family centred on the
mother. It is as though this regressive fixation leaves him
sexually retarded: sex can only be business for him, it has to be
kept apart from his deepest emotional feelings. This blocked
sexual energy leads eventually to violence and murder.

Alice Trilogy (2005) is a new theatrical departure for Murphy.
In the past his concern has been with one time of crisis for his
characters, a day, a night, 'a crucial week', in which they must
come to terms with who they are and what they are. In the
Trilogy, three linked plays capture different moments across half
a lifespan from 1980 to 2005. In the first play, 'In the Apiary',
it might seem as though this is an updated version of *A Doll's
House*: Alice, like Ibsen's Nora, is a housewife with three
children married to a terminally dull bank-manager husband.
But for Alice there will be no miraculous liberation from
patriarchal bondage when she discovers that her highest duty is
to herself. This is not a play about social issues but a drama of
the interior, theatrically rendered in the attic/roof space 'in the
apiary' where Alice debates with her alternative self Al. And
the second play, 'By the Gasworks Wall' – the title simultaneously reminiscent of Ewan McColl's song 'Dirty Old Town'
and Joyce's short story 'The Dead' – makes it clear that Alice's
difficulties are not gender-specific. Her old boyfriend Jimmy,
paranoid in spite of his successful career in television, uses the
memory of Alice's seventeen-year-old self as an illusory idyll,
their brief adolescent romance as some sort of road not
travelled to which he might now return. Women have no
monopoly on the sense of entrapment, the need to rerun their
lives.

In 'At the Airport', when the worst has happened to Alice,
she observes the scene in numb alienation, as though outside
herself and the limbo-like situation she occupies. She is, she
feels, in 'a place as from a nightmare that is pretending to be a
dream, where a party, or indeed a wake, will never really
begin'. The terms are significant for this play and for the other

plays in this volume. This is Murphy's dramatic territory, Christopher's necessarily impossible dream quest in *Too Late for Logic*, the nightmare action that follows Vera's return home in *The Wake*, or Christy's in *The House*. The characters all seek the social release of festivity if only in the ritualised mourning of the wake. But that healing is not to be had within communities that are as directionless as the individual characters themselves. In place of the wake that never begins, what frees Alice at last out of paralysed self-absorption into feeling, is a shared solidarity of sorrow in the chance encounter with a stranger. It is a very moving moment and a fitting conclusion to this collection of plays.

Nicholas Grene, 2006

Too Late for Logic

Too Late for Logic was first performed at the Abbey Theatre, Dublin, during the Dublin Theatre Festival, on 3 October 1989. The cast was as follows:

Christopher	Tony Doyle
Petra	Michèle Forbes
Jack	Darragh Kelly
Patricia	Kate Flynn
Monica	Deirdre Donnelly
Michael	Des Cave
Geoffrey	Godfrey Quigley
Tony	Garret Keogh
Maud	Doreen Keogh
Wally	Pat Laffan
Moreva	Gabrielle Reidy
Susie	Brid Ní Neachtain
Young Dennis	Jim Bruton
Figures	Kathy Downes
	Kate Hyland
	Patti Roche
	David Keane
	Davóg Rynne

Director Patrick Mason
Set and Costume Designer Monica Frawley
Lighting Tony Wakefield
Sound Dave Nolan
Stage Director Finola Eustace

Characters

Christopher
Petra
Jack
Patricia
Monica
Michael
Geoffrey
Tony
Maud
Wally
Moreva

The roles of **Maud** and **Wally** can be doubled by the actors playing **Patricia** and **Geoffrey**.

Scene One

'J'ai Perdu Mon Eurydice' sung by Maria Callas has introduced the piece and continues into this scene.

Christopher, *isolated, fifty, looks bedraggled in his overcoat, an unlit cigarette in one hand and, now from his pocket, a gun in the other hand: a man with a problem.*

The shadows about the place are like figures. They are figures, come to invade his space. He doesn't yet appear to notice them – nor they him – though they start to circle him, close on him . . . And there is a report from a gun.

The figures now are like a group talking sadly at a graveside. What they are saying makes no sense; gibberish (e.g. **Petra**'s *'Cigarette a like you would Mum': Mum, would you like a cigarette? – etc. with other character lines, spoken backwards, taken from later in the play) . . .*

Christopher, *minus cigarette and gun, has emerged from among them, smiling, denying that he has done anything: he shakes his head, then checks it to see if it's still there . . .*

Christopher   What has happened here? . . . Not at all. I mean, I am I, you are you, whatever we were to each other we are, still. *Nothing* is what's happened here.

*The figures are about to leave. Now they are making sense: 'A drink, everybody?' (***Michael***) 'Yeah!' (***Petra***) and appreciative sounds from the others.*

Christopher   Wait a minute – Hold on! . . . I mean, this is pretty desperate stuff. Oho! . . . I am very well thank you. Hold on – hold on! – We can work this one out! All I was doing was – what was I doing? – was trying to write something – a speech for God's sake, that's all! While trying to give up – (*'smoking': he holds up his cigarette hand*). That's all. I'm very well thank you. I'll prove it! Let's go back a few days, backtrack a little, and I bet you I will. OK? OK. O-righty!

He removes his overcoat to become his former self of a few days ago. In his room: his table, table lamp, telephone and answering machine, small tape recorder, some writing materials and a remote control which he uses to kill the music. His speech is more or less continuous from the above.

Yes, he's writing a speech, preparing a lecture and he goes to his desk with *confidence*! With *confidence*! Never felt better in his life, at the height of his powers – (*He has picked up his recorder to dictate:*) Draft one: Ahmmm . . . Yes. President, fellow acolytes of IASA, ladies and gentlemen, distinguished guests, viewers, and students of course. Schopenhauer: His Phenomenology of Reproduction, and, Did he Hypostasise the *Ding an sich*? (*To himself:*) Good. Now what? Yes. (*Dictates:*) But, before giving my paper, it would be crass of me if I did not pay tribute to . . . (*To himself:*) Crass of me? *Crass? Tck!*

'Tck!' in reaction to the phone that has started to ring. He lifts the receiver and replaces it on the cradle, terminating the call.

What was I saying? Crass, crass – *remiss*! (*Dictates:*) But, before giving my paper, it would be remiss of me if I did not pay tribute to the head of our department here at Trinity, whose place I take today. I refer of course to my distinguished colleague – and *friend* – Dr Wuzzler who cannot be with us. Unfortunately. Indeed, who is extremely ill in hospital. Alas. (*To himself:*) Knocked down by a bus alas-and-indeed – Yep? (*Dictates:*) The election of this venue by IASA for its second international conference is due in no small measure to the efforts of Professor Wuzzler, to his scholarship and to his remarkable – truly, truly remarkable discovery only last year: the previously unknown-about two-day visit by the young Schopenhauer to the little scenic town of Cobh in Co. Cork, in 1802. (*To himself:*) Pause for applause. (*Dictates:*) Woozy, if by any chance you are looking in, thoughts with you, get well soon. (*To himself:*) Good, Christopher. Now what? (*Dictates:*) Here, it may be appropriate to give a rapid summary of the age Schopenhauer was born into – in consideration of our lay brethren (*the viewers*). Arthur Schopenhauer 1788–1860. An age where things were happening? Yes. French Revolution – Concept of Human Rights – man's freedom at last?

Came the Terror. Disillusionment. An age begun in hope, an age of reason: for nothing. *Egalité, liberté, fraternité,* said the bishops and princes, our royal arse. (*To himself:*) No-no-no-no-no. Our royal, our royal . . . ? Bottoms for the moment, don't spoil my flow now. (*Dictates:*) Bottoms for the moment which they replanked up on thrones. A Bourbon –

The doorbell rings. He listens:

A Bourbon? . . . A Bourbon back in France, who had learned nothing, forgotten nothing.

The doorbell again.

Tck, Jack Daniel's himself! (*Listening, hoping it won't ring again*) . . . And as for Napoleon –

The doorbell rings –

(*Going off.*) They took Napoleon to distillers and put a cork to his spirit. Further . . .

He has gone off to answer the door, dictating as he goes.

Jack *and* **Petra** *are at (what is meant to be)* **Christopher**'s *front door.* **Jack**'s *finger is pressing the doorbell.*

Jack *is eighteen, old top coat, hanging open, as is the fashion. He has a close bond with* **Christopher**, *though the slow, single nod of the head, that he is given to, doesn't necessarily mean that he agrees. He is caught in the middle and is probably trying to hold a balance between his parents.*

Petra *is making a roll-up. Her conflict with* **Christopher** *is ongoing. She tries to be polite with him – dainty syllable-by-syllable delivery – but it doesn't come out right. And she resents* **Christopher**'s *giving so much attention to* **Jack** *to her exclusion. (Also, the usual sibling rivalry between her and* **Jack**.) *Her dress is colourful, rag-trade stuff, as is the fashion. She is capable of great tenderness and great rage: a child-woman. She is sixteen.*

Petra   He's in there. (*She's containing her anger.*)

Jack   How d'you know that?

Petra   He's in there!

Jack   How d'you know that?!

Petra   Why's your hand still on the fucking bell then?! (*And to herself:*) Geeeesss!

Christopher (*arriving, dictating*)   I thank the devil said Goethe I'm no longer a nipper in so thoroughly a dicked-up world.

Jack (*shyly*)   Hi!

Christopher (*greeting them with up-held hand*)   The masses turned back to religion: feed the birds, tuppence a bag.

Jack   Can we come in a minute?

Christopher (*beckoning them to follow him off, returning to his room*)   Man had lost himself again. (*Off.*) Hard to visualise it so unlike our own times. (*Entering:*) So it became a time of demoralisation and debilitation reverie. (*To* **Jack**, *for* **Jack**'s *admiration of his words:*) Hmm?

Jack   What's? (*Meaning 'what are you preparing?'*)

Christopher   Speech – I – Shh! Hence, hence . . .

Petra   Are we dis-turbing you?

Christopher   Hence the melancholy of the writers, the – oh – the Pushkins! Byrons, Lermontovs. The melancholy of the composers: Schubert, Schumann, Chopin. (*To* **Petra**:) Hmm?

Petra   Mozark?

Christopher   Mozart?

Petra   Mozark!

Christopher (*a little triumph*)   Ah! (*Dictates:*) While Mozart was dancing in the depression of his day as a Shirley Temple in hers. (*He puts the recorder aside.*) Nice, the common touch, humour – But we'll put it away.

Jack   Your rooms are nice.

Christopher (*to* **Jack**)   A speech, it's going to be televised.

Jack   Yeh?!

Christopher   But – my progeny! – tea, a coffee? Long time – Hi!

Jack   Hi!

Christopher (*to* **Petra**)   Hello?

Petra *replies with a sharp nod of her head.*

Christopher   The character or will says Schopenhauer comes from the father, the intellect from the mother.

Petra   Where's Chokki?

Christopher   Hmm? (*Vaguely.*)

Petra   The dog.

Christopher   Oh, fine, I had to have her put down. (*To* **Jack**:) Big, big opportunity. I'm not going to do the usual dry old academic stuff on it: I'm going for the reality principle, all-embracing life and what it means. I have missed our conversations, Jack. Are you reconsidering returning to university?

An apologetic 'no' from **Jack**.

Petra (*to* **Jack**)   Give us a light. (*For her rollie.*)

Jack   D'you mind if we smoke?

Christopher (*doesn't mind, and absently accepts a cigarette from* **Jack***'s packet*)   You know, to find the harmonies of words that will present the contradictions in man, and . . . (*Only now wondering why have they called.*) But, I mean, surprise visit.

Jack *looks at* **Petra**. **Petra**, *smoking, now affects her superiority, waiting to see how the men will deal with the next.*

Jack   Cornelia died at lunchtime, Uncle Michael is going to commit suicide, Mum said would you take care of it.

Christopher   . . . Say that again.

Petra   Cornelia died at lunchtime, *yesterday*.

Jack (*taking her correction*)   Yesterday.

Petra   *In* hos-pit-al.

Christopher   I know she was in hospital.

Petra   Your brother's wife, Mum's sister, she's dead.

Christopher   I'm not disputing the matter.

Jack   Uncle Michael is going to – (*Nods/gestures, meaning commit suicide.*) Mum's been trying to phone you.

Petra   To kill himself: do-you-under-stand?

Christopher   The always open door.

Jack   What?

Christopher   Epictetus. Phone him.

Jack   He isn't answering either.

Christopher   Call to his house.

Jack   We called.

Petra   Sev-er-al times.

Jack   He's disappeared . . . Dad?

Christopher (*to himself, meaning he is not getting involved*)   No. (*Then pacing, waving his arms.*) Maybe he's dead already, I don't care!

Jack   No!

Christopher   What?

Jack   He said Saturday.

Christopher   Today is . . . He said what?

Jack   Mum got the news and, because he isn't answering, we drove over. He put on his coat – we thought he was coming with us to the hospital. No. He nodded, did that (*'put a finger like a gun to his head'*) – said 'Saturday, D-Day' and – Phith!

Christopher   Left. (*And nods to himself 'yes, that would be Michael'.*)

Petra   We have been looking for him since.

Christopher   What are the arrangements?

Jack   That's it!

Christopher   What is?

Jack   Mum can't make them without him. (**Christopher** *doesn't understand.*) He's the husband.

Christopher   (*'Oh yes.' Then*)   Saturday, why Saturday?

Jack   He didn't give us time to – (*'ask'*). Phith! It's a good question though.

Petra   Try your philosophy on it.

Jack   D'you think he will?

Petra   Grandad did it.

Christopher   (*sharply*)   He was shell-shocked. (*Blows a heavy sigh.*) Michael!

Jack   Didn't he swim too far out to sea one time?

Christopher   And I was the one who nearly got drowned.

Petra   Can-you-help-us?

Christopher   And what about me?

Petra   Do you have any idea where he might be then?

Christopher   (*has an idea, but*)   No. (*He's pacing, cigarette in an out of his mouth, his hands in a flap for a light.*) I'm not getting involved.

Petra   Oh that's great! –

Christopher   Immaterial to me! –

Petra   That's smashing! –

Christopher   I left all this kind of thing behind me six months ago! –

Petra (*to* **Jack**)   Do you hear?!

Christopher   Just when things are beginning to fall into place –

Jack   Wrong end –

Petra ('*You*') Left 'all this kind of thing' behind you: US!

Christopher   Just when I'm finding some *meaning*, some answers –

Petra   You're his brother –

Jack   Wrong –

Petra   His bloodywell, bloodywell, bloodywell brother!

Christopher   No.

Petra   . . . For Mum's sake then?

Christopher   And just when this crucial piece of work –

Petra   For Mum's sake then? –

Christopher   Comes along, that I must prepare –

Petra   At her wits' bloody end –

Christopher   That will most likely be the making of me –

Petra   Run off her bloodywell bloodywell feet! Do you ever pick up that phone or listen to messages on that machine?

Christopher *shakes his head, 'No', he's not getting involved and turns to* **Jack** *for a light.*

Jack   Wrong end.

Christopher   Oh. No thanks, I gave them up. (*Absently, he keeps the cigarette.*)

Jack   Did you?! (*Impressed.*)

Christopher   And drink.

Jack   When?

Christopher   Two days ago.

Jack   New life.

Petra (*to herself*)   Geeesssstupid!

Christopher   Yes, new life! Look! (*Look at his rooms.*) *This* is where I belong. *My* place. I've had twenty *terrifying* years as caretaker of your troubles. Frightening, fossilising years of domesticity. No more. So: young philosopher – all right, middle-aged. Middle-aged philosopher now working purposefully and alone: He has things to say because he has suffered. He's no longer a victim because he's coming up with the answers. The moment he's been waiting for arrives. Head of the department – ('*that*') old Wuzzler – is knocked over by a bus. He has to step into the breach at short notice and make a singularly meaningful speech. Will he write that speech *and* deliver it *and* on television? Yes, he will – even if it kills him. At last he's recognised as somebody-who-counts, as somebody-who-matters in this world. Enough to be going on? So no Michael thank you, or those other complicated thorns of kindred in my side. (*He gets his tape recorder and dictates:*) Enter Schopenhauer to take to his rooms and have a think about it all.

Petra (*to* **Jack**)   Let's go.

Christopher (*to them*)   Find Michael: d'you think the matter would be as simple as that?

Petra   Are you coming, Jack?

Christopher (*to* **Petra**)   The *friends* he picks up!

Petra   Kind of you to ask how Mum is. (*She leaves.*)

Christopher (*dictating*)   Ahmmm . . . He sees the world as strife, a never-ending mess. He . . . (*To* **Jack**:) How is your mother?

Jack (*holds a shrug, then completes it with a solemn nod. And:*)   Not great.

Christopher ... Is his car there?

Jack (*'Oh!'*)   We forgot to check the garage. (*He's about to leave.*) Will we – keep you informed?

Christopher *holds a shrug, then completes it with a nod, 'Yes'.* **Jack** *leaves. (Joins* **Petra** *who is outside and they go off on their mission.)*

Christopher   O-righty! Enter Schopenhauer. (*He doesn't sound so'o-righty'. Dictates:*) He sits down, yes he sits down to write his masterpiece, *The World as Will and Idea*, which he begins – which he begins modestly enough! – 'The world is my idea.'

The phone is ringing again. He looks at it for a moment, then lifts it fearfully, then replaces it gently.

The world is my idea – (*dictates:*) by which he does not mean of course that life is a dream, though we can safely say – I think! – that it is akin to dreams. The terms Will and Idea: Let us take Idea first . . .

The lights have been changing during the above – and continue to change – for a passage of time. While **Christopher***, now in dumbshow, continues dictating and making notes . . . He has become engrossed in himself to such degree that he is unaware that the phone has rung again; indeed, the caller,* **Patricia***, is speaking before he registers it (and it is too late to terminate the message).*

Patricia *materialises gradually. She is a woman so exhausted and unhappy that she is unaware of her own confusion – has she phoned* **Christopher** *or* **Michael***? – or that she is at times talking to herself.*

Patricia   Christopher ... Christopher? ... Michael? ... (*Smiles.*) Which of you have I dialled? ... Christopher, this is Patricia again. I'm sorry to bother you, but we still can't find Michael. I've phoned and phoned. I don't know what to do. Doesn't he want to see her? Before they, before they ... Doesn't he want to say goodbye ... I've left messages on his machine, bloody machine ... your bloody machine. I've left messages everywhere ... Bloodywell machines ... I

thought love was stronger than death. Doesn't he want to
kiss her? ... (*Smiles.*) Isn't there anybody there? ... Come
away my love my dove my fair one come away with me
... My beloved is mine and I am his. I thought love was
stronger than separation ... I do not understand ...
Michael? Christopher? ... Michael, this is Patricia again.
I've told them at the hospital that you are abroad, but that
I've contacted you and that you are returning. But they are
getting very cross. I've written the ad, the death notice to
put in the papers. Does it suit? I don't know. That the
remains will be taken to St Helen's five pm. That's
tomorrow. That the burial will be on Friday at eleven.
Does that suit? I hope that suits ... My love my dove my
fair one come away with me ... I'm taking it in by hand
or else it won't appear. To the newspaper office. And to
see the undertakers again. *Caskets*, they keep calling them
caskets ... I don't know ... And do you want a limousine?
And there are papers to be signed. Always bloody papers.
Certificates, affidavits, bloody papers, when someone dies,
walks out. Dies ... I thought that if matters could not be
altogether lovely ever again between us, they could at least
be pleasant. At least that ... *Michael*: There are matters I
am not allowed to discharge on your behalf. I have enough
bloodywell matters of my own in any case. Cornelia was
my sister but she was your wife. For twenty years. Does
that not matter – does that not mean something? Does
anything matter? ... I'm sorry. (*And a sob escapes. Then:*) But
I thought I was getting over another kind of grief. I
thought that winter was past, the rain was over and gone.
(*She's weeping. She smiles as she weeps.*) I sat down in his
shadow with great delight. (*And she apologises.*) I'm sorry, I'm
so sorry. I'm sorry.

And she's gone. (The call over, she becomes a figure/dematerialises.)
Jack *and* **Petra** *have returned. They have heard the very last of the
above.*

Jack   Mum? (*'Was that Mum?'*) How d'you work this
thing? (*The telephone-answering-machine.*)

Petra (*angry*)   Just lift the receiver-fucking-thing and dial.

(*She takes charge.*)

Jack (*as* **Petra** *dials*)   His car isn't there.

Christopher   Mm.

Petra   Mum, hi-yih, hi-yih! . . . Yeah, we got your message just now . . . No, not yet, but we're *sure* to find him, *certain* . . . Where will you be? . . . And after that? . . . Gotcha! I'll phone you . . . Mum-Mum-Mum, don't cry, don't cry, shhhhh . . . *That's* better! Oh, d'you know who we met? Olivia Morley. She's home, she's back, she's fine, she said to thank you again for letting her sleep in the spare room when her father threw her out. For *all* your kindness . . . She's had it, eight pounds one ounce, she's keeping it! . . . I'm glad too . . . Guess . . . No-o, I'll give you one more guess. Yeah, a little girl. *Beautiful*, she said . . . Yeah, he's here, d'you want a word? . . . (*'Well'*) D'you want a word with Jack? . . . Well, chin up, what-o, whack-o, heigh-ho! – Here's Jack. (*She hands the phone to* **Jack** *and her anger is back immediately. To herself:*) Gsssss . . .

Jack   Hi . . . Yeah . . . No . . . We had . . . A very *big* meal.

Petra   Has she bloodywell eaten?

Jack   Have you eaten?

Petra   Has she?

Jack   Have you?

Petra   Promise.

Jack   Promise . . . Yeah. Just as soon as . . . yeah, we find him . . . You too. Oh! Dad sends his love and to say how sorry he is about Cornelia . . . Bye.

He feels self-conscious about having spoken for his father; he replaces the phone.

Silence.

Petra   Where to now?

Jack   We've tried everywhere . . . Dad?

Christopher   The Abbey, Monica's new nightclub-hotel-place: I hear he goes there. I'll be with you in a minute.

Jack *and* **Petra** *move aside – as to wait for him outside.*

Christopher, *isolated, has put on his overcoat. (All very brief.) He finds he has a cigarette in one hand; he looks at his other hand: it's empty.*

Christopher   You see: no gun!

He collects up his tape recorder, earphones and some notes and is putting them in his pockets as he leaves.

Jack *and* **Petra** *– and the other figures – follow him. The lights changing and disco music, piped, has come up.*

Scene Two

An anteroom (in what is meant to be a converted Gothic building) in 'the Abbey'. Red light and beat music coming from a nightclub type of bar immediately off it.

Petra *has gone into the nightclub.* **Jack** *has begun to make up a song, 'The Man Comes to See Me'; his body is responding to the music; unconsciously, he is beginning to enjoy the adventure – until later, when his patience and humour are exceeded.* **Christopher** *is like a man entering a trap – hell: the red light – but can do nothing about it.*

Petra *returns, delighted, now magnanimous of* **Christopher** *(and will continue as such until her generosity is repulsed, later).*

Petra   Found him! Brilliant, brilliant, well done!

Jack   Is he still alive? (*Sniggering at his own wit.*)

Petra   Brill! Anybody got any ten ps? I'll phone Mum.

Petra *and* **Jack**, *in the manner of youngsters, swapping coins.*

Jack   'The man comes to see me, says the tree shimmer.'

Christopher   Did he see you?

Petra   No. The obvious, the Abbey! It's nice, isn't it? (*The decor.*)

Jack   'The man *he* comes to see me.'

Christopher   Who else is in there?

Petra   Geriatrics! How do we go about getting him home?

Jack   We know, we know! (*Sibling superiority. To* **Christopher**:) Will we go in?

Christopher   Ahmm.

Petra   The best thing would be to make and keep the bastard footless until the morning. Where's the phone? (*She's moving off.*)

Christopher   Petra! Don't − either of you! − say we were looking for him and we might get him home without a drama.

They nod to his instructions. She beams at him.

Petra   Brilliant! Mum will be pleased. (*She goes.*)

Jack   D'you not want to go in there?

Christopher   Monica has seen us. Don't leave my side tonight, Jack.

Jack   Sure. (*As he moves off:*) Just having a peep. 'The man he comes to see me, says the trees shimmer *red* . . .'

Monica *is joining* **Christopher**. *She's about forty; a laughing, welcoming woman (ideally, big; as generous as she is large). She is remarkably, innocently forthright; and with a capacity to alternate seamlessly and fluently from celebration to concern. It's difficult not to respond to her warmth.*

Monica   Christopher! My *dear*! My dear, my dear, how are you, how are you, how on earth are you!

Christopher   I'm −

Monica   My dear – My *dear* – always lovely to see you!

Christopher   And you.

Monica   Now! And it was only the other day I was saying to Big Dennis we hadn't seen you in an age. But maybe that's because we've moved to our new premises? I hope so. *How* are you, *how* are you!

Christopher   I'm – (*and he's pleased to find himself laughing*) – fine! And Dennis?

Monica   Oh Big Dennis, my dear, is! Well, a little depressed. He can't bask in himself, he can't bask in his family. What is the solution? But *who* is free to play anything but the role allotted them? And he knows it? Male intelligence. And how is Patricia?

Christopher   Well –

Monica   You haven't seen her in a while, I understand. Jack! My dear – My *dear* – standing back!

Jack (*returning*)   Monica.

Monica   But you're not so slow in other matters. I saw him the other day, his arm around a gorgeous girl – what's her name? He's not telling – up by the park – But you didn't see me – Thursday! But why would you see me: the beautiful people.

Jack   The place is lovely.

Monica   You like our new premises, Jack?

Jack   It's lovely.

Monica   Well, if banks and building societies can turn churches into – marketplaces? – might we not in dueness convert an abbey into a hotel-cum-place-of-relaxation, keeping as many of the old features as possible of course and, I can tell you, I can tell you, I am more than happy to sleep in the abbot's cell down there when Big Dennis's mystery moods descend. And how is Cornelia?

Christopher (*puzzled that she has not heard about*

Cornelia)   Well –

Monica   You don't know, of course. (*'She understands.'*) And the lovely Petra?

Jack   She's here.

Monica   Wonderful! A little reunion! You haven't eaten. Tck! The kitchen is closed, but wait ... Yes I can. We had lovely turbot on this evening and if you would like? ... I mean, as you please.

Christopher   Actually –

Monica   No trouble whatsoever. And for Jack?

Jack   Yeah!

Monica   And what about Michael? Soup ... You're right, Christopher, better that you all have the same thing.

Jack (*to* **Christopher**)   I'll tell him we're here if you like?

Monica   Do, Jack, do.

Jack *goes into the club.*

Monica   I know why you're here. He's in a state.

Christopher   We'll get him home shortly. (*Laughs.*) Can't force things with our Michael, what! You know Michael.

Monica   I know Michael, but I don't know so much about that – with respect, Christopher.

Christopher   Talking wild, is he? It's a way of life rather than a way of death.

Monica   Killing someone?

Christopher   Everyone talks-thinks about suicide at some time.

Monica   Suicide?

Christopher   ... He's *not* going to commit suicide?

Monica   He's going to shoot Walter Peters.

Christopher Who is Walter Peters?

Monica I don't know.

Christopher (*to himself*) Walter Peters.

Monica Walter Peters. Saturday.

Christopher *laughs.*

Monica Christopher?

Christopher Nonsense!

Monica No, my dear. Because when he came in this evening and showed me the gun. Yes! Like, I would have dismissed the matter out of hand, but to walk in here like that? What! When did you see him last?

Christopher A gun?

Monica You see! It's been building up. Just look at him! He's been in here I-don't-know-how-many nights running. Trying to make him eat? – Picking at it. Trying to refuse him drink – you try with your brother. And he's so nice: gorgeous in his pinstripes last week: this week? – what can one say?

Christopher Ahmm.

Monica But last night, honestly! I tried to persuade him to stay – number seven, no charge. My dear! (*'The futility of trying to persuade* **Michael** *of anything.'*) I had to call Big Dennis down – and good enough of him? – he came down and took the car keys and drove him home and *stayed* with him for a while, in case, because, as Big Dennis said – mind you he didn't have to say it to me – there's something brewing there, my dear, he said.

Christopher Being under the strain of Cornelia's –

Monica Illness for so long, I know, and my heart bleeds and I'm sorry for interrupting you again, but the child is really crying wolf.

Christopher (*wants to tell her – but how to tell her? – that Cornelia is dead*) Monica.

Monica   Yes, Christopher, I know: men simply do not face reality: And I sympathise with your gender, but women have to do it all the time. He hasn't been near the hospital to visit her in a week – Are there signs? (I was out there myself – when was it? She was expecting Patricia – poor Patricia. But they are so close, sisters, unlike brothers.) I'm racking my brains to think of what to do but really and truly I think you are the only one who can stop it.

Christopher   Stop what?

Monica   Stop it happening. Petra! My dear – My *dear* – Another lovely surprise!

Petra (*returning*)   Hi-yih, hi-yih, hi-yih, Monica!

Monica   The lovely attire!

Petra   And yours!

Monica   D'you like it?

Petra   Wow!

They continue to admire each other. While **Christopher**, *to himself:*

Christopher   Stop what happening? (*Turns to* **Jack**, *who is returning.*) He's going to shoot himself, he's going to shoot Walter Peters, who is Walter Peters?

Jack *doesn't understand. He has returned, a pint of lager in his hand.*

Christopher   Cornelia is dead, isn't she?

Jack (*a silent 'what?' Then:*)   Yeh.

Christopher   He hasn't told Monica about Cornelia.

Jack   He isn't going to do it.

Christopher   I don't know what he's going to do! Is he coming out or what?

Jack   I thought we were going in?

Monica (*hand in hand with* **Petra**, *joining them*)   Wonderful! Now, a little something on the house to take to your table. What would you like, Christopher?

Petra (*protective of him*)   He's off it.

Monica   And is that why we haven't seen you?! Fresh orange juice.

Petra   I'll have a pint of Bud.

Christopher   Could you bring us a bottle of your burgundy.

Monica   Are you sure?

Christopher   Yes, I'm sure.

Monica   Life is short. You try to cut yourself off from the herd but you always come back to us. And Jack is all right for the moment. (*He's got a drink.*) Now, let us find the naughty Michael.

They are moving towards the club. **Christopher** *steeling himself.*

Petra   How is Young Dennis?

Monica *stops – all a bit dramatic – and points a finger at the club (that Young Dennis is in there).* **Jack** *and* **Petra** *go into the club. Monica holds the increasingly bemused* **Christopher** *back.*

Monica   You are the very man. Do you know, our struggles never cease. Young Dennis, his studies, a blank wall. I have him working in there for the interim. Big Dennis says he had better pull himself together or he's leaving this house. But what about Big Dennis himself?! My dear! And when I don't have to sleep down there in the abbot's cell he's climbing all over and on top of me! And I don't know, is he that interested? But I do my best. And we were thinking if he had someone like you to sit down with him for half an hour. I don't mean tonight of course.

Christopher   Mmmah! (*Total agreement, though it's likely he doesn't know that she's talking about.*)

Monica   You're very good. We are unhappy married and

unmarried we are unhappy. Now let us celebrate it.

They go into the club. Louder music, lights changing, figures moving about again.

Scene Three

A table and table lamp (reminiscent of **Christopher***'s room) in the deeper light of the club. Nearby, in denser light, figures at a bar – or perhaps the bar is just off. The scene is a bit unreal.*

Christopher *is at the table. He has a bottle of wine.* **Petra** *is with him. She now, like* **Jack***, has a pint of lager. She's pleased to be with* **Christopher***. She rolls a cigarette.*

Petra   Those are nice shoes, Dad.

Christopher (*absently*)   Hmm?

Petra   Are they new, Dad? Very nice. I haven't seen nicer on you before.

Christopher   Who are those people with Michael?

Petra   The geriatrics, Dad?

Jack (*coming to join them, singing*)   'So you go for a swim – so you go for a swim in the stagnant pool.' Monica is bringing him over.

Christopher (*to* **Jack**)   Who are those people with him?

Jack (*shrugs. Then:*)   I'm making up a song. 'And there you see, and there you see . . .'

Christopher   Hmm?

Jack   They're talking about their schoolboy days.

Petra   Ger-i-atric wankers.

Jack   The terrible things that used to happen to them at school, forty years ago.

Christopher   In the playground?

Jack   Yeh.

Petra   D'you want a rollie, Dad?

Christopher   In the playground, in the schoolyard? (*A degree of urgency to* **Jack**, *to elaborate.*)

Jack   Yeh. 'And-there-you-see' – *mermaids*!

Petra   Piss-art-ists. Want it, Dad? (*The rollie.*)

Christopher (*turns on her*)   Why aren't you at home with your mother?

Petra (*affronted; her gesture repulsed*)   . . . I could ask the same of you, couldn't I?

Christopher   I asked you a question!

Petra   She's out! You know: out? I phoned! You know: the telephone?

Christopher (*to* **Jack**)   Yes?

Petra   Geessssstupid! (*She moves away, to sit / stand at a remove from them.*)

Christopher (*to* **Jack**)   Yes?!

Jack   She was holding out a hand to you.

Christopher   Schooldays – schoolboys – schoolyards – the terrible things that used to happen to them: is that what they're talking about?

Jack   Yeh.

Christopher   Bullies?

Jack *nods.* ('*Is my father going loopy?*')

Christopher   Aaa! Wally. Walter Peters. It's all making sense! (*He laughs, he drinks.*)

Petra (*from her remove*)   I just didn't want to miss the fun!

Michael *and retinue are coming from the bar.* **Michael** *is laughing, messing with* **Monica**, *grinning into her ear,* ('*Monica, do I love you?*'), *his arm around her: a glass of whiskey in his other* *hand.* **Geoffrey** *and* **Tony** *follow for a little, briefly, before returning to the bar.*

Michael *is a handsome man, elegant, late forties. (Perhaps a little emaciated.) But he's been drinking for a few days. His suit is rumpled, he's probably slept in it. His impeccable manners under other conditions are not entirely absent. But swings of mood: boyish charm, suspicion, moroseness, hilarity; laughter perversely expressing pain; a man who would like to smash his glass, but doesn't.*

Michael   Monica, do I love you? –

Monica   Michael, Michael, stop it, stop it! Oh dear – My *dear* – Unhand me! Be good! Look at who we have over here for you! Michael is the great old flirt.

Michael, *in this first moment, sees* **Christopher** *as some kind of long-lost friend and comes to him expansively.*

Michael   Christopher!

Christopher   I'm sorry about –

Michael (*now recognising him, wheels about, rejecting* **Christopher** *and the outstretched hand*)   Fucking brother!

Monica   Jack, another chair over here for your uncle!

Michael   Jack! What precisely – exactly! – is our relationship?

Monica   Come now, Michael, sit over here.

Michael   Jack!

Jack   Friends!

Michael   Friends! Did you hear, everybody?!

Monica   Now, sit down, Michael.

Michael   This calls for a celebration. (*To* **Christopher**:) What are you having?

Christopher   I've got a drink.

Michael (*suspiciously*)   Pardon?

Christopher (*shows him the bottle of wine*)   I'm fine.

Michael   And is everyone else a leper? Jack, speak up!

Jack   Pint!

Michael   Three large whiskeys!

Monica   And is it serious, Jack, that gorgeous girl?

Michael   Monica, three large –

Monica   He won't tell us her name, Michael.

Jack   I don't know her name.

Michael   Pardon?

Monica   Where is she from then?

Jack   Frankfurt.

Michael   Frankfurt! Grrrrrr, good at English, Jack, is she? Jack takes after his uncle Michael.

Christopher   Jack does *not* take after his uncle Michael.

Michael   Pardon? (*Suspicious again; his eyes fixed on* **Christopher**. *Then:*) I'm not going home.

Christopher *affects a shrug and sits.*

Michael (*laughs*)   Friends! Monica, do I love you?

Monica   You do, Michael – Now asparagus soup for three and three turbots. (*She has cutlery for the table.*)

Michael   What's this? (*'What's the cutlery for?'*)

Monica   Oh and what about Petra? –

Michael   What-is-this?!

Monica   Asparagus –

Michael   No food!

Monica   Soup of the day –

Michael   Are we friends?

Monica You haven't eaten for –

Michael Do you respect a hunger-striker?

Monica Stop being tragic now.

Michael Do you respect the rights of man, do you respect – I ask you! – a hunger-striker?

Jack (*to* **Christopher**)   Tell her it's OK.

Michael Since there are no other bloody rights.

Jack 'We've eaten.' (*To* **Christopher**, *meaning 'Tell her'.*)

Michael Well, Michael has that right.

Christopher We're fine, Monica.

Michael Pardon? Settled. The man of letters has spoken.

Monica *nods/winks at* **Christopher** *and leaves.*

Michael (*calls*)   And thank you, Monica! That woman would strip well, what? Cheers! Wouldn't she, Christopher?

Christopher Cheers. (*They drink.*)

Petra, *at a remove from them – excluded – is concerned for* **Michael**. *She is also pursuing her own tactic of getting him 'footless' and she goes purposefully to the bar.*

Christopher . . . But isn't there something we have to talk about?

Michael And I heard about what you did to Chokki.

Christopher Michael –

Michael Man's-best-friend. I ask you, Mummy's dog! Did you hear, everybody?

Christopher That is neither here nor there, we have something to –

Michael Why'd you do it?! Why-did-you-do-it! Neither here nor?! I met a vet! If I had known you were going to do such a thing! Bloody Christopher. Does he have any feelings? Jack?

Jack   You were offered the dog.

Michael   Sorry, Jack?

Jack   You were offered . . . (*He gestures the rest of it.*)

Petra *returns during this and stands by with a glass of whiskey, waiting her chance.*

Michael   I do not have a spare room for a fucking dog! What would Mummy have said?! Jack?! No point in asking him.

Jack (*to* **Christopher**)   Isn't it against college rules to keep a dog in –

Michael   She would have said – dreadful. That is what she would have, Jack, said.

Petra   It's sad, Uncle Michael, but –

Michael   She would have, Christopher, written another novel. Your grandmother, Jack, Mummy. ('*She*') Didn't like him. Two geniuses, I suppose, couldn't live in the same house. That is what she would have, Christopher, said.

Petra'*s chance has arrived. She takes the empty glass out of* **Michael**'*s hand and replaces it with her glass of whiskey.*

Petra   It's sad, Uncle Michael, but Chokki was old.

Michael (*absently*)   It's what, love? (*Note: It's doubtful if Michael recognises/registers* **Petra** *as* **Petra** *in this scene.*)

Jack (*to* **Christopher**)   And she was eating the furniture, wasn't she?

Michael   I do not bloody care what she was eating! It is a dog's nature to eat college furniture!

Christopher   And it's my nature to put her down if she does!

Michael   . . . Good grief! Did you hear that? (*Asking* **Jack** *to share his disbelief.*)

Jack   No! (*His solidarity with* **Christopher**.)

Michael   The man is an idiot.

Christopher   There is a matter of urgency we have to talk about –

Michael   A donkey –

Christopher   Michael –

Michael   Corridors of learning for you! Golden letters after their names, rounded humps from carrying all they know. But you mark my words, one of these days a golden stiletto in the back from on of your colleagues will soon pull your shoulder blades back together again. (*And he drinks his whiskey. And sighs.*)

Jack   Ask him about the arrangements.

Christopher (*gestures to **Jack** not to interfere*)   Michael, I have to go soon.

Michael *sighs heavily again to himself.*

Christopher   I've work to do.

Michael (*wearily*)   And I suppose I shall be phoning everybody in the morning to apologise.

Christopher   And your apology will be accepted, but now we must talk about –

Michael (*revived, attacking again*)   Why should you accept it, why should you? D'you see what I mean, everybody? A donkey!

Petra *purposefully to the bar again.*

Michael   You know absolutely, Christopher, *nothing.* I'm the one who has discovered things: Michael. Meaning of life? Answer please? All you've done is made an unholy botch of things – without even knowing it! And a shambles of the lives of those about you. The meaning of life: the spirit and the flesh. The flesh? – How many women have you screwed in your life, Jack, your entire life – usefully? No point in asking him. (*To **Christopher***:) All you have only ever had are your wife, and mine, and Monica, I suppose. So, you see! And the spirit? God is up there, isn't he? What-is-he-doing up there? Answer, please? I'm down here. D'you see what I mean? So, you see: what more is there to say? (*Morosely, to himself:*) Enough is enough.

Petra (*returns, and puts another glass of whiskey into his hand*) Drink hearty!

Jack He's indulging himself.

Christopher (*perversely sitting back in his chair*) No!

Michael (*absently, morosely, sighing*) That's love, thanks, love, cheers. (*And he drinks.*)

Jack He's –

Christopher No, this is most constructive! Cheers, everybody! (*As if luxuriating in the situation.*)

Monica (*coming in, professionally*) And how are we getting along here? Wonderful! Jack, I haven't forgotten you: your drink on the house when you've finished that one. Oh, and, Christopher, that little matter we were discussing?

Christopher Mmmah!

Monica I'm taking steps. (*She nods/winks and goes out again.*)

Jack *has moved aside to* **Petra**.

Jack They're indulging themselves.

Petra Bastards.

Jack Where are you getting the whiskey?

Petra Young Dennis in there.

Jack I'm starving.

Both of them are aware that **Geoffrey** *and* **Tony** *have put in another appearance (to check on* **Michael** *from a distance).* **Jack** *sees potential danger in them.*

Jack I think we should get out of here now.

Petra I'll try the phone again for Mum. (*She goes.*)

Tony   Girlie? Girlie? (*Calling to her; plaintive, foolish.*)

Geoffrey (*who has returned to the bar, off*)   Tony!

Tony   Geoffrey! Oft in the stilly night! (*He has gone off again, too.*)

Michael   I took a year off – sabbatical, Christopher?

Christopher   Ah!

Michael   Where's Jack?

Jack   Here I am!

Michael   Permanent fucking sabbatical, Jack, as far as I am concerned.

Christopher   Dropping out?

Jack   Let's go somewhere else!

Michael   Party, Jack?

Jack   Yeah! – Where's your coat?

Michael *stands to point to somewhere off* – **Jack** *goes off for the coat – and to finish his drink.*

Michael   Finish this. (*Drinks. And:*) Yes, Christopher: dropping out. But when Michael says dropping out he means business. But you don't know what I'm talking about. South America?

Christopher   Saturday?

Michael   Pardon?

Christopher   Suicide, South America?

Michael   What on earth are you –

Christopher   Walter Peters? (*All mock-casually.*)

Michael *starts laughing, laughing at length, laughing and coughing, highly amused.*

Michael   Do you remember *him*?!

Christopher   Oh yes.

Michael   Wally!

Christopher   Oh yes.

Jack, *returning with* **Michael**'s *overcoat, meets* **Petra**, *who is returning from the phone.*

Jack   Did you get through to Mum?

She didn't. **Jack**, *through the following, succeeds in getting* **Michael** *into the overcoat: quite a business.*

Michael (*laughing*)   At school?! – Wally, Walter Peters! – Do you?!

Christopher   Yes.

Jack   Coat, Michael.

Michael   He picked on the brilliant Christopher too?!

Christopher   You, though a slob, were the brilliant one.

Jack   Coat, Michael, here we are –

Michael   Why'd he pick on you?

Christopher   I was innocent of the charge. Why'd he pick on you?

Michael   Prank? Called him a bollix? An anonymous letter to his childhood sweetheart's mother? It didn't take much in those good old days to incur the awful wrath of Walter, did it?

Christopher   His tyranny, in those good old days, outdistanced God's.

Michael   I saw him walking in the street two days ago: a white suit – *white*, I ask you, Jack! Wally! (*Points.*) Going into the pink house down there – *pink*, I ask you, Christopher! I thought he was dead or at least had gone abroad, but you cannot mistake an ox. We ready, Jack?

Jack   Yeah!

Michael   Party!?

Jack   Yeah! (*Takes his arm and is leading him off.*)

Christopher   Excuse me! (*Continues seated.*) When is the funeral?

Michael   Someone say something?

Jack   Let's go, everybody!

Christopher   When is the funeral?

Jack (*aside to* **Christopher**)   Let's get him out of here first.

Christopher   No-no-no –

Jack   He's ready to go.

Christopher   No, I'm enjoying this.

Michael   Is this – private conversation?

Christopher   When is the funeral?

Michael   When is?

Christopher   When is the funeral?

Michael   *What* fucking funeral?! Sorry, Jack, you wanted to – (*To* **Christopher**:) There are fucking funerals every day of the week! I beg your pardon, Jack, you wanted to say?

Christopher   What about the arrangements for the funeral?

Michael   And! – Christopher? – In my opinion – I ask a simple question! – Is that any of your fucking business? (*And turns again to* **Jack**.) Sorry, Jack?

Christopher   It has been *made* my business, unfortunately.

Geoffrey *and* **Tony** *have re-emerged.* **Jack** *has registered them.*

Jack   Dad, let's go –

Christopher   Be quiet!

Michael (*to* **Christopher**)   Pardon? – (*To* **Jack**:) Pardon?

Jack (*offended, sits down/gives up; shrugs*)   How're things?

Christopher   We understand how you must feel, but –

Michael   How are? – (*To* **Christopher**:) Pardon? – (*To* **Jack**:) *Things?* (*To* **Christopher**) Did you hear that?! (*He's now trying to get out of his overcoat.*) That is worse than –

Christopher   I've work to do, I must go soon –

Michael   Worse than – the piped music she uses here!

Geoffrey   You ride shotgun, Tony son.

Geoffrey *and* **Tony** *join the scene.*

Geoffrey *is seventy – thereabouts. Physically, he can carry his drink but it induces a romantic nonsense. Sober, he is an everyday, decent businessman.*

Tony *is forty. He's in business with* **Geoffrey**. *He isn't at all bright; there isn't much of a difference, if any, when he's sober; really, he doesn't understand his own catchphrases: they come out automatically or are barked in response to his name. An innocence that can be physically threatening; a stocky, muscular frame; perhaps a bright pullover under his jacket with a paunch in the middle. He probably still plays club rugby.*

Geoffrey   Everything OK, pal? Because we're just in here.

Michael   I beg your pardon?

Geoffrey   Tony!

Tony   A dry finger can't lick salt!

Geoffrey   Who are your friends?

Michael   What is he talking about?

Geoffrey   These guys, pal.

Jack   Who are you?

Geoffrey   Checking it out for you, Mike.

Michael   Did you not hear the young gentleman request your credentials?

Geoffrey   Geoff Williams. (*'Wyatt Earp'*) Casing matters, Mike.

Michael   Casing Matters Mike – What on earth is he?!

Geoffrey   Understood, amigos?

Michael   Piss off!

Geoffrey   Understood, amigo. We're in here. Tony!

Tony   You supply the birds, we'll provide the cages!

And they return to the bar.

Michael   *In there?* (*He wrestling with his coat again to get out of it.*) Two minutes, Jack: Gents.

Monica   (*comes in, a pint of lager for* **Jack**) Now, Jack!

Michael   Monica, who is that man?

Monica   (*helps* **Michael** *out of his coat / takes it off for him*) Geoffrey. You have been with him all afternoon and evening and Tony.

Michael   I know I've been with him all afternoon and evening and Tony: what does he mean he's 'in there'? (*He goes off to the Gents.*) Bloody hell.

Petra   Is there a window in the loo? I don't trust him.

Jack *follows* **Michael** *off.* **Monica**, *who has been ostensibly dusting down* **Michael**'s *coat, calls* **Christopher** *aside for a private word.*

Monica   Christopher?

Christopher   Mmmah! (*Joining her.*)

Monica   Only be a moment, Petra sweetheart!

Petra   Not at all, Monica love! (*Inwardly fuming at this further exclusion.*)

Monica   Is the wine to your liking? (*She produces a gun from underneath* **Michael**'s *coat.*) You see! In his pocket. I put a rubber-toy thing of Young Dennis's from the attic in its place: the state he is in he won't know the difference.

Christopher (*alarmed*)   My father's.

Monica   Honestly, I wouldn't sleep.

Christopher   He was a lieutenant colonel in the war.

Monica   I mean, if one does the right thing in taking a person's car keys?

Christopher   I took his fob watch as a memento, Michael took that.

Monica   It probably doesn't work but to be on the safe side. Here.

Christopher   I don't want it.

Monica   Christopher?

Christopher   What do I do with it?

Monica   I don't know . . . Put it away.

Christopher *takes it. Clumsily, to get it to fit in his pocket, he has to take out his tape recorder.*

Monica   Now I can breathe.

Jack (*returning; to* **Petra**)   He can't escape, there's no window in there.

Monica (*leaving*)   Quite lovely, my dears – my *dears* – to see you all!

Christopher *is left isolated, tape recorder in his hand, the gun in his pocket.*

Petra (*for* **Christopher**'s *benefit*)   Two girls, Jack – children – from my school attempted suicide last year!

Jack   What?

Petra   Both of them are permanently damaged!

Jack   Take it easy.

Petra (*daintily*)   Fuck! Five girls – I know them personally – have done the trip to London for *that* little operation.

Jack   Take it easy –

Petra   Some of them didn't come back! Will you excuse me? I shall now try phoning Mum again. (*She goes off.*) Fuck!

Christopher *returns to the table.* **Jack** *smiles a gentle smile, indicating the departed* **Petra**, *hoping* **Christopher** *will find her personality simply amusing.*

Christopher   Is there something funny?

Jack   No! . . . She's trying to help . . . She's –

Christopher   Jack, *Jack*, I've a lot on my mind, we've never had a row as far as I remember and if at all possible could we avoid one now?

Jack *nods to the sense of this.*

Christopher   You were saying?

Jack   Petra. She doesn't hate you. (*Gentle smile.*) Neither do I. She's been fighting Mum's battle.

Christopher   What battle?

Jack   You walked out.

Christopher   What battle?

Jack   I watched and heard the rows! You walked out six months ago, you left.

Christopher   Consigned you to anonymity and illegitimacy?

Jack   Is that another quotation?

Christopher (*points after* **Petra**)   Her language, her staying out late, her – sixteen years of age! – how many of those things – pints! – does she drink?

Jack   Everyone's doing it!

Christopher   Because they're fighting their mothers' battles?

Jack   You walked out! Look, I'm only saying – I'm a man too, you know?

Christopher   Your mother and I agreed –

Jack   She didn't agree, you agreed! To start your new life, pursue your whatever. But it's reprehensible to deny the truth.

Christopher   Oh? 'Reprehensible'.

Jack   OK. The reprehensible thing then is not that you walked out or that you deny it but that you did it to bury your head deeper in a book, and that makes no sense to me.

Christopher (*turns away*)   I don't have to listen to – (*Turns back.*) You've let *me* down: I'm disappointed in *you*. You're aimless, dressed in rags, no job. And, like everyone else, you blame me for it. You've caused me great sorrow, Jack – you're all punishing me. You have caused me woe.

Jack   These aren't rags!

Christopher   You're the one who walks out on things.

Jack   You're facing them – in *Trinity*? University has nothing to do with life.

Christopher   This after the two terms you spent there?

Jack   Yes.

Christopher   You will publish your findings no doubt?

Jack   And! From the general to the specific, the very best way to stop thinking is to become a philosopher – or shoot yourself in the head! (*He regrets it. But he has been hurt too . . . A silent gesture of apology. Then:*) You're pressed for time: I understand: Petra and I have it in hand now: *we'll* get him home.

Christopher   No! I finish things, Jack, people can depend on me –

Jack   I only said –

Christopher   I'm not a parasite, I don't tell lies. When I say I'm going to do a thing I see it through, not like you, for better or worse . . . (*He turns away, he can't do anything right, he's caught in a nightmare. Hand to his pocket, the gun is there; to his other pocket, finds the cigarette; toys with it.*)

Jack   . . . D'you want to light that thing? . . . Dad?

Christopher   No, I don't want to light that thing! (*And, like a man of action, pulls his earphones out of a pocket and switches on his tape recorder.*)

Christopher's recorded voice   But whereas other philosophers declare that the world as phenomenon is known to us, they assert that the numenon, that is, the *Ding an sich*, is unknown. Schopenhauer, however, maintains that it is known . . . (*Etc., if required: 'Indeed, far from being unknown, it is known to Schopenhauer as a unitary principle. And he calls his principle will.'*)

Geoffrey, *the sheriff, has come in during this.*

Geoffrey   Everything OK in here?

Christopher *plugs in his earphones, thus terminating his recorded voice and sits, listening to his tape in private.* **Geoffrey** *notices* **Michael***'s absence.*

Geoffrey   Mike? (*To* **Jack***:*) Hey, where's Mike?

Jack   Fuck off.

Tony (*entering, following* **Petra**)   Girlie?

Petra   Fuck off.

Jack   Did you get through to Mum?

Petra   Yeh. Get him out of the loo.

Jack *collects* **Michael***'s overcoat and is heading for the Gents: But* **Geoffrey** *and* **Tony** *feel that they have been insulted.*

Geoffrey   Tony!

Tony (*excited, stays* **Jack** *with an upraised hand and indicates that the room is now an arena for battle*)   No problem! Geoffrey: was it sonny here or four-ears over there? (*He decides to deal with 'four-ears',* **Christopher**.) Want to play ball, friend? ... I've had two trials on the possibles for my country! You? (*'How many trials have you had?'*) Compared with rugby, boxing is a puff's game! (*He's running out of ideas.*) ... Stand up! (*Tips of his fingers under* **Christopher**'s *arm, he assists* **Christopher** *to rise.*) ... It's the highest body-contact sport! ... Multiply mass by acceleration and what've you got? Rugby! (*He doesn't know what his next move should be.*) ... Take off the earphones.

Christopher, *petrified, obeys. And:*

Christopher's recorded voice   So: The body is the appearance, the phenomenon, of which the will, that is the *Ding an sich*, is the reality. And the focus of the will lies in the reproductive system. Sex. Now: Sex and the sexual drive –

This has taxed **Tony**'s *mind, momentarily. Now he takes the recorder and, not knowing what else to do with it, he throws it away. And:*

Tony   Your play, friend!

A movement from **Jack** *to catch/field the recorder, but it's gone (possibly out a window). Immediately following,* **Petra** *intervenes herself between* **Tony** *and* **Christopher** – *to protect* **Christopher**.

Petra (*face to face with* **Tony**)   You bloodywell stupid person! Do you want to hit someone? Do you?! Hit me then, go on, I dare you, hit me!

A melee has started. (The following is all one fluent action.) **Jack** *has joined in* –

Jack (*swinging* **Michael**'s *coat at* **Tony** *and* **Geoffrey**)   Hey! Hey! Hey! –

All become involved, in ways appropriate to character.

Geoffrey   Run with it, Tony!

Tony   No problem! –

Geoffrey   Heel, heel! –

Petra *is swept aside and comes unceremoniously sprawling out of it. (Out of what looks like a scrum?)* **Jack** *is grappling with* **Tony** –

Petra   Gssssss . . . !

Geoffrey   Take him down, Tony son!

Tony   No problem! –

Christopher *watches horrified. And* **Michael** *is making a staggering, joyful, expansive return:*

Michael   Geoffrey! Tony! Amigos!

Geoffrey   Step aside, Mike, leave it to Tony!

Jack *now has* **Tony** *in a neck-hold, rendering* **Tony** *ineffective providing he does not release him* –

Geoffrey   Aw, down him, Tony, take him down!

Tony (*half-strangled voice*)   No problem.

Christopher   Let him go, Jack.

Jack   Jesus, let him go?!

Michael   My coat! (*His coat is being trampled on.*)

Petra   Beat the shit out of him, Jack!

Geoffrey   The blind side, Tony!

Tony   No prob – (*He's choking.*)

Michael (*retrieving his coat*)   Bloody hell! Bloody hell!

Geoffrey   Aw, wheel him!

Petra   Take his fucking head off!

Michael (*dusting his coat*)   Dreadful! Dreadful!

Monica (*coming in*)   What is going on? Boys, boys, boys!

Michael (*searching his pockets*)   Car keys, anybody?

Monica   *Boys!* What a din!

Geoffrey   Foul language, insulting behaviour –

Petra   Get the bloodywell pig!

Monica   Petra! My dear – My *dears*! Geoffrey, Tony –

Geoffrey   We were having a quiet drink in there –

Petra   Oh yes, oh yes, a quiet drink –

Monica   A family reunion, Geoffrey!

Geoffrey   Eh?

Monica   A little family get-together! A father and his children and their uncle.

Geoffrey   Jack son, Tony son –

Monica   Geoffrey and Tony: two of our regulars, businessmen down from the North on business, Geoffrey-and-Tony, G-and-T!

During the above, **Michael** *– searching for his car keys – finds something in his pocket that puzzles him. It looks like a gun but it doesn't work, it even bends – 'Bloody hell!' – and when he throws it on the floor it bounces – 'Good grief!' ... And, unobserved by the others, he leaves – 'Dreadful!'*

Geoffrey   Family confab, Tony, Jack son, let him go.

Jack   I'm letting you go now. (*Releases him.*)

Monica   My *dears*!

Tony   No problem.

Monica, **Geoffrey** *and* **Tony** *go to the bar or they retire a little. (***Monica***: 'a family reunion',* **Geoffrey***: 'all a mistake',* **Tony***: 'family confab'.)*

Jack, *adrenalin going, is moving about, sing-songing 'The man he* *comes to see me, says the trees shimmer red –' He sees the stunned (?) ***Christopher*** *and shouts angrily at him:*

Jack   'Was that necessary?' – Still disappointed in me? – I've let you down again? – Petra didn't make another gesture to you?!

While **Petra** *has registered* **Michael**'*s absence: she circles the room, looking this way and that for him. She comes to a stop.*

Petra   So now, the bastard's gone! Shhhit! Jack! (*'Follow me.'*) Shit. (*The last, daintily, as she goes.*)

Jack, *follows, to search for* **Michael**.

Monica *sees them leave and follows enquiringly.* **Geoffrey** *and* **Tony** *follow* **Monica**.

Music up, lights down to a single light, the table lamp. We are back in **Christopher**'*s room. He has a cigarette in one hand, a gun in the other.*

Scene Four

Christopher, *isolated, stands watching the scene. It could be a deserted street or a deserted parking lot: the pathetic figure of* **Michael** *moves along it. He appears lost and he is crying to himself. He comes to a halt. He is literally twisted in pain (from repressed grief more than from drink).*

The others arrive gradually: **Petra** *and* **Jack**, *then* **Monica**, *then* **Geoffrey** *and* **Tony** . . . *And* **Petra** *comes forward, approaching* **Michael**, *cautiously, caring.*

Petra   Uncle Michael?

Michael   Can't find my car, love.

Petra   Uncle Michael?

Michael   Can't even find my car keys.

Petra   It's all right, it's all right. But you're going home now, aren't you? Uncle Michael?

Michael (*looks at her; a slow dawning*) . . . Petra. Where on earth did you . . . (*'come out of'*)? I haven't seen you in . . . (*'months'*)!

Petra   Oho!

Laughing-crying, he embraces her.

Michael   Darling little niece.

Petra   Darling Uncle Michael.

Michael   Little tittle titties growing.

Petra   Now-now, Uncle . . . *Uncle*!

Michael (*clenched, pained face*)   Come home with me.

Petra   Oho, oho, gerron!

She eases him to arm's length, holding both of his hands, to circle with him, as one might with a child, in a game, a slow dance.

I just wanted to see you . . . To look at you . . . To behold you . . . To say how much I love you . . . And Cornelia . . . And that you're going to be all right . . . Aren't you? Uncle Michael? . . . Because you mean so much to us . . . Because we are so precious to each other, because we love one another so much.

He has sunk to his knees, in tears at her feet, his arms around her legs. She strokes his hair.

There there, there there . . . (*She assists him up.*) And you have something to tell us before you go home with Jack, haven't you? Uncle Michael?

He nods.

Monica   Cornelia: Is she? (*Her hand to her mouth.*)

Petra   . . . Nite-nite, everybody! Nite!

She has to leave. (Hides in the shadows.) The tears she's been restraining all day, all night, are about to break. **Christopher**'s *eyes follow her.*

Monica (*to herself*) Oh dear. Oh my dear.

Geoffrey Misunderstanding.

Tony Misunderstanding.

Monica If there's anything at all that we can do.

Geoffrey When is the funeral, Mike?

Michael (*doesn't know, but he's good for a tragic line*) I stand before you a widower and childless.

Geoffrey We'll be there.

Monica She sang at my wedding. (*She leaves.*)

Geoffrey Tony.

Tony (*shakes hands with* **Jack**) Keep in touch.

Jack *leaves with* **Michael**. **Geoffrey** *and* **Tony** *follow* **Monica**.

Christopher'*s eyes on the shadowy place. Now we hear* **Petra** *weeping.* **Christopher** *approaches, cautiously, caring.*

Christopher . . . Petra?

Petra *emerges. The child-woman explodes, circling him, spitting it at him through her tears:*

Petra Did I get pregnant, did I commit suicide, did I have to go away to have an abortion? Did I get my Junior Cert, will I get my Leaving – Does any of it matter – Does anything matter to you but *you*? Will I drop out of college, will I drop out of life, will I walk out on my family when I have them, will I know how to be a parent? *Man!* Do I know the meaning of trust-trust-trust? Big deal, the man of letters, the speech-maker, the professor! Oh! And Jack – Jack-Jack-Jack – is gone off that way for you! You shit! You nothing! . . . Mum is at home now. Nite!

She's gone. He is still, head bowed. (Figures appearing?) 'O Silver Moon' from Rusalka *by Dvořák.*

Scene Five

A table, a table lamp and **Maud**, *seated, posed, watching her
reflection in a cheval mirror. She's about sixty; a sad, elegant
anachronism in dress and lost dreams. (Apart from once, at the end of
the scene when she looks at* **Christopher** *directly, she looks at the
mirror; the pitch at which she holds her head acknowledges the person
she is addressing. And it does not appear to matter that*
Christopher *does not answer her questions; it's as if she knows
the answers.) On a record player (which we don't have to see): 'O
Silver Moon'; she has a remote control for adjusting the volume, as
she requires, and for switching off and on.*

A second table and table lamp at which **Christopher** *is sitting, a
glass of port in one hand the gun in the other in his lap.*

Maud   ... She is singing to the moon ... because she
has fallen in love with the handsome prince, who came to
bathe in the limpid pool, her home ... she longs for a
mortal body in order that she might know the warmth of
union with him ... to share the wonder of life with a
human being ... Are you married?

Christopher   ... Is that you? (*'Singing'*)

Maud   No. Because then, for very good reason, I stopped
... And her wish is granted. But there is a condition. If he
proves false, both she and he will be damned for ever ...
The decision is irrevocably taken ... Do you love her?

Christopher   ... Does he keep guns? (*He holds up the gun.*)

Maud   No. You are quite safe ... He won't be much
longer. He likes to look neat without being helped.

Christopher   Sorry?

Maud   He has a bad ear for music. But he's proud of his
memory ... And she leaves the limpid pool, her home, to
love her prince and be loved in return.

Wally (*off*) ... Wo-ho-ho, wo-ho-ho!

Maud   That will be Walter now.

Christopher *stands, nervously, gun behind his back.*

Wally *comes (careering?) in in a wheelchair. He doesn't need a wheelchair but it stands him greater odds, he reckons, against being shot by callers. Mostly, he affects to be quadriplegic; 'Ouch!' or 'Arrgh!' when he realises he has moved a limb too much, dropped the pretence. Blazer-and-cravat type or maybe an off-white game-hunter's kind of tunic. He's younger than* **Maud**. *Practically everything he says is an exclamation. He's too hearty-sounding by half. He is terrified.*

Christopher's *underlying emotional state and confusion is not helped by* **Wally**'s *wheelchair.*

Wally   Wo-ho-ho, wo-ho-ho, talking about me, someone talking about me?! (*He brakes to a halt.*) Catalani, Maud? Cat-a-lani?! Is this the way to entertain a guest? Switch'm off, switch'm off! Bloody Catalani. (**Maud** *switches off the music.*) That's better! Old boy, old boy, good of you to call, good of you to call! What?! Don't get up, no need to stand! Good of you to call, I appreciate it, I do, good of you to call! What's that? (*Did* **Christopher** *say something?*) . . . Nothing? To be sure! (*He didn't say anything and that's perfect.*) Long time. Long time? Long time. And! . . . She give you nothing stiffer than?! Ouch! (*To* **Maud**:) Get up! (*To* **Christopher**:) T'be sure yeh will, t'be sure yeh will, won't take no for an – (*To* **Maud**:) Get up! Cognac, whiskey, this's an old friend, wo-ho-ho!

Christopher   This is fine.

Wally   Eh?

Christopher   No.

Wally   If y'say so, if y'say so, if that's yer tipple, if that's your choice. It's what I drink m'self. – (*To* **Maud**:) Get up! Haven't much say in these things now, since my – (*Taps his legs. Then:*) Ouch! Arrgh! My ration, Maud.

While **Maud** *holds a glass of port to* **Wally**'s *lips,* **Christopher** *sits, stands, sits . . . Inner agitation. The gun is visible in his hand, yet no one comments on it.*

Wally (*to* **Maud**)   Enough! . . . So! So! How're things, how're – Good? Good! Good! So things're good, things're good? Good of you to call! Hang about, elephant's brain: Christopher.

Christopher   Yesss.

Wally   Eh? . . . Hang about, younger brother, don't tell me his name.

Christopher   Michael.

Wally   I would've got it! Ouch! . . . Yes?

Christopher, *fixed on* **Wally**, *shakes his head, absently.*

Wally   Been back that ways since?

Christopher   Ahmmm . . .

Wally (*to* **Maud**, *who has moved; terrified that she will leave the room*)   Where you off to? Sit! She's like a hen. Been back that ways since, Christopher?

Christopher   Yesss, no.

Wally   Y'have?

Christopher   No.

Wally   Remember the beak?

Christopher   No –

Wally   Y'do, y'do! The headmaster, was fond of you –

Christopher   I don't –

Wally   Y'do –

Christopher   I don't –

Wally   Y'do! – You cared for him a lot!

Christopher   I don't!

Wally   Top him up, Maud.

Christopher   I don't, Wally. (*To* **Maud**:) No, thank you.

Wally (*to* **Maud**)   Up, get up! (*To* **Christopher**:) Y'don't mind if I do?

Christopher (*to himself*)   I never cared for anyone.

And, while **Maud** *feeds* **Wally** *another sip of port, he starts to pace (?), the gun held tight against his body.*

Wally (*eyes screwed sideways, watching* **Christopher***, whispers to* **Maud**)   Enough. Sit . . . (*And to* **Christopher** *when he comes to a halt:*) Eh?

Christopher   I called about a matter.

Wally   And that brother of yours – Bit of a lad, what?!

Christopher   I called about – ahmmm! –

Wally   But weren't we all, weren't we all! –

Christopher   A matter that has started to bother me.

Wally   Boys will be boys!

Christopher   But, aren't you surprised, I called rather late.

Wally   So what? Ouch!

Christopher   It's two o'clock in the morning.

Wally   Lights were on, Maud sits up, what're old friends for?!

Christopher   . . . And I'm surprised that . . .

Wally   Yes? (*Aside to* **Maud**:) Chip in.

Maud   And he's surprised that you're not surprised to see him, Walter.

Wally   Surprised?! – No! – I mean I'm – Yes! If he says so!

Maud   And *he* (*meaning* **Wally**) is surprised at where you found our address.

Wally   Immaterial! – Not at all! – But if, y'know?! (*'If he wishes to tell us.'*)

Christopher   The book.

Wally   We're not in it.

Christopher   You are.

Wally   If y'say so – but we're not in it. Maud – ex – chip in.

Maud   We are ex-directory. Because when we returned from abroad, Walter had two other callers –

Wally   Eh?

Maud   Old school friends too, come to call late at night, like you. So Walter had us removed from the book.

Wally   Kind of people to call on me, Christopher?

Christopher   No. (*To himself; it doesn't explain matters.*)

Maud   Perhaps it was a very old directory.

Wally   There – she has it – mystery solved – First sensible thing y've said in yer life! I bet you've nothing like hcr at home? (*He taps his head, meaning* **Maud** *has a screw loose, then is about to go 'Ouch!' but* **Christopher** *is buried in himself.*)

Short silence. Short as it is, it becomes too much for **Wally**.

Oh, put on the bloody Catalani again, I know that's all yer itching for.

Maud   Dvořák, Walter.

Wally   Dvořák, Catalani, elephant's brain but I keep mixing the twisters up.

Maud   Do you mind hearing it again?

Christopher (*absently*) No.

Wally   Where are you, oh where are you my beloved – same old thing.

Christopher *looks at him; fixes on him.*

Wally   Eh? . . . Music man yourself, Christopher? . . .

Work going well? . . . I'm retired – you retired? – I'm retired.

Christopher   Yesss, yesss!

Wally   Eh?

Christopher   And I'm surprised at that.

Wally   Which – What?

Christopher   *That*, the wheelchair – Recent?

Wally (*taps the chair*)   This?

Christopher   Yesss!

Wally   No! Funniest thing, comes and goes. (*He half stands – with a touch of 'watch me, no hands' – to demonstrate his point, and sits again.*) Neurological stuff, the experts tell me.

'O Silver Moon' again. (Or the resumption of it.) And **Maud** *is talking to the mirror again.*

Maud   How warm and gentle her kisses . . . How she tries to speak to him with her eyes, so that he might learn to live.

Wally   Fish out of water, what! . . .

Maud   But the prince is unable to learn . . . He is unkind to her . . . He betrays her trust . . . She wants to die.

Christopher (*emotionally, to himself*)   . . . What's her name?

Wally   You interested in? (*'this kind of music?'*) He's interested in (*'this kind of music'*) – Speak up!

Maud   Rusalka . . . And she returns to the limpid pool, to sink alone back into the water . . . But she knows that he, too, will never be free of her. And she waits for him to follow, to die, in understanding at last, in her arms. (*She rises.*)

Wally   Eh? . . . Sit!

She remains standing. She looks at **Christopher**.

Maud   Would you like me to leave?

Wally   What's that?

Christopher *rises. He is trembling, highly agitated, the gun pointed directly at* **Wally**.

Wally   . . . Steady on, old boy.

Christopher   I didn't find you in directories, new or old –

Wally   Please –

Christopher   You were observed walking heartily in the street!

Wally (*rising*)   Was I? Well, if you say so –

Christopher   Yesss, I say so! – No, sit!

Wally   No, please, Chris, Christopher – You in any financial bother? –

Christopher   No, no –

Wally   D'you know what I mean? – Money! – She has plenty –

Christopher   No! Sit! Sit! I never played a prank on you or called you names but I've begun to remember a matter that has started to bother me, an incident that happened in class in school one day.

Wally   Was there? Wo-ho –

Christopher   Ho!

Wally   If y'say so –

Christopher   Indeed I do say so, wo-ho-ho and ouch, elephant's brain, old boy!

Wally   Maud? (*A plea for help.*)

Maud (*quietly*)   Shoot him.

Christopher   Whilst you were standing up in class one day someone placed a drawing pin on your seat for you to sit on. Without any evidence whatsoever you decided I had put it there and then cruelly made of me another subject of your reign of terror. I told you then a hundred times and over as many days that I did not put the drawing pin there, if drawing pin there ever was that day, and I have called tonight to tell you for one last time.

Wally   T'be sure, t'be –

Christopher   No, you be sure –

Wally   If y'say so –

Christopher   No, you be sure, you say so, yes or no, to *what* I *now de*clare up*on* my *word* of *hon*our!

Wally   Accept!

Christopher (*sobbing*)   I'm sorry for calling so late and unannounced, Mrs Peters!

He stumbles off, gun in hand, sobbing.

The music and the figures follow him.

Scene Six

Table and the table lamp, unlit.

Christopher, *dishevelled, overcoat; a sense of futility. The earphones dangle from his hands.*

The table lamp comes on of itself. He wonders about this. A bright light falls on the table. Then another. (Lights as for television purposes.) A mike is lowered over the table. He is terrified.

Christopher   He goes to the podium with confidence. (*He stands at the table and stuffs the earphones into a pocket. Then:*) Testing: One, two, three, four, seven. (*He mouths the word, as to a television crew, off.*) More? Schopenhauer: His phenomenology of Reproduction. (*Mouths it.*) More? And Did He Hypostatise the *Ding an sich*?

During the following, he holds a fascinated horror of himself; he has to pretend that what he's saying makes sense; and he cannot stop himself. Terror makes him smile.

He nods, having received his cue to begin. He smiles.

Christopher   President. Fellow acolytes of IASA, distinguished guests, distinguished colleagues, distinguished viewers, friends, distinguished students . . . (*He gathers speed.*) The spatio-temporal world consisting of individual objects subject to the law of causality bound together by the cause-effect relation which is an a-priori form of existence though pertaining to the mind is phenomenon, is idea, but the thing-in-itself, the reality, the everything, is will, and its focus lies in the reproductive system, the ding-a-dong. (*There is something he has just said that doesn't quite make sense.*) Which gives us pought for thause . . . But! – Before! – Yes! – Because! – Before I go further – Exactly! Crass – remiss. I refer of course to my colleague and friend Dr Wuzzler who is extremely ill in . . . Actually, who passed away this morning. Alas. Speaking personally of his distinguished career and of his remarkable discovery only last year I fear no contradiction when I say I do not for a single moment believe that the young Arthur Schopenhauer ever came next or near that little scenic port of Cobh in Co. Cork in 1802. (*There is something there too that he shouldn't have said.*) Another year, yes, but o two, no. And it was certainly no mean achievement of his to hold that chair at Trinity for twenty-eight years and a bit. But now he has a throne. (*He acknowledges heaven.*)

Here it may be appropriate to take a look at the age Schopenhauer was born into. The guillotine was not at all essential. Suicide. Suicide went rampant – so unlike our own times. Self-destruction to such an extent that records down-through-the-ages were looked up in search of possible causes and cures. Suicide, the incidence of *mass* suicide! Oh yes, those have-a-happy-go-lucky-Californian-day caperers did not create a precedent in the avocado or banana fields of – Orange County, was it? Yes, there are seats up here at the front, boys and girls. (*Gesturing the student section of his 'audience' to come forward.*) Ah, the insidious appeal of suicide to the young romantic mind!

I do not wish to overemphasise this suicide business because I am very much against it, very much, and because – Sorry, President? – (*He nods.*) – and because we have to push on.

So, enter Arthur Schopenhauer to take to his rooms and have a think about it all. Did he help matters? The brevity of life which we so lament may be its greatest virtue, he said. Man is a thing that ought not to be, he said. Worse, he said: Man is a flaw containing a bigger flaw within himself, which is the will to reproduce, blind will, the thing-in-itself, the ding-a-dong. (*There is something again that isn't right; an aside to himself.*) Ding-a-dong? (*No, it's fine.*) Ding-a-dong.

And *that's* why we feel guilty about doing it.

But there is a way out, because all this is very sad. And the way out is? Knowledge. The way to stop this all-too-active, mindless and erroneous business and get blind autonomous willie off reproductive duty is to take matters by the head. 'For what bridle and bit are to the unmanageable horse, the intellect is for the will of man.' In a nutshell, if only we thought about it we'd think again.

But wait a minute, knowledge is an illusion, isn't it? So where does that leave the intellect? What is he talking about? Further – exactly! The intellect comes from the mother, will from the father. He *hated* his mother. And she was a bad novelist, wasn't she? She pushed him down the stairs, didn't she? – She was a *terrible* novelist. You will say forget the staircase, what is meant is that the intellect is inherited *genetically*, from the mother: that is what I would've said too but *so-and-therefore*! the same must apply to the will coming from the father. His father was a suicide! D'you see what I mean? Died by his own hand – well, he pushed himself into the river, didn't he? – 1805, April – August then, September – probably on a Saturday. And! His paternal granny was crazy as a Danzigger coot.

Need I mention his brother? D'you see what I mean? I
mean, if he says there's never to be contentment, no love
lost, knowledge only an illusion, will wicked, without any
ability to know, suffering the true destiny, why does *he* go
on and on? For seventy-two years. Why didn't he kill
himself, instead of leaving it to me? Or you. And I don't
think he can have liked himself very much.

*Through the above he has been searching his pockets, absently
producing various items in turn and putting them on the table: a book,
earphones, the gun, the cigarette, a handkerchief . . .*

He must have found something to keep him going, some
harmony. Sorry, President? (*He holds up the book.*) This? (*The
earphones.*) These? (*The gun.*) This? (*The cigarette.*) This? (*Nods,
and puts the cigarette away.*) And because we have to push on.

*The bright lights, in turn, go out on him during the following and his
voice, if miked, is unmiked, until he becomes a man, lost, alone in a
room, talking to himself.*

He lived alone, kept his distance. Loaded guns beside his
bed at night. For burglars? Cheph! His career at university?
Hegel had the chair. Hegel had a suite of chairs. He had a
dog of course, called . . . forget. Atma, yes. Atma, meaning
world soul. A poodle – a toy one maybe, and not big
enough to be of threat to property, a young one and,
therefore, not have to be put down like Chokki. Chokki,
meaning . . . gentleness. What else had he? (*Cigarette is out
again and he is searching for matches.*) A pipe, yes he smoked a
pipe – what else? Tears, self-pity – yeh, they were a great
help – what else? Women. That narrow-shouldered, broad-
hipped short-legged race he called them. Still, it didn't stop
him having his one-night stands and casual amours. But of
sufficient duration, of such effect, as to produce children.
Children: thorns of kindred. All of whom he managed to
consign to anonymity and illegitimacy. Or did he manage
that so well? . . . And though he could not see how they
could possibly love him, could it be possible that they did?
(*He can't find matches.*) Hasn't anybody got a light? . . . Why
did he take to his rooms in the first place? He didn't care?

... That Jack might come home late one night mortally wounded by a blade. That Petra, too, waylaid, innocence defiled, mouth open, eyes dilated in the grass. Never to be found? Or that they would take their own lives down into the earth. Thorns of kindred? *Beloved* thorns of kindred. Yes. Yes, and that she, too, his casual amour, water-sprite and temporary wife – Was that what she was? Patricia ... too, would (*nods: 'die'*) ... or drown. And when they stopped, the kisses of that casual amour of twenty years' duration, instead of love letters, did he send to her for signing, affidavits, orders, papers, to achieve that right of man to be left alone. For what? To escape, *ease* the pain of boundless love. For what? In order, in isolation, to achieve that other state, the terror of memories and guilt mocking the impotence and failure of a jumble of words.

Mind you, he did, genuinely, like animals. Could that have kept him going? And he wrote something about porcupines, didn't he? What was it? Porcupines – hedgehogs – What was it? (*He can't remember.*)

What is the resolution, boys and girls? (*Sighs.*) Does it have to be suicide? Reconciliation: Too late? Blasted hedgehogs? ... Bury Cornelia first.

Music up, figures gathering, babble of voices.

Scene Seven

A post-funeral feast at **Michael**'s *place.* **Michael** *looks well and he is impeccably dressed.* **Patricia** *is present, happy and relaxed.* **Petra** *in a long Arab-type wedding dress (the square of bodice done in coloured threads and beads). An issue isn't made of it but she is unforgiving of* **Tony**: *she ignores him.* **Jack** *is enthusiastic, it's like Christmas to him; he has drink and a cigar.* **Geoffrey** *and* **Tony** *are on their best behaviour;* **Tony**, *as before, is cued into action by* **Geoffrey**. **Monica** *has a new hairdo – or maybe it's a hat. And there is* **Moreva**, *a new girlfriend of* **Jack**'s *who wears jeans with a man's check shirt hanging outside them; almost throughout, she reads a thick paperback.*

They are drinking wine and there's beer for later for those who want it. And **Michael** *is going to open a bottle of champagne.*

Christopher, *in his overcoat, at a remove from them, watches for a while before joining the scene.*

Jack   That was *lovely* lamb.

Monica   Did you like it, Jack?

Jack   Oh God it was lovely!

Monica   Did you have enough, Geoffrey?

Geoffrey   First rate, a sufficiency! Tony!

Tony   Top class!

Geoffrey   Thank you!

Tony   Full marks!

Michael   Well, you can thank Monica! (*He is undoing the champagne.*)

Monica   Good heavens – heavens – he cooked it himself!

Patricia   Oh! Michael, I'd forgotten. (*A bottle of champagne from her feet in a paper bag.*)

Michael   You shouldn't have, Patricia! (*See:*) I'd got some in.

Monica   He's a wonderful cook.

Michael   Are you all right, love?

Patricia   Yes!

Michael   Should I call over one evening?

Patricia   No!

Tony   That's a very peculiar dress – Petra. (*He means 'lovely'.*)

Petra   Uncle Michael, is there a pint glass in the house?

Michael   Everybody! Wait for it ... (*Champagne cork pops.*)

Jack   An angel's fart!

Michael *starts to circle the table, pouring the champagne.* **Monica** *and* **Patricia** *start to clear things away.*

Monica   Let us make a little space for you.

Patricia   No, you sit down, Monica –

Monica   I'll do no such thing, Patricia! –

Patricia   You've been on your feet all morning!

Geoffrey   Tony! (*'Help with the clearing away.'*)

Monica   Shall we leave it to Tony then? (*The women laugh as they clear up.*)

Jack   The champagne is going to take all day – Petra, pass us down that bottle there!

Patricia   Easy does it now, m'boy!

Petra (*to* **Jack**)   D'you want beer?

Patricia   And m'girl! You didn't do very well with your plate, Monica.

Monica   Tummy. (*A lie.*) Have the men all had enough now?

Tony (*clearing* **Petra**'s *plate*)   Allow me – Petra. You have a very peculiar name.

Petra   Uncle Michael, can we open the beer?

Michael   Good grief!

Christopher *has joined them.*

Monica   Christopher, my dear!

Patricia   Christopher!

Monica   My dear, my *dear*!

Patricia   Come in, come in, so pleased you could make it!

Monica   Always lovely to see you!

Patricia   Where shall we put you?

Petra   Pint bloody glass anywhere?

Michael (*sighing;* **Christopher**'s *arrival is most inconvenient to his management*)   Have you eaten, because as you can see we are clearing things away?

Christopher   I have.

Michael   Pardon?

Monica   Are you sure?

Christopher   I've eaten.

Patricia   Where would you like to sit?

Michael   Anywhere! (*And he continues his round with the champagne.*)

Christopher   I've eaten.

Monica   I understand.

Michael   Everybody! *Please* hold your champagne for the toast, there's plenty of it but don't-drink-it-yet!

Monica *and* **Patricia**, *chatting, go off (to the kitchen) with lunch things.*

Jack (*self-consciously*)   Hi!

Christopher (*self-conscious of* **Jack**, *nodding, smiling*)   How're you?

Jack (*nodding*)   Would you like a glass of wine?

Christopher   Yeh.

Geoffrey   The hard man! (*Shakes hands with* **Christopher**.) A bit of high spirits the other evening. (*Calls:*) Tony son, don't you have something for someone?

Tony   Geoffrey! (*He has a present for* **Christopher** *and as he goes out to fetch it:*) Privilege to be here!

Geoffrey   He's my nephew, we're in business together. He's a university man too, you know? Oh yes, he was a student for years and years.

Jack   Dad? (*A glass of wine to* **Christopher**.)

Geoffrey   Studied to be an architect, but he never practised, so we're in animal feed together.

Jack   Dad? (*He has pulled up a chair for* **Christopher**.)

Michael   Now, would everyone mind sitting down again, please!

Geoffrey   So, when we came down here on Wednesday and swung a big one: bit of high spirits.

Jack   Good luck?

Christopher   Cheers! (*They clink glasses.*)

Michael   Is she all right, Jack? – Are you all right, love?

Moreva *looks up, smiles-nods, and returns to her book.*

Jack   Did you smoke?

Christopher   No. (**Jack** *smiles, dubious.*) I didn't.

Jack   Would you like a cigar? (*He laughs.*)

Michael   Everybody, please! (*'Be seated.'*) Patricia, Monica! Where's Tony?

Geoffrey   Tony!

Tony (*returning*)   You supply the birds, we'll provide the cages! (*He has a small box.*)

Geoffrey   D'you get it? He studied architecture –

Petra (*calling*)   Mum, Monica, speech! –

Geoffrey   Y'don't get it? – It's an architect's joke!

Christopher   Mmmah!

Michael   Christopher, *please*! Geoffrey, Jack.

Geoffrey   OK, Mike. (*And a finger to his lips to* **Tony**, *to leave the presentation of the box until later.*)

Monica *and* **Patricia** *are returning to their seats.*

Monica   No, the lamb was Michael's idea. I hope I'm not speaking out of turn, Patricia, but turkey, poultry for a funeral; meat, flesh: no. Or is that just me?

And they laugh and sit.

Michael   Now, has everyone got a glass of –

Jack   Silence! Michael is going to make a speech!

Michael   Champagne, everybody?

Geoffrey   OK, Mike.

Michael   Ladies and –

Jack   Silence, everybody!

Patricia   Jack.

Tony   OK, Mike.

Michael   The service was short. That is how Cornelia would have liked it. This feast which we have just had is how she would have liked it: family, friends, acquaintances around her own table. Thank you all again for coming. The reason why the Reverend Lavelle isn't here to say a few words which I asked him to prepare is because he had to go off and bury somebody else.

Jack   Pass down that bottle again.

Michael   I have no way of knowing what those words would have been –

Jack   D'you want some?

Tony   No thank you –

Michael   But I should like to say –

Tony   Jack.

Michael   But I should like to say, everybody, that Cornelia's death was not in vain. I am not a churchgoer myself, but I believe in immortality. Whatever others might believe in. My brother, for instance. Death, everybody, is not the end. Is *not* the end. Nor is it a disintegration. Death opens unknown doors. It is most grand to die.

Christopher   John Masefield.

Michael   . . . John Masefield. How wonderful is death. Death and its brother, death and its brother –

Christopher   Sleep.

Michael   Sleep.

Christopher   Shelley.

Michael (*nods, grudgingly*) Shelley. And how wonderful – how wonderful Cornelia feels now, seeing her sleep bringing families and friends and acquaintances together – bringing families together who-God-knows should be together! That her sleep can transform *acquaintances* into lasting, lifelong friends. Witness: Tony, Geoffrey and – sorry, Jack's girlfriend, name please?

Jack   What's your name?

Moreva   Moreva.

Michael   Pardon?

Jack   Moreva.

Michael   And Moreva from Frankfurt.

Jack   No!

Michael   Pardon?

Jack   She's gone back.

Michael   Pardon?

Jack   That was someone else.

Michael   I see.

Petra   Would you like a cigarette, Mum? (*She's making a rollie.*)

Patricia   Thank you, love, thank you.

Michael Speaking of friendship, I should like to make an especial word of thanks to Monica for –

Monica He cooked it himself! – Good heavens! – He's a wonderful, wonderful cook! He's –

Michael Monica – Monica! Monica kindly offered her place, the Abbey, for this – celebration.

Monica Oh! I understand.

Michael But this is how Cornelia would have liked it.

Geoffrey Around her own table, Mike.

Michael *nods solemnly.*

Tony And his – Geoffrey.

Petra Mum? (*Cigarette to* **Patricia**.)

Monica But wasn't it a long hold-over, Michael?

Michael Pardon?

Monica Big Dennis himself commented. Cornelia's waiting all that time to be interred.

Michael Her generosity, love. (*Such a well-told lie that he believes it himself.*)

Monica Michael?

Geoffrey Son?

Petra Shit! (*Her lighter doesn't work.*)

Michael She donated everything.

Geoffrey Parts.

Michael Though she was ill –

Petra The fucking thing was new.

Patricia Love.

Tony (*fervently*) I wish I'd known her.

Michael Though she was ill, everybody –

Geoffrey   Her words, Mike, were?

Petra   Give a poxy light to Mum, Jack.

Michael   Her words were: Take any part of me that's good that will benefit mankind.

Jack   Mum? (*And gives her a light.*)

Geoffrey   And that's generosity.

Tony   Generosity.

Michael   And that takes time.

Patricia   That colour suits you, Jack.

Monica   Any part, any organ: that would be Cornelia.

Michael   Signed on the dotted line.

Patricia (*to* **Jack**) Very, very nice.

Petra   She loved parties, didn't she? – Jack, give us your matches here! –

Michael   Further –

Petra   Shouldn't we have some music?

Michael   Further –

Monica   She *adored* parties! Oh the things Cornelia got up to! My *dear*! You don't have to tell me, Petra! If only we could sit down and write a book, Patricia!

Monica, **Petra** *and* **Patricia** *laughing.*

Michael   A moment please! Further, everybody, Cornelia's dying this very week cannot be written away to coincidence. She could have died any week she liked. But her dying this week, I cannot help believing, was another mark of her generosity. And thoughtfulness. She was very well aware that I had taken a year off work: that year ends tomorrow, Saturday, and I must, I simply must return to work on Monday.

Petra   Uncle Michael –

Jack   The toast! – (*'For God's sake get on with it!'*)

Petra   Uncle Michael –

Geoffrey   To Cornelia! –

Tony   To –

Michael   Geoffrey, Jack, Tony! – What, love?

Petra   Wasn't there a guitar in the house?

Michael   Banjo, love? Bedroom somewhere? (*Vaguely; though he indicates the direction of the bedroom.*)

Jack   'The man he comes to see me, says the trees shimmer red –'

Michael   A moment please, Jack –

Petra   Would that be in order, Mum?

Patricia   Quite in order.

Michael   Very much in order, but – Petra! (**Petra** *has gone to the bedroom.*) She left a final message: I want everyone to hear.

He has produced a slip of paper, Cornelia's final message. It induces a silence. **Patricia** *smokes her cigarette. When they speak, they talk in whispers while awaiting* **Petra**'*s return.*

Jack   ... (*sotto voce*) 'And outside the night deepens ...' (*He continues to mouth the words of his song.*)

Monica   ... Did you design that yourself, Patricia?

Patricia (*nods that she designed her own dress. Then, smiles 'are you'*)   All right, Christopher?

He nods, smiles that he is.

Monica   And you're opening a business.

Patricia   Next week. I found a premises.

Monica   You're so clever.

Geoffrey   ... Tony. (*Cueing* **Tony** *to make his presentation.*)

Tony *tiptoes to* **Christopher** *to present him with the box.*

Tony (*whispering*)   It'll record at fifty paces. Ultra-sleek model.

Christopher   Thank you.

Geoffrey   It's got – (*He demonstrates that it's got earphones.*)

Tony   Batteries. (*Separately.*) And if you ever need a load of bran nuggets. Any quantity. (*He tiptoes back to his place.*)

Jack   . . . 'The man he comes to see me.'

Patricia (*calls*)   Petra, come at once, Michael is waiting!

Petra (*off*)   Found it! Coming!

Michael   Is she all right, Jack? Are you all right, love?

Moreva *smiles and puts down her book.*

Petra (*returns, blowing dust off a guitar/banjo/bouzouki*)   I think the strings are bolixed.

Jack   Show it here.

Patricia   Just a little longer now, children.

Michael   A last message from Cornelia. (*He reads.*) 'Death is . . . Death is . . .' (*He has become emotional, contains it suitably, and:*) Perhaps it would be more fitting coming from her sister. Would you mind very much, love?

Patricia (*reads*)   'Death is nothing at all. I have only slipped away into the next room. I am I, you are you, whatever we were to each other we are still. Call me by my own familiar name, speak to me in the easy way we always used. Put no sadness into your tone, wear no air of sorrow, laugh as we always laughed at the little jokes together. Play, smile, think of me. Life means all that it ever meant, it is the same that it ever was. There is absolute unbroken continuity. What is this death but a negligible accident? Why should I be out of mind because I am out of sight? I am but waiting for you for an interval, somewhere very near, just around the corner. All is well.'

Tears, embraces, handshakes, kisses.

Monica (*dabbing her eyes*)   Oh my dear, oh my dears I am so happy.

Petra   Mum, I love you.

Patricia   I know, love.

Petra *kisses* **Michael**. **Patricia** *holds up her hand in a gentle wave to* **Christopher**. *He smiles, bows.*

Tony   Jack? (*A handshake.*)

Jack   Would you like a cigar?

Tony   Never use them, I don't have television and I'm about to take up hang-gliding.

Monica   Such wonderful, wonderful sentiments, what can one say?

Patricia *hands the slip of paper back to* **Michael**. **Michael** *holds it up before pocketing it and, then, to* **Christopher**.

Michael   So, you see!

Christopher   Cornelia? (*'Cornelia wrote that?'*)

Michael (*nods solemnly, as is his wont; then*)   *In*-correct! Canon Henry Scott Holland, 1847–1919. So, you don't know everything. (*And, now, he laughs.*) Drink up, everybody! – Open house! – Drink up! What's your name again, love? (*And he starts to chat up* **Moreva**.)

Patricia   Michael! The toast!

Michael   To Canon Henry Scott Holland!

Patricia   To Cornelia, to my sister!

Others   To Cornelia!

Patricia   And to everyone here present.

They drink. There's laughter. **Jack** (*mends/has mended the 'bolixed' strings*) *tunes and strums the guitar.* **Petra** *has a pint glass and fills it with beer.*

Michael   To love, Moreva! Good grief, she is reading *War and Peace*! Good grief, she has nearly finished it!

Jack (*plays and sings*)   'The Man he comes to see me / Says the trees shimmer red / And reflect big yellow leaves in light / That laugh at us in fadin' beauty.'

Petra   Jack, d'you mind!

Jack   'So yeh go for a swim in the limpid pool / And there you see mermaids –'

Petra   It was my idea! (*She wants to sing.*)

Jack   Push off! 'Slivers of blue translucent fins / Turn to the crimson sun.' (*Strums/finer tuning.*)

Christopher (*has moved to* **Petra**)   How many of those can you drink? (*Pints.*)

Petra   Nine. Ten. (*Defiant glance:*) Eleven?

He nods, as if impressed. He has a flower in his hand, a red rose, but he is unsure of how to present it. And, though it would appear to be for her, she cannot be sure of it.

It just goes through you. ('*Beer just goes through you.*')

He nods. He puts the flower down somewhere nearby and moves on.

Jack   'Struttin' girls with tinsel hair / lavish misery on screamin' hounds / Tear from the moon a silver shroud / A misty veil of sick-stained air.'

Christopher   Not bad.

Jack   Author?

Christopher   Askey?

Jack (*laughs*)   'Your mind rips through the tangled room / Bodies emanatin' filthy smoke / Twistin' carcasses writhin' wet / Your head explodes, you can't forget.' (*And strums a little.*) 'So yeh pick up your clothes, walk out the door / Your feet leave impressions on red bits of floor.' (*Strums.*)

Christopher   Good stuff. I'd watch my back over there if

I were you: your uncle Michael would tip a cat going out a skylight.

Jack, *still strumming, laughs, then shrugs 'Moreva is just a friend'.*

Christopher   But are my quotations improving? (*He is moving on again.*)

Jack   Dad? . . . I'm sorry about the other night.

Christopher   No, I'm sorry, Jack.

Jack   I'm the one who has to prove something.

Christopher   I think you're getting there. (*He moves on.*)

Jack (*is pleased*) 'And outside the night deepens, darkness descends / The man says your head is right / The man says your head's now right, the nightmare begins!' (*Which song is a bit of a triumph for* **Jack**.)

And, indeed, somewhere around here, **Michael**, *with* **Moreva** *in tow and a bottle of champagne, slips off to the bedroom.*

Geoffrey *and* **Tony** *are putting on their coats.*

Geoffrey   Well, God bless, all! God bless! Tony.

Tony   Privilege!

Geoffrey   God bless!

Tony   Privilege!

Goodbyes. They leave. **Monica** *and* **Patricia** *have done more clearing away.* **Monica**, *too, is putting on her coat.*

Monica   Well, do you know, Patricia, honestly and truly, people are wonderful, they're so nice. And do you know it is all about love. Honestly, I'm still crying inside.

Patricia   Jack, give Petra a hand to replace those tables to where they belong.

Monica   And I'll see you soon again, please God. (*Fingering* **Patricia**'s *dress.*) So clever. Jack, Petra: sweetheart, sweetheart. (*She kisses them.*) I must be getting home to my treasure. He's holding the fort, he can be very good at times, 'the chiefest among ten thousand'.

Patricia 'I sat down in his shadow with great delight'!

Monica I sat down in his shadow – Isn't it wonderful? – The Song of Solomon!

And the two women celebrate it with a laugh, together.

And my dear Christopher! *(Kisses him. Then:)* But *you* should be able to write a book – or a play? Have you ever tried? *(And she tweeks his cheek:)* Oh, if we could only simply keep you as pets! *(And she's gone.)*

Christopher *and Patricia, together, now find they are shy of each other.*

Christopher How are you? *(She smiles.)* Hmm?

Patricia No, how are *you*, which is more important.

Christopher No, how are *you*? Which is more important.

Patricia I'm fine.

Christopher You've lost weight.

Patricia I've gained! Women put it on when things go . . . *('wrong')*; men lose it. And Michael is like a skeleton. Where is he?

Christopher I think I saw him go into the – out for a breath of fresh air.

Patricia We have to be going in a minute.

'Yes,' he nods. They'll be going their separate ways in a moment.

. . . Like a nightmare, wasn't it? The past six months.

He nods.

. . . How did we arrive at this point in time?

He nods.

. . . But I'm fine now. And you?

Christopher Yeh!

Patricia   Are you looking after yourself?

Christopher   Yeh!

Patricia   Oh! And Petra was saying you're working on something very important.

Christopher   Mmm!

Patricia   Yes?

Christopher   No, you were saying earlier – I overheard you saying you've got a shop?

Patricia (*'yes'*) I'm looking forward to it. And I wanted to apologise.

Christopher   For what?

Patricia   Oh . . . (*'lots of things'*). And those papers from the solicitor that I've been neglecting to sign.

Christopher   I haven't been pushing them. I *haven't*! I mean, that was – that was the solicitor. (*He has an inclination to laugh.*) I mean, there's no hurry . . . Is there?

Patricia   I was in his office yesterday and I took the opportunity. And I find I'm at peace now. You've been extraordinarily kind to me. Thank you.

Petra *and* **Jack** – *singing, laughing, perhaps, swapping snatches of* **Jack**'s *song – have been 'replacing' the furniture, until there is only a single table and table lamp, phone and answering machine left.*

Patricia   Well done, children! Now get your coats. (*To* **Christopher**:) But they're great, aren't they?

Christopher   I didn't know how great.

Patricia   Wherever we got them from.

Christopher   Blind will.

Patricia (*laughs 'What?'*)   Well, take care now, won't you? All the best.

Christopher   Bye.

Jack *waves to him from the door.* **Petra**, **Patricia** *and* **Jack** *leave.*

Lights changing. **Christopher**, *alone, isolated, feels his pockets. He finds the gun and the cigarette. He has a choice to make. But he has no light.*

Christopher (*whispers*)   Help . . . Help.

Petra *returns, ostensibly to collect her hat. (He holds the gun behind his back.)*

Petra   My bloodywell hat. Oh, I thought everyone had gone. (*Then, the flower:*) Is this for me? (*He nods.*) An olive branch?

Christopher   No, it's a rose.

*She takes the rose, smiles to herself, dumps a box of matches (***Jack***'s) on the table and leaves, putting on her hat.*

Nothing is what's happened here.

He lights the cigarette and draws deeply on it.

Instead, after long and penitential abstinence, he rejoined the persecuted minority of smokers in slow death. Draft two. President, fellow acolytes of IASA, ladies and –

The phone is ringing. He lifts it and replaces it on the cradle.

But, here, before giving my paper, it might be appropriate to take a preamble from the *Paralipomena*. A group of porcupines – hedgehogs – on a winter's day crowded close together to save themselves from the cold by their mutual warmth. Soon, however, they felt each other's spines and this drove them apart again. Whenever their need brought them back together, this discomfort intervened until, thrown this way and that between the cold and the spines, they found a moderate distance from one another at which they could survive best.

The figures have returned, music comes up, the figures are circling him. He looks at the gun.

It probably didn't work anyway.

As the figures close on him, he appears to be tossing the gun away and there is a bang.

The Wake

à
mon agent provocateur extraordinaire
alexandra cann

The Wake was first performed at the Abbey Theatre, Dublin, on 28 January 1998. The cast was as follows:

Vera	Jane Brennan
Mrs Conneeley	Pat Leavy
Finbar	David Herlihy
Henry	Stanley Townsend
Marcia	Anna Healy
Mary Jane	Olwen Fouere
Tom	Phelim Drew
Caitriona	Jennifer O'Dea
Father Billy	Seán Rocks
Norman	Simon Jewell/Brian Martin

Director Patrick Mason
Set Designer Francis O'Connor
Costume Designer Joan O'Clery
Music Conor Linehan
Lighting Ben Ormerod
Sound Dave Nolan
Stage Director Colette Morris

In subsequent performances of *The Wake* at the Abbey Theatre, Dublin (23 July to 12 August 1999), and the Edinburgh International Festival (16 to 21 August 1999), the part of **Henry** was played by Stephen Brennan.

Scene One

An open space: the country. Night.

Off, in the distance, a light. The purr of an engine, a car. It stops. The engine is switched off, then the lights.

And **Vera** *comes in, as one might to an empty church, warily. To stop, hold her breath, as if listening. Now she moves about silently. She comes to a stop, fixing on a memory of something or someone. A sigh overtakes her, she catches it back, holds it. And now releases it, her face moving into a smile of acceptance.*

She's thirty-seven. (Ideally, she is a large, handsome woman.) Urban dress: a wig, a mackintosh coat hangs open over a tan, suede suit; the skirt is a bit short . . . perhaps she hasn't quite got the hang of dress.

There is someone approaching. Not knowing what else to do, **Vera** *moves into the shadows.*

And **Mrs Conneeley** *arrives. She is unsure whether to stop or pass by . . .*

Mrs Conneeley *is in her sixties. A country woman. She is holding her long, unbuttoned coat about her: a long, man's type of coat. She is an unassuming woman; she has a lot of integrity, a lot of what used to be called 'nature'.*

Mrs Conneeley . . . Is it Vera?

Vera . . . Mrs Conneeley?

Mrs Conneeley Is it Vera? . . . D'you know we were saying it might be you – Aw, is it Vera! Paddy was above with the sheep while ago and saw the car, so I came over just in case. How are you, how are you!

Vera Mrs Conneeley.

Mrs Conneeley How are you? (*Her two hands are on top of* **Vera**'s.)

Vera Fine.

Mrs Conneeley You came home to pay your respects.

Vera   I did.

Mrs Conneeley   You did. Your poor grandmother. I wish we were meeting under different circumstances. Poor Winnie.

Vera   When I got the news I came home as quickly as I could arrange things. I! (*She flaps her hands to her sides, awkwardly.*)

Mrs Conneeley   I understand. But d'you know I'm so pleased to see you. And how are they all in town, your family?

Vera   Oh, they're all – I haven't seen them yet! They don't know I'm coming.

Mrs Conneeley   You didn't tell them!

Vera   No! Faster than a letter just to arrive.

Mrs Conneeley   That's going to be a great surprise for them.

Vera   It is.

Mrs Conneeley   'Tis. You'll come over for a cup of tea? No! – No now! No, you will! No! No!

Vera *laughs, responding to the warmth of the invitation.*

Mrs Conneeley   Leave – leave the car.

Vera   The air here!

Mrs Conneeley   Yes.

They are moving off together.

Vera   And I have another niece.

Mrs Conneeley   You have. And what's her name?

Vera   Carol.

Mrs Conneeley   That's a nice name . . .

Scene Two

Mrs Conneeley's *house: two chairs and a cooker.*

Vera *and* **Mrs Conneeley** *are coming in. (They have two cups of tea – this to avoid the fuss/business of making tea during the scene.) They are still in their overcoats.* **Vera** *is intoxicated by* **Mrs Conneeley**'s *warmth, house, conversation. And* **Mrs Conneeley** *is no less pleased with* **Vera**'s *company.*

Vera   They're good to me in all sorts of ways.

Mrs Conneeley   They send you all the news.

Vera   They're great like that. The house is lovely.

Mrs Conneeley   It's not bad – Oh, give me your coat, you'll be cold when you go out! Paddy and Julia are here with me. They're gone up to make the last hour in Melody's for a drink. Julia, his wife, she's nice. One of the Tierneys below? (*Meaning: 'Do you remember the Tierneys?'*) I've four grandchildren sleeping in there so I haven't many complaints in her. (*Going out with the coats:*) You're staying in the hotel?

Vera (*calls*)   It's closed down! They recommended that I sell it – (*Which, privately, casually, she finds odd, and she shrugs to herself.*) – and they're auctioning it for me.

Mrs Conneeley (*returning*)   I didn't know that – pull down to the fire. Fire? I miss the open hearth, d'you know, but if you open the door to the grate on this gazebo you at least have a place to spit.

Vera   And your other son?

Mrs Conneeley   Francis?

Vera   Francis.

Mrs Conneeley   Isn't he a solicitor. . . ? (*She is surprised and a little amused at Francis's success: what does* **Vera** *think of it.*)

Vera's *face expresses appreciation.*

Mrs Conneeley He's married too sure and has a practice in Newcastle.

Vera Mmm!

Mrs Conneeley And yourself?

Vera Oh!

Mrs Conneeley You haven't found him yet.

Vera Well, *some* relationships.

Mrs Conneeley Yes?

Vera I'm all right the way I am.

Mrs Conneeley Indeed and maybe you are and as well off! New York you're in all the time?

Vera Yes.

Mrs Conneeley Hah?

Vera Mainly.

Mrs Conneeley Now. And you're doing well?

Vera Quite well.

Mrs Conneeley Yes?

Vera Oh! – 'I've been a rover'.

Mrs Conneeley (*laughing*) Yes! – 'I've been a rover'.

Vera Still looking for myself.

Mrs Conneeley You are! 'I've been a rover.' I know. Lord, she was a powerful strong woman in her time. Mighty. (*She smiles shyly.*) She was very fond of you.

Vera *smiles.*

Mrs Conneeley You were a long time living with her.

Vera Eleven years.

Mrs Conneeley Eleven. Now. And she was lonely for you when they took you home again.

Vera I was lonely for her too. But I used to – long – to be with my family.

Mrs Conneeley I know.

Vera My brother and sisters.

Mrs Conneeley I understand.

Vera I used to – wonder – what had I done wrong for them to send me out here to live with grandma.

Mrs Conneeley It's a strange thing, isn't it? Loneliness. (*And she begins to laugh at loneliness.*) Well, isn't it? What does it mean? Sometimes, d'you know, I think about it and I have to laugh. What!? Married or single or widowed or as children – or married six times over maybe! – it's all the same, that's the way we are.

They smile at each other.

What'll we talk about next? (*Appreciatively; the cooker again:*) It makes great bread though. Paddy and Julia I know want me to sign this place over to them, but what's the hurry on them. I'm not dead yet. Well, I'm so pleased to see you.

They smile at each other.

Oh, and she could be cross?

Vera (*laughs*) She could.

Mrs Conneeley She had her ways. And not much loss in her, mind you, towards the end. The sight was what troubled her most. Oh now, when the sight begins to go, Vera. And you're not unlike her, God bless you: I can see the resemblance.

Vera What age did they put on the coffin?

Mrs Conneeley We were talking about that all right. Eighty-six?

Vera . . . Yes. That would be about right. She told me she was born . . . (**Vera** *smiles:*) About a half a dozen years after the century, she said.

Mrs Conneeley   That'd be about right then. Eighty-six. (*And they are pleased that no mistake was made on the breastplate of the coffin.*) . . . And sure you must be . . . Thirty-four?

Vera   The last time I saw thirty-four, Mrs Conneeley, was on top of a bus.

And they laugh at age until **Mrs Conneeley***, remembering her grandchildren, puts a finger to her lips.*

Vera   What day did she die?

Mrs Conneeley   What *day*? . . . Was it about the middle of February?

Vera   *Feb*ruary?

A dream is about to move into a nightmare.

Mrs Conneeley   Hah? . . . It's a terrible month for death.

Vera   I had thought . . .

Mrs Conneeley   . . . We thought all right when you weren't home for the funeral that maybe they forgot to tell you.

Vera   No! They write, they – We've been in constant touch – Well, about the hotel, the – Other matters. (*Smiles:*) It slipped their minds.

But **Mrs Conneeley** *has begun to smile painfully.*

Mrs Conneeley   . . . And sure she'd have lasted another ten years.

The smile closing on **Vera***'s face.*

Mrs Conneeley   Aw, God, Vera.

Vera*'s waiting apprehension.*

Mrs Conneeley   Sure she'd have lasted another ten years if someone got to her . . . (*She is waiting for permission to continue.*) I'd be ashamed if people were to think us bad neighbours.

Vera *nods, or half nods, slowly.*

Mrs Conneeley   She was very strong d'you know. But I knew for a good while the sight was going. You'd know it the way she wouldn't recognise you sometimes 'til you spoke. And I started to go over to see her? And tell Paddy, any time he was passing, to call in. Or I'd bring her over the drop of soup or whatever was going in the saucepan. That way. Because she was good. And I know well about that. And Paddy'd go over to give her the lift in the car to Mass of a Sunday, and home again afterwards. Or at least he'd ask, because sometimes she liked the walk. Or to take her to the village for her pension of a Friday. And the few groceries. But your brother didn't like it. Tom. Oh, I don't know. Maybe, I suppose, he thought we were after the farm. It happens. Well, it's his now. He has it stocked these two months. (*To herself:*) Hah?

Vera, *waiting, holding her breath.*

Mrs Conneeley *has been painfully smiling the above. Now the smile dissolving and hardening into anger, to stare at* **Vera**, *as if* **Vera** *were the enemy.*

Mrs Conneeley   But how much land does anyone need? I know how much land – *and* property – a person needs. How much land does your grandmother need now? Or the man who used to be my husband need? Or anyone else for that matter ... (*The anger dissolves the way it came, until she becomes soft again. To herself:*) You wouldn't know what's wrong with people. Unless it's something greatly innocent. (*Smiles at* **Vera**:) Hah? ... But your brother came out one evening and one of your sisters was with him. Paddy was in with her. And your brother followed Paddy out as Paddy was leaving to come home. And he said to Paddy: I'm sure you have more things to be doing than visiting old women. And tell your mother the same, he said. What could we do? Paddy was shaking telling me. What could we do? ... Poor Winnie.

Vera *nods.*

Mrs Conneeley   I think it was a Wednesday and Paddy

came in. Julia was there, feeding the youngest. I don't see
any smoke he said coming from Winnie Lally's, did ye see
her at all since Sunday? We left Julia there and went over
the road the two of us. First, to pass by, then look in the
windows. But it was hard to see in, d'you know. And I
called out her name? And Paddy tried the door, but it was
bolted from inside. I don't care he said then and I nodded
to him to go ahead.

Mrs Conneeley *has begun to weep, silently.*

Vera, *increasingly, has become upright in her chair. Now she is
nodding, positively, to continue.*

Mrs Conneeley   Oh she was dead. Oh she was dead,
Vera. (*Her mouth is dry: she is trying to swallow.*)

Vera, *bolt upright, waiting for her to continue.*

Mrs Conneeley   . . . She'd fell. She was there for a few
days, d'you know. She'd fell into the fire. But she got out
of it. She got out of it someway, the creature, crawled. But
couldn't get up. What could we do?

*She continues to weep. She emits a single wail. One hand, now, is
covering her eyes, the other is held out and back to* **Vera**. **Vera**
*takes the hand, holds it, absently. She is frowning-smiling. She shakes
her head to deny what she has heard; it won't go away: the frown-
smile keeps returning.*

Mrs Conneeley   . . . You're staying where? In the hotel?

Vera   Ahmmm . . .

Mrs Conneeley   That place is yours, isn't it?

Vera   It's, ahmmm, yes. It's closed down. It doesn't mean
anything to me. I have to, have to go now, the plane, get
away. (*She has risen. A vague movement/gesture for something – her
coat.*)

Mrs Conneeley   Hah? Sure you can't! Drive all that way
is it back to Dublin again tonight? Stay in the front room.
Do!

Vera No, I'll ... They're all I ... No, thanks.

Mrs Conneeley *goes out for* **Vera***'s coat.* **Vera***, alone, does not know what she is going to do, where she is going to go. A stifled sob.*

Vera They're all I have.

Mrs Conneeley *returns with* **Vera***'s coat: did* **Vera** *say something?* **Vera** *shakes her head.*

Mrs Conneeley I'm sorry. (*Her two hands on top of* **Vera***'s.*) But I'd be ashamed if people were to think us bad neighbours.

Vera There was no wake.

Mrs Conneeley There was no wake. There was an inquest.

Vera Heigh-ho!

Mrs Conneeley Will you call again before you go back? ...

She is showing **Vera** *out. The lights have faded to nothing.*

Scene Three

Someone lights a candle. **Finbar***. He has just got out of bed.*

Finbar*'s place: a single bed and a broken armchair. (Maybe, just out of the light, some bentwood chairs and a bastard table – 'A composite'.)*

Finbar *is forty-one, lives alone in squalor, a bachelor. A mess of hang-ups to do with class and sex. He is a product of a culture. (Lifted as a boy by 'the authorities' and put into care, brutalised there and sexually abused by the Christian Brothers.) He sells second-hand furniture and holy medals. 'Fuckin'!': a squeak, a nervous, vocal tic. Quick flash-point. A frightened scavenger.*

Finbar (*to himself*) What, what, who, Jesus? (*Feeble call:*) Is there someone there? ... (*To himself:*) Half past one in the morning. (*Calls:*) Just a! (*Coughs.*) Just a, just a! (*He turns it into a bout of coughing. Calls:*) Just a minute! (*To himself:*) I'll have to go out. Will I? . . . Fuckin'!

He pulls on his trousers, takes the candle and goes out to (what is meant to be) the front door.

Finbar (*en route or inside the front door*)   Yes?

Vera *is outside, mackintosh over her arm, overnight bag beside her, smiling.*

Vera   Hi!

Finbar   Yes?

Vera   Hi!

Finbar   Who?

Vera   Me! Vera!

Finbar (*to himself*)   Vera? . . . Vera. What are you doing here? (*He has 'opened the door'.*)

Vera   Hi!

Finbar   You put the!

Vera   Can I come in?

Finbar   Put the heart crossways in me!

Vera   Can I come in?

Finbar   . . . Liberty Hall as the fella says. Watch your step. Wait'll I light the way. Stick close to the wall. My antiques. The lights are gone . . . (*He has led her back to his room.*) Well! Well! This is a surprise! This is – how shall I put it? – a total surprise! Is that your car out there? – Sit down. And it was only the other day that I – No! sit on this: (*The bed.*) If you don't mind. The fuckin' springs are gone in that. And it was only the other – You'll excuse the French. And it was only the other day that I was thinking about you – You're welcome, sit down, you're welcome.

Vera   Thanks.

Finbar   What?

Vera   Nothing.

Finbar   The electricity. (*Is cut off.*)

Vera   Romantic.

Finbar   What?

Vera   No! (*Meaning, 'it's fine'.*)

Finbar   And I'm afraid it's the maid's day off.

Vera   It's great! (*The room is great.*) Would you like a drink?

Finbar   Now, that might not be!

The might not be a bad idea, and he goes out. Now that she is alone: her tired confusion and what on earth is she doing here.

Finbar (*off*)   A social call?

Vera   Yeh! . . . Is that okay?

Finbar   . . . Only be a sec!

Vera   No hurry!

She opens her jacket, the top button of her blouse, considers the next one down. She produces a bottle from her overnight bag. He returns with two wet glasses.

Finbar   Here we are. Well! Well! What's new?

Vera   Oh!

Finbar   Not much. I didn't know you were home – Did you feel the touch of frost out there? – When did you arrive?

Vera   Just now.

Finbar   Just? Did you!

Vera   Yeh. (*She is pouring the drinks.*)

Finbar   Speak your word said the guard at the gate, yes but bear it to Caesar straight!

Vera   Nice glasses.

Finbar   Now, they're special. They, would you believe, came out of a castle in Scotland.

Vera   Down the hatch!

Finbar   Down the!

They drink.

State of the place.

Vera   On the contrary.

Finbar   What?

Vera   On the contrary, Finbar.

Finbar (*nods. Then*)   And you only just arrived this minute?

Vera   Yeh.

Finbar   You came home for the auction, the hotel – saw the ad.

Vera   Yeh.

Finbar   Heard a good one. Fella goes into the doctor's yeh see and the doctor examines him anyway. I'm afraid says the doctor I've bad news for you, you've only three minutes to live, do you have a last request. And says your man: a soft-boiled egg? . . . What?

Vera *starts laughing.*

Finbar   Jesus! Jesus! A soft-boiled egg!

Vera   I drove into town of course. You know? Driving round: Where *is* everyone? Where *is* the place? It's like a ghost town down there.

Finbar   Yeh?! Jesus, this's lovely, what is it?

Vera   Bourbon.

Finbar   You're not serious! Humphrey Bogart!

Vera   Here's lookin' at you, kid!

Finbar   And at you!

Vera   Driving round the town: where will I go, where *can* I go? No place in my *own* home town to go to?! Had a bottle, didn't have a message, yeh? (*Then:*) Bingo! A name from the past, I thought what the hell, what the hell I thought, I'll try him, I'll *ask*, what can he do to you, the boy can only eat you for God's sake! I hope you don't mind?

Finbar   No, I don't –

Vera   I hope you don't mind, Finbar?

Finbar   No, I –

Vera   After all – Ah-haa! – that famous romance we had one time?

Finbar   Oh yes! (*Though it is not at this stage the foremost memory in his mind.*)

Vera   Wasn't that something – Wasn't-that-something! – Wasn't it, just!

Finbar   Yeh.

Vera   Ah-haa! How are you, Finbar?

Finbar   Not a bother.

Vera   You're okay?

Finbar   Living it up – as you can see.

Vera   You're okay?

Finbar   You can't take it with you.

Vera   You cannot take it with you, Finbar, and you can't come back for it either. (*Would he like his drink topped up:*) Hmm?

Finbar   I don't mind.

He draws his overcoat from among the bedclothes to drape it across his knees, to search the pockets.

Vera   Business?

Finbar   Would you like a gross or two of them glasses? Business, Vera? *Comme ci, comme ça,* up and down – Where did I leave them? Or a combination of canaries and stuffed parrots in a nice glass case? Can't find a fuckin' thing in the place since they cut me off. I'll do a deal for you. Yes, they cut the electricity on me. Oh, I'd pay them, no problem, *and* for the reconnection fee, but they're saying there's going to be a sudden general election and if that is to be the case, won't there be amnesties flying for everyone and anything from Mephisto O'Flynn our local politician. Where did I?

Vera   Cigarettes?

Finbar   D'you have some?

Vera   I have come prepared.

She is unzipping her overnight bag again, her head is down.
Finbar*'s misgivings/interest/calculation, watching her.*

Finbar   (*humourlessly*)   I must have left mine on the piano. Yes, I was thinking about you there lately.

Vera   Nothing good I hope, something bad I hope sincerely.

Finbar   No but, were you due another visit. We don't see you very often.

Vera   (*looks up: something childlike*)   But I think of here.

Finbar   What?

Vera   (*producing carton of cigarettes*)   Now we have all the essentials. Almost.

Finbar   Your mother's funeral, Lord have mercy on the soul of the woman, was the last time (*'you were home'.*), wasn't it?

Vera   There's been another death in the family since.

Finbar   They come in threes. Who?

Vera My grandmother. (*She gives him a pack of cigarettes.*)

Finbar Oh yes!

Vera She damn near brought me up.

Finbar Out the country. Thanks. (*For cigarettes.*) That was when we met. You weren't that long back in from the country.

Vera Wasn't that something – Ah-haa! – when we met, wasn't it, just, Finbar!

Finbar Jesus! (*And laughs: there is, now, a bitterness entering the memory.*)

Vera (*childlike again for a moment*) They say that I resemble her?

Finbar Yeh? Jesus!

Vera My grandmother. We shared the big bed – (*He is returning the pack of cigarettes to her.*) Keep them. Her bed. Sometimes I didn't have to go to school at all. 'Ah stay there, child, it's too cold to get up.' The two of us – I ask you! – my grandmother and myself, sitting up in bed for half the day – singing! (*Sings:*) 'Carry me back to ol' –' I ask you, Finbar, singing songs!

Finbar Sorry to hear that.

Vera For God's sake, eighty-six years of age – A good innings: Isn't that what you'd say yourself? – she's dead since February. (*She is searching for and finds her cigarette lighter.*) People used to say that she was cross: she *wasn't* cross: she was shy. (*Then, as she lights his cigarette:*) Can I stay?

Finbar Thanks. (*For the light.*)

Vera The hotel is closed down.

Finbar 'Tis.

Vera Can I stay?

Finbar . . . Why?

Vera   I need to – Just somewhere to crash. For a few hours.

Finbar   Sleep?

Vera   Yeh. Whatever.

Finbar   Is this what you do in America?

Vera   Yeh! (*And laughs.*)

Finbar (*laughs. Then*)   But! The place: chock-a-block. Furniture, my antiques – You saw them out there yourself: The hall, the! (*The rest of the house.*) They haven't been shifting too fast lately. So, there's only here. (*This room.*) And! (*Points:*) Backkitchen.

Vera   This is fine.

Finbar   A dealer – You would not believe it, Vera – can leave nothing outside his door any more. There's no respect left for law and order. Why should there be! The tinkers? – The rich are worse! – Pick up the papers! And there's only a few of them caught! And *they* get off! They're given presents of Mercs to get off in! And fuckin' quarter-million-pound handshakes! I think things have become so bad there's no one any more that knows how bad they are. So where do you go?

Vera   The rich will always be with us.

Finbar   What? . . . They will! Can't leave a blessed, single, fuckin' thing out there! Well, at least nothing that's portable. Did you see anything in my garden as you were coming in that you could lift? You'd have to be a very strong man. No the only things I keep out there are heavy. That out there is my hernia department, rupture land, and let any or all enter it at their peril to test their strength. So, yeh see, chock-a-block. Nice lighter. (*He is toying with her lighter.*)

Vera   This is fine if it's all right with you.

Finbar (*shrugs that it's all right with him – but he won't say it*)   . . . What would your family think, your brother say, your sisters?

Vera Who's to know?

Finbar Because – can I be frank? Though it's a well-known fact that these are not the Middle Ages, the authorities in this town can be very serious people. *I'm* the one they say is the danger, an enemy to their order? I'll tell you. Because, unlike my colleague in the antique business up the road there, John-John McNulty, who can say fuck them, *and mean it*, the reason why I say fuck them is because I'm frightened of every single one of them. D'you get my drift?

Vera D'you want me to leave?

Finbar Did *I*?! (*Did he say that.*) Would *I*! . . . I'm only a simple man, that's all I'm saying. (*'You'*) Can stay as long as you like as far as I'm concerned.

Vera (*a silent*) Thanks.

Finbar *shrugs 'Not at all'. He sips. He is still toying with her lighter. Now, a resentment is growing in him.*

Finbar That's settled then. Haven't a thing in my stomach. No but, what I was thinking back there was, you gave me one of these, one something like this one, one time.

Vera Did I?

Finbar You did.

Vera A lighter?

He nods.

You gave me a fountain pen.

Finbar I know I did. But!

She waits.

I know I did.

Vera (*'It was'*) A long time ago.

Finbar   A long time ago, yes.

Vera   We were kids.

Finbar   We were kids – I know we were. We were children. But I stole that fucking thing for you, yeh know.

Vera   You did not!

Finbar   Ooh! your people never stole anything?

Vera   Did you?

Finbar   Can I have another drink? (*As she pours it:*) Stole that fuckin' pen out of Mooney's.

Vera (*extends the freedom of the bottle*)   Help yourself.

Finbar   Thanks. And you wrote me off.

Vera   . . . No.

Finbar   No?

Vera   *You* were the –

Finbar   No! – Vera! – Now! – You!

Vera   *You* were the one who –

Finbar   Oh-ho Jesus, that family of yours!

Vera   There is nothing wrong with my . . . (*Automatic defence of her family that tails off into a silent 'well'.*)

Finbar   What? (*And laughs harshly at her.*)

Vera (*to herself*)   Heigh-ho! (*To him:*) Yes?

Finbar   They didn't like you – consorting? – with the likes of me?

Vera   Yes?

Finbar   Protecting you from me?

Vera   Yes?

Finbar   There never was such a tale of woe than that of Juliet and her Romeo! They were scandalised.

Vera But you were the one who gave in to them.

Finbar *I* was the one? – I wasn't the one!

Vera Oh-you-were.

Finbar Well, you can bet your sweet – Why wouldn't I be the one?!

Vera Do you know the defiance a schoolgirl is capable of?

Finbar . . . What?

Vera This is childish.

She appears to dismiss the matter. But, on reflection, her stand against her family in childhood interests her. She gestures **Finbar** *to continue while she* tries *to work it out: perhaps she will defy her family again, with* **Finbar***: perhaps this is why she came here.* **Finbar** *laughs:*

Finbar The pressures! Your father, Char*les* P. O'Toole, your mother, your – the fucking sheriff: they even got the superintendent of the guards in to have a word with me! Because we were *walking* out the road together! What? They brought in what-was-his-name? – Bollicky Bill – rubbing the lapels of his holy black jacket – who summoned me to the presbytery for a serious interview. If you'd had been a skivvy, a maid, he'd have made me marry you! Me, all of sixteen years of age!

Vera They called the doctor for me to examine – my tonsils! (*And she starts laughing.*)

Finbar They became very serious. I don't know if they considered assassination.

Vera My mother pulled my hair –

Finbar (*laughing harshly*) Nickerdepazze!

Vera The nuns sprinkled holy water – (*She demonstrates how they did it.*) – Ah-haa!

Finbar Aw but *you* missed out on the Christian Brothers: Wait'll I tell you –

Vera   They didn't have to assassinate you. Someone got you a job: Mac – Goozelum's – messenger boy, the butcher shop. That's how they got *you*. But, a schoolgirl: I would've died for you then to go on defying them.

Finbar   . . . What's up? What're you at?

Vera   Nothing that I know of as yet.

Finbar   Help me make it through the night.

Vera   Can I stay for two nights? I'm booked to go back Wednesday morning. (*Shrugs:*) I'd prefer not to have to check in anywhere. And – twenty-four years later? – we take up where we left off. What d'you like? Anyway you like. And, bob's your uncle. D'you get *my* drift?

He nods.

D'you know what I mean, Finbar?

Finbar   Yeh.

Vera   Settled then?

Finbar   No problem.

She nods, 'settled'. They sip. Something beginning to worry him: a problem.

The car. (*She doesn't understand.*) What about your car out there? The Punjab: This is the Punjab you're in now, i.e., the New Estate!

Vera   Does it matter?

Finbar   As it is, there mightn't be a wheel left under it already. No, let me think this one out.

Vera   Leave it until morning.

Finbar (*reflectively*)   I'd better do it now while I'm drunk.

She laughs at him. Then he laughs too.

Vera   Don't leave it near the hotel.

Finbar   Give me the keys.

Vera Can you drive?

Finbar Ooh! Is it an aeroplane then? (*He has put on a jacket, is putting on his old overcoat.*) I'll think of some place safe. Yeh. Though I know someone will spot me: This town! (*Takes up his glass.*) What d'you think of me now is it any harm to ask?

Vera I couldn't give a fuck about you.

Finbar Here's lookin' at you, kid. (*And knocks back his drink.*) Back in a tick.

Vera We'll have a nice time.

Finbar In case you're interested: that's a candle, and my place of ablutions is out there.

He's gone.

Vera's *private self. Her gathering depression. She takes off her wig. The broken armchair, the small bed: she bows to them. She starts to undress, down to her slip. She takes something from her overnight bag, takes the candle and goes out.*

Scene Four

A long, dining-room table, antique, and some chairs: **Henry Locke-Browne**'s.

A child, seated at the table over his homework, looks lost in this space. His head comes up to think, and continues up, becoming frozen in a mystery that perhaps has no answer: **Norman**, *aged eleven.*

At a remove from **Norman**, *his back to us, standing, looking at nothing,* **Henry**.

Norman Dad?

Henry *does not register* **Norman**'s *whisper for a moment. He too is lost in this moment of time. He looks at his watch as if he were puzzled by it. He is middle-aged, a drop-out lawyer who does not practise; disillusioned, an alcoholic, an urbane one. The culture has defeated him. He does not know who he is. This evening – and* *perhaps yesterday – he is playing the role of father. His concentration span in causes/interests is short-lived. Today is his third day on the dry.*

Norman   Dad?

He goes to **Norman**. **Norman** *has a problem with his homework.* **Henry** *refers him to an earlier page in a textbook for the answer. He hears his wife arriving – a minor movement of his head. He refuses to be impressed by his wife.*

And **Marcia** *comes in, drawing a pushchair/pram behind her. She looks like* **Vera** *but she's bigger. Overcoat. Almost invariably her expression is one of alarm. She's not the brightest. She is trying not to make any unnecessary noise, but her face is pregnant with news. She likes to get the most out of telling a story in order to distress herself the more. She is in awe of her* **Henry**; *she loves him.*

Marcia   ... You'll never guess what.

Henry   You're late.

Marcia   I've good reason to be.

Henry   Tck!

Marcia   No, wait'll you hear.

Henry   Pram?

Marcia (*silent 'oh!' then*)   Sorry.

And she pushes the pushchair/pram out of the room. The pushchair/pram and its contents are not allowed in this room.

Henry (*to* **Norman** *who was interested in his mother's news*)   Twenty-five minutes.

Norman *resumes working.* **Henry** *sits with a book and* **Marcia** *returns.*

Marcia   ... Vera.

Henry   Yes.

Marcia (*disappointed*)   Did you hear?

Henry   I didn't! (*And a warning/checking glance in* **Norman**'s *direction.*)

Marcia (*distressed for a moment*)   Lord!

Henry (*casually*)   Is she dead?

Marcia*'s superstition of his last.*
He blows a silent sigh.

Marcia   She's back!

Henry   Yes?

Marcia   Since Monday.

Henry   Yes?

Marcia   Four days! – No, wait'll I tell you. And d'you
know what she's doing? . . . Living with the tinkers. Henry!
With that old thing, with that old sponger, that old
layabout, Reilly, Finbar Reilly, the medal man, up in the
New Estate.

Henry   In the Punjab? (*He's interested.*)

Marcia   In this town, our Vera!

Henry   Norman, apply yourself!

Marcia   With that old trick-o'-the-loop, that old –

Henry   In the Punjab?

Marcia   In the Punjab, up in the Punjab! Weren't the
guards up there! Because of the car. Someone reported it –
Didn't I see them myself walking round it, writing down
the number!

Henry   What car?

Marcia   Oh, stop, Henry! The car, the car, the car sure!

Henry   Hold, child. (*Then a glance at* **Norman** *to check on
him:*) Twenty minutes. What car?

Marcia   The big silver one! Isn't it parked in the street
up the road round the corner. Four days! No one knowing
whose it was or how it came to be there, someone reported

it to the guards and they traced it to Dublin – Hertz! They found out it was rented to Vera in Dublin. Don't you know the way she is and sure it must've cost her the earth. How could the guards or anyone have known if she was alive or dead or kidnapped, Tom said. Tom is in a desperate state. Then someone saw Finbar Reilly skulking the back streets early the other morning and the guards drove up to him and there she was. But wait'll you hear. Because then the guards thought Tom would like to know. You know the way he worries and tries to be a father to us all.

Henry (*irritably*)   Yes-yes.

Marcia   And Tom drove up there and knocked at the door. But d'you know what she did? 'How yeh doin':' That was all he said to her! 'I only want to talk to you for a minute.'

Henry   Yes?

Marcia   She was in her underwear.

Henry   Yes?

Marcia   Slammed the door in his face. She nearly took the nose off him he said.

Henry   She was frightened of him.

Marcia (*through her tears*)   Pardon?

Henry   He frightens me.

Marcia   Tom?

Henry   Is that it?

Marcia   I thought you were going out to play bridge?

Henry   Is-that-it?!

Marcia   No. Tom and Mary Jane will be here in a minute to see Norman.

Henry   Norman?

Marcia   They want to talk to Vera.

Henry   What has Norman got to do with it?

Marcia (*licks her lip for the answer*)   Vera has always given him money?

Henry *shakes his head.*

Marcia   The Tintin comics she sends him that she reads herself?

Henry *shakes his head.*

Marcia   They were writing a letter when I left them?

Henry *nods.*

Marcia   It's urgent – it's very urgent – That must be them arriving now. And they were saying that if Norman took it up to her she wouldn't slam the door in *his* face. (*She is moving off.*)

Henry   A moment. (*Wait a moment.*)

Marcia   What is she trying to do to us?

Henry (*angrily*)   Marcia!

Marcia   Sorry. (*Returning obediently.*)

Henry   If a child is required for this diplomatic manoeuvre why cannot one of Tom's be engaged for the purpose?

Marcia   They're in Newcastle, being looked after by their granny: Caitriona's nerves are gone again.

Henry   I'm not surprised.

He dismisses her and she goes out. **Henry** *has a new interest. He becomes conscious of* **Norman** *who, now, smiles at him. There is gentleness, regret in* **Henry**'s *voice:*

Twenty minutes, my son.

Mary Jane, **Marcia** *and* **Tom** *come in.*

Mary Jane *is the (smallest and) cleverest of the O'Tooles. She and* **Henry** *had a romance one time: she dropped him. Something she has* *lost or betrayed has made her hard, cynical, impatient – and innocent. On this occasion she tries to rein herself, putting up with* **Tom**. *(She and* **Tom** *have done a deal and she does not want to lose her part of it.) Refer* **Henry***'s description of her, Scene Six.*

Tom. *Refer* **Henry***'s and* **Vera***'s remarks, Scene Six. He looks an inoffensive type. His jacket is never unbuttoned. It is difficult to insult him. (Or this is a defence mechanism, now ingrained in him, adopted from the culture.) Almost invariably he is professionally jolly or professionally sad/concerned/angry. At the moment he is sad.*

Mary Jane   Oh?! (*She did not expect to find* **Henry** *in.*)

Henry (*a charming host*)   Ah! Mary Jane!

Mary Jane   How are you, Henry!

Henry   I am very well, thank you! And you?

Mary Jane   I am very well! Norman!

Tom   My friend. (*His hand out for a handshake.*)

Henry (*bows, but keeps his hands behind his back*)   The Irish family O'Toole! And your good husband Declan, Mary Jane?

Mary Jane   He's fine! Do you have change, Tom?

Tom (*producing his wallet*)   We thought we'd find you out.

Henry   No, oh ho-ho, I'm in!

Tom   You're a gas man.

Henry   And your good wife Caitriona?

Tom   But we're disturbing this man (**Norman**) in his work.

Henry   Ara what! (**Henry***'s brogue: meaning 'not at all'.*)

Tom   Now: For Norman. (*A fiver to* **Mary Jane**.)

Mary Jane   Norman.

Norman *looks at his father.*

Henry   Accept. And give it (*'to'*) your mother, and she will give you a thruppence for it.

Norman   Thanks. (*And pockets the fiver.*)

Henry   I have undertaken his tutelage.

Tom   I's wonderful.

Henry   You'll take a drink: Tom, Mary Jane?

Marcia   Henry! (*Alarmed.*)

Henry (*gestures his freedom from alcohol*)   I am completing day three! I shall never again take a drink in this life: Perhaps not even in the next. Tea, woman of the house.

Tom   I can see the difference in you already.

Henry   True as Our Lady is in heaven.

Tom   Gas.

Marcia, *relieved, has gone out.* **Norman** *resumes his homework.*

Tom (*sad, sits*)   Yeh heard.

Henry   I'm sorry?

Tom *shakes his head, sadly.*

Henry (*shrugs to himself his feigned incomprehension, then brightly*)   Well, Mary Jane, you don't *look* very well!

Mary Jane   No? How are you?

Henry   Beano! Groceries selling well?

Mary Jane   Dandy!

Tom (*becomes a good sport*)   Well, ye're a nice pair the three of ye! (*He warms to himself:*) 'Twas morning last night when ye came in. Now if this's to continue it'll have to stop cause if ye want to stay here ye'll have to find somewhere else! The landlady bejakers! (*But he grows solemn again: he has produced an envelope – the letter.*) Well if this's what the world is coming to, I don't know where it's going; if this's what we're bringing up our children for: Can anyone explain that to me, Henry?

Henry   Excuse me? (*And, then, he looks at* **Mary Jane** *for an explanation or interpretation.*)

Mary Jane   Vera.

Tom   Vera.

Henry (*to himself*)   Vera?

Mary Jane   Marcia told you! (*Trace of annoyance, impatience.*)

Henry   Yes. That Vera has returned from – New York? – and something about delivering a letter – Is that the one? – and everyday, common-or-garden matters, but – Lost: what has produced this air of grief?

Tom   Did Marcia not tell you where our sister is presently residing?

Henry   Did Marcia not tell me where . . . ?

Tom   For the past four days!

Henry   I believe she – (*Thinks.*) – Yes, she did. But what is the problem?

Tom*'s mouth growing a silent, smiling 'what?'*

Mary Jane   Oh come on, Henry.

Henry   Mary Jane?

Tom   Ve-ra! Ve-ra! –

Mary Jane (*to calm him*)   Tom –

Tom   'What's the problem?'! She's us in a flaming pickle, we're in a moral fix.

Mary Jane (*to* **Tom**)   Just a sec –

Tom   Vera! When morality goes out the door anything can happen!

Mary Jane   Tom –

Henry   Not bad. (**Tom***'s near epigram.*)

Tom   What's *your* problem, Henry?

Mary Jane   Just a sec. May I smoke?

Henry   Please.

Mary Jane   But the point now is –

Henry   What age is she? – Excuse me, Mary Jane. Would you care to sit down? She must be forty years of age if she's a day?

Mary Jane   She's –

Tom   I don't know and I don't care what age she is but she's old enough to know better than go disgracing herself and her family and her morals in this manner. Is this what our father and mother worked hard for all their lives? What's she trying to do to us? Can she have so completely forgotten her upbringing? New York indeed and I'm sure is New York but a name means something here. It may be the nineties, (*but*) what's wrong is wrong – Even if it was the year two thousand, i's diabolical – The twenty-first century for that matter, I would be astonished and – Henry – I, for one, refuse – cannot-cannot – refuse to turn a blind eye – my conscience.

Henry   Don't follow.

Mary Jane   She's pushing thirty-eight.

Tom   All that we've been trying to do for her – for how long, Mary Jane? – Trying to look after her affairs. And now – I've a responsible government job to mind and children to rear in proper manner. And now, when her affairs are about to be finalised – and there was never any mention in the correspondence, from her or from us, about coming home, was there?

Mary Jane   No –

Tom   She arrives out of the blue and goes to live up there with your man! D'you not flaming see?

Henry   Well, when you put it that way. She must have a reason.

Tom   What?!

Henry Yes. And, come to think of it, it is odd, strange behaviour from Vera because, I must say, I have always found her rather – shy? No?

Mary Jane We're concerned about her, Henry.

Henry Mary Jane? (*He's trying to bait* **Mary Jane**.) Why, I almost called her – backward. No?

Mary Jane, *refusing bait, lights her cigarette at this point.*

Henry These affairs of hers that you've been looking after: Has anything gone awry in that department that might have upset her?

Tom What?!

Henry This setting up of the auction of the hotel –

Mary Jane It's going to be a *public* auction.

Henry Oh, I know that.

Tom Everyone knows that!

Henry 'Deed they do, man dear alive!

Mary Jane (*to* **Tom**) Just a second! (*To* **Henry**:) Vera isn't shy *or* backward. (*To* **Tom** *again*:) Excuse me! I think I detect something here. (*To* **Henry**:) Yes?

Henry You're concerned about Vera, Mary Jane.

Mary Jane We're concerned about the hotel.

Tom (*quietly*) Yes, and –

Mary Jane (*still to* **Henry**) We want it. Now, do you find anything odd, strange, questionable – aberrant? – in *our* behaviour!

Henry *gestures: Take the floor.*

Mary Jane Because if you do, I'll have to say that you are frankly dafter than I thought.

Tom We're only, Henry, trying to –

Mary Jane   Look! Look, we are not going to insult
anybody's intelligence by explaining or discussing what is
natural, reasonable, commonsensical – Excuse me, Tom!
Next thing, we'd end up discussing American, hippy, gutter
– mysticism! Excuse me, Tom! We want the hotel. We
want to get our sister out of that place. We must. And, as
it happens, we need your help. Okay so far?

Henry *gestures: She has the floor.*

Mary Jane   Well, it may surprise you or it may not,
Vera is a very difficult woman. I'd like to have done with
this one because it's pfff-rubbish! Yes, people always
commented on her shyness, even among the rest of us, the
family –

Tom   She wasn't like one of us at all.

Mary Jane   Excuse me! Reticent nature? It's so-called.
Where is she at this moment? I have always known it.
Father on about her lack of 'go'. Who high-tailed it out of
here – whenever she liked – Did we? Mother ranting on
about her not pushing herself, taking a lead, what was to
become of her. *Ranting.* Maybe that's why mother – to our
surprise – left her the hotel.

Tom   The woman was a saint sure –

Mary Jane   Just – (*A second.*)

Tom   But she wasn't right in the head towards the end.

Mary Jane   For a shy person, Vera has always managed
to get an extraordinary amount of attention and managed
extraordinarily to do anything she liked. (*Silently:*) Oh! And
the rumour – maybe you've heard it, maybe you've not –
about our Vera's 'line of business' in America?

Tom   What?

Mary Jane   I know that Marcia hasn't heard it and I
wouldn't like to be the one to mention it to her, let alone
mention it in a room where there is a child.

Tom   What?

Mary Jane (*angrily*)   I told you!

Tom (*to himself; he refuses to believe the rumour*)   No.

Mary Jane (*to* **Henry**)   I'm not being uncharitable.

Tom (*to himself*)   No.

Mary Jane (*continues to* **Henry**)   She's not ungenerous – oh boy can she be generous! And she's intelligent – She's not backward: That's the maddening thing. Look! Look, I didn't want to get into this – pfff! – at all.

Tom (*sympathetically*)   Mary Jane.

Mary Jane   I'm telling you what-we're-dealing-with: She cannot be trusted.

Tom   She's a messer, Henry.

Mary Jane   Too many contradictions and surprises from our Vera. And d'you know what it's all about? She thinks she's special. Oh she *knows* that she is special. (*As if* **Henry** *had contradicted her*:) But I know it! It's enough for the rest of us to realise we have only one life to live and try to make the best of it, Vera has to go one better. There's only one Vera, there will never be another: not 'til or after kingdom-come or ever. And she is being 'true' to her – uniqueness. And while she's working out this extraordinary individuality of hers, whatever comes into her head she's going to do it, be it sink or swim for everyone around her. Without thought, fear of consequences – Be it sink or swim for *herself*! That's what we're dealing with. She's capable of anything. Now, I don't know what her next surprise in this present circumstance is going to be – could be a big one! – but, if I can help it, it's not going to happen at my expense. Or his. (**Tom***'s*.)

Tom   Or Marcia's.

Mary Jane   Okay, Henry?

Henry   I could wait on your company (**Mary Jane***'s*) for ever.

Tom   Okay, Henry?

Henry   I begin to follow.

Tom (*touched*)   Do you?

Norman   Dad?

Henry (*to* **Norman**)   Five minutes.

Mary Jane   Questions?

Henry   The Imperial Hotel, this jewel in the crown of the family fortunes. (*To* **Tom**.) You will buy it at the auction.

Mary Jane   Absolutely.

Henry   Any price.

Tom   Birthright.

Mary Jane   She won't be left go short. She will get what she deserves.

Henry   I see. And the letter, Mary Jane?

Mary Jane   It's a request, simply, for her to come out and sit down with us, calmly, at a table.

Tom   Since we can't go into that 'No-Go' area.

Henry   And you want it delivered.

Mary Jane   In view of the reception she gave earlier today to Tom, his going up there again is unlikely to succeed.

Henry   Mary Jane.

Mary Jane   Marcia won't.

Henry   Yes. And?

Mary Jane   Well, I'm hardly the one to do it. I mean, to stand on some knacker's doorstep, talking to my sister in her underwear? I'd die.

Henry   Ah!

Mary Jane   So, with your permission of course, Norman.

Tom   Because whatever else about her, you were saying, Mary Jane, she responds to children.

Mary Jane   Frankly, she does.

Tom   And she's always, you were saying, Mary Jane, had a special affection for Norman.

Mary Jane   Who would blame her. Frankly.

Henry   Check! Norman, it is time!

Tom   And there are articles in the hotel that Marcia wants and should have.

Henry   Now I follow.

Norman *is tidying up his books.* **Marcia** *is coming in with a tray of tea things.*

Tom   The solidarity of a family in trouble.

Henry   Indeed.

Tom   I's moving.

Henry   Oh pull back there bejesus and mind the dresser! (*Make room for* **Marcia**.) And from as far back as my young manhood I considered that family O'Toole was warmth itself. Remember, I tried not one but two of your sisters for membership. Ah, as we roved the grove summer evenings, Mary Jane's enthusiasms about Daddy and Mammy, Tom and her sisters, loyalties and sibling rivalries, innocent banter 'cross the table, storytelling round the hearth at night, domesticity full of simple pleasures to scald the lonely heart of this orphan boy.

Tom   Gas man.

Henry   I first plied Mary Jane here with my earnest suit. Admission denied.

Tom   Gas.

Henry   My perseverence, bejesus, and persistence! I knocked upon Marcia's door and she took me in.

Tom   Gas.

Henry   You may leave.

Norman *leaves.*

Henry   No, Norman.

Tom   But?

Henry *smiles a 'Hmm?' to him, a 'Hmm?' to* **Mary Jane**.

Mary Jane   I understand. It is always difficult for in-laws in these little family affairs. Tom, Marcia and I, somehow, the immediate family are of course the ones to deal with it.

Henry   ('*T*') Protest! Your attentiveness in bringing this matter to my home and including me in the family conference: Solidarity. As a first step towards resolution an interview with Finbar Reilly is crucial. Put yourselves in my hands. I shall see to it personally and at once.

Mary Jane   No –

Henry   Not at all! My father the colonel died in the Punjab, in a house owned by a Mrs Scarry, I believe.

Tom   But – (*He has the letter in his hand.*)

Henry (*takes the letter*)   That too: I shall deliver it. Brave men lived before Agamemnon, and still.

And he leaves purposefully, removing his jacket – as for a change of dress. **Marcia** *looks alarmed,* **Mary Jane** *has misgivings but it is too late,* **Tom***'s smile is widening and beginning to freeze.*

Scene Five

Finbar*'s. Candlelight. A couple of bentwood chairs and a rickety table have been called into play. (The table is 'a composite': component parts are stylistically at odds, salvaged pieces from other furniture.)*

Another light, off, in the back-kitchen – candle or flashlamp – where **Finbar** *is doing something.*

And **Vera** *is in bed, smoking, depressed, singing. Her slip, now, is dirty and she has not brushed her hair in four days. She has decided, it appears, that as long as* **Finbar** *keeps talking she will keep singing: 'Carry me back home to Old Virginia'. (The song, though no issue is made of it, was one of her grandmother's songs.)*

Vera　'Carry me back to Old Virginia . . .'

Finbar *(off)*　Oh but nice clean people are the O'Tooles!

Finbar *comes in with plates, bread, mugs, a tin of beans for the table. Then:*

Finbar　Wouldn't you think she'd get up! Wouldn't you think she'd! Get dressed! Wash herself! *(Going out again.)* Wouldn't you think she'd!

Finbar *is back with a tin-opener to open the tin of beans. A beat. And:*

Finbar　Two nights you asked for –

Vera　'Carry me back . . .'

Finbar　Two nights! you asked for for to stay here –

Vera　'To ol' Virginie, that's where the cotton –'

Finbar　Now there's four gone –

Vera　'An the corn an' taties grow –'

Finbar　Now the fifth starting! –

Vera　'That's where the birds warble sweet in the springtime –'

Finbar　Uff! *(He throws down the tin-opener – he's hurt his finger – and goes out again.)* Fuckin'!

Vera　'That's where this ol' darky's heart am long to go.' *(And she blows a sigh to herself.)*

Finbar *returns with a box of new tin-openers. He unwraps one.*

Finbar　And bringing the red-necks up here to me in their uniforms and squad car. Fuckin' guards watching every hands turn I make all my life already, and Mr Tom

O'Toole after that on his BMW. Is it that you want to go bringing them up here to me again?

Vera (*to herself*)   Yeh.

Finbar   And aul' ones out there this evening, coming up here for a gawk at my house when the news had broke. Linking one another for safety: the way aul' ones like to take a look at a place where a man has hanged himself.

Vera (*reasonably*)   You fucked me twenty minutes ago.

Finbar . . . (*an astonished whisper*)   What?!

Vera   He fucked me twenty minutes ago so what is he complaining about?

Finbar   Oh nice clean – Wouldn't you think she'd – And I've a man in the morning calling early about a lock of bentwood chairs! (*Completing opening the tin:*) Neglecting my business. (*And off to dump the box of tin-openers:*) Fuckin' Taiwan!

Vera (*sighs to herself*)   Oh fuck off.

Finbar (*returning*)   Nice clean people and they at one another's throats after the mother dying last year when it became known that the one in America had inherited the hotel over all their heads.

Vera (*to herself*)   Oh fuck off.

Finbar   The town is delighted. (*Then, hearing in retrospect what she said, another astonished whisper:*) What?!

Vera   Oh fuck off.

Finbar   . . . *You* fuck off!

Vera   Oh fuck off.

Finbar   *You* fuck off – *You* fuck off!

Vera   'Carry me back to ol' Virginie!'

Finbar   By Jesus, by Jesus, it's hard to credit it was from the nuns that you learned your manners!

Vera   'Wouldn't you think she'd.'

Finbar   What?

Vera   Wash herself.

Finbar   Wouldn't you think she would!

Vera   Look at the place! Look at the place!

Finbar   I'm looking.

Vera   How does anyone live like this?

Finbar   Ooh! –

Vera   Woodlice!

Finbar   What?

Vera   Woodlice! The place is infested with them! –

Finbar   No –

Vera   Out there – Woodlice! – waddling their lives in the dark in the damp across that floor out there! –

Finbar   No! –

Vera   Over there then – look at them *now*! – doing pilgrimages by candlelight up the fucking walls!

Finbar   Ooh! but the O'Tooles set the highest standards –

Vera   'Carry me back! –'

Finbar   Fighting like cats and dogs over property!

Vera   Fuck off!

Finbar   *You* fuck off, *you* fuck off, that's what *I'm* saying to *you*!

Vera   How! do people live like this?

Finbar   There's the door for you there!

Vera   *starts whistling her song, crosses her arms – whatever: A gesture that she's staying put.*

Finbar   But methinks they've come to some arrangement

of late, the O'Tooles, because the tempest has died down among them. And Tom O'Toole, short of going on the radio to broadcast it, has made it known to all and sundry that he'll be bidding for the hotel at the auction. A hotel, yes, but once the family home as well and, with the clergy behind him and considering our history against the English, who will bid against an honest man attempting to get back the homestead? He'll get the place for nothing.

Vera (*blankly/blandly*)   Yeh? (*But it's further news and hurt.*)

Finbar   Yeh! Them are the rules. That's the way it goes.

Vera   And there's a rat about the place.

Finbar   A?

Vera   There's a rat about the place.

Finbar   No.

Vera   There's a rat about, in, the place!

Finbar   No rat –

Vera   I saw him!

Finbar   No rat in –

Vera   Several times!

Finbar   No rat in this!

Vera   A rat, a fucking pet, a pet fucking rat!

Finbar   A fucking –

Vera   I feel sorry for him! – he doesn't even bother to run –

Finbar   A fucking mouse!

Vera   I don't think he's able to run!

Finbar   Keep your voice down –

Vera   He's lost heart! – who would blame him?

Finbar   Oh but they're –

Vera   Only waiting for someone to bring the back of a shovel down on his head!

Finbar   Oh but they're getting the one from America, no half measures.

Vera   How – WHY – do people live like this?

Finbar   Rooking her, screwing her – They are!

Vera (*swings her legs out of the bed*)   Heigh-fucking-why-ho! (*Slips on her shoes.*) And if you move anything: tawny, yellow, almost see-through, fast-moving strings of evil-looking fucking things that move in and out precisely.

Finbar   They are!

Vera   And this poxy little bed that would cripple you. (*She stands.*)

He watches her suspiciously. (He's frightened of her.) She gets her handbag without knowing what she wants from it. She produces an aerosol tin of something from it and throws it aside onto the floor. She turns her bag upside down, spilling the contents onto the bed and she stares with puzzlement down at them.

Finbar (*through the above*)   They are! . . . So they are . . . I don't know yet where the in-laws fit in.

Vera   Cockroaches in New York?

Finbar   But I'm working on it.

Vera   All this place needs is seagulls. (*She takes a mug from the table and she goes out.*)

Finbar (*calls after her*)   His majesty, Mr Henry Locke-Browne, Lord Henry, barrister-at-law who doesn't practise and friend of the working classes! (*He picks up the aerosol tin, returns it to the contents of her bag. To himself:*) No rat in this. (*Calls:*) Or 'The doctor's daughter', Caitriona, Mr Tom O'Toole's missus, Caitriona! (*The contents of her bag are on the bed in front of him. He steals some money out of her wallet.*) But I'm working on it. So I am. But I'm the one in all this is going to end up in handcuffs. (*Calls:*) Or the other fella,

Mary Jane's fella, Mr Declan Mansfield, the wanker with
the supermarket and the straight white eyelashes!

Vera *returns, sipping water from the mug. A quietness, a 'politeness',
about her, a new mood. (Perhaps she smiles – winks broadly – at him,
which frightens him even more.) She sits on the bed, raking a finger
through the contents of her bag. A feel, just a touch, to her wallet.*

Finbar   Because it's my business to know the O'Tooles'
business and everybody else's business in this town. And
that's for sure.

Vera   Today is Thursday, yeh? *(She has taken up an airline
ticket.)*

Finbar   All day.

Vera *(reading airline ticket)*   Dublin–New York, 'OK, OK.'
This was for yesterday morning. Okay. *(And she tears it up.)*
So that one's okay.

Finbar *(indicates the table)*   If she wants something to eat.

Vera *(absently)*   Hmm?

Finbar   Oh well, if she doesn't want it. *(The food.)*

Vera   No thanks. *(Like talking to herself:)* You're making
statements about my family: I want you to stop. Okay?
Okay. They mean an awful lot to me. So they do. They
keep me going. Lifelong fear that I might be on my own.
Out there in space like a fucking astronaut with his tube
cut. Did you see that one? *(She's probably talking about a film.)*
Lifelong fear of just going to sleep, afraid to let go. So
they've been a great help. *(A second airline ticket, looking at it:)*
Thursday, you say, Finbar. This one's for tomorrow. New
York–Atlanta, 'OK, OK.' Some hope Atlanta now. *(Tears
up second ticket:)* So that one's okay too. So what am I do?
Because I was meant to be in Atlanta, Georgia, tomorrow
to entertain some cavalry. A weekend-long affair. It was on
the strength of that *(job)* that I came home. I got an
advance from the man because the man likes me. Still, the
man would throw you out a window or in the river if a
cavalry party he set up went short of meat. 'Specially paid-

for meat. Maybe I would do the same to him or better.
Caviare and a little mercury. So I want you to stop making
statements about my family because now I've got problems
both sides of the Atlantic. (*She has an impulse to laugh.*) Okay?

Finbar   What did *I* say?

Vera   My family keep me going. I've been in situations
you cannot even imagine. That *I* cannot even imagine. Up
there, down there. (*Highs and lows.*) Did anyone ever tell you
to eat shit? Human excrement, shit. No? But I survived –
up there, down there – came out on top of! – situations
because of – y'know? So I want you to stop. Okay . . . See
these? (*A small container of pills.*) My Xanadus I call them.
These can ease things. Human excrement, shit, shits,
become more palatable with these. Working girls, friends of
mine, use them on themselves. I don't much use them on
myself. I prefer to use them more for the purpose of
taming a difficult client, anaesthetising an animal. And not
for all the fucking tea in China, the coffee in Brazil would
I take one of them now.

Finbar   If I hurt your feelings.

Vera (*rises*)   One of these'd put manners on a mustang.
(*She puts them on the table.*) So I keep these in reserve. I could
tell you things if I wanted to.

Finbar   I said I'm sorry if I –

Vera   How to kill someone? (*Turns on him.*) Caviare and a
little mercury? I learned more at school from the nuns than
loving chastity above all things. D'you read me? – God
bless yeh! – D'you get my drift?

Finbar   Don't come near me – !

Vera   Who d'you think you're dealing with?

Finbar   Stay where –

Vera   Who is the whore?

Finbar   I never called you a –

Vera   Who is the whore? –

Finbar   I don't know what you're talking about! –

Vera   Okay? Okay? –

Finbar   Stop! – Fuckin'! – Jesus! –

He is retreating, she keeps following. Though her attack on him is blind it is slow-moving – at least it is at first. She follows with her face thrust out. Now she is swinging her hands at him:

Vera   Okay? Okay? . . .

Finbar   Fuckin'! Jesus! Stop!

Vera *hits him a few clatters. She is going to hit him again:*

Finbar (*hits her. Then*)   You cunt! (*A beat, and he hits her again.*) You cunt! . . . (*Frightened:*) I told you! . . . That's what you get . . . I warned you.

She is hurt – holding her head and doubled over. But now she starts laughing – terrible laughter – and now she is pursuing him again, for more, laughing, her face thrust out. He gets out of the room, to the front of the house, to the hall. She behaves as if he had never been in the room.

Vera   Okay? . . . Fuck me, screw me, rook me – if-you-are-able! – but don't anyone of you insult me like this! Okay? . . . I'm someone, amn't I? . . . Who-what *am* I? A hole between my legs? . . . I'm not a cunt . . . (*'I'm'*) Someone. Okay, (*'I'm'*) someone on my own then – I'm not going to be afraid of that. Lifelong fucking fear of – are you kiddin'?! Okay . . . *Who* is the whore? – Quem, cunt, ghee, box, slash, gash, cock-sucking, grandmother-fucking piece of shit, daff, crap, excrement? *Me*?! . . . (*Asking herself:*) Look, what do you want? Tell me. This? (**Finbar**'*s place.*) Revenge: is that what you want? The hotel? More hotel-fucking-rooms? Fucking family? (*She doesn't know. She sits.*) All dirt and lies. Well, look at it: Dirt. Lies. All fucked. All over. There: buy a child for a dollar, cheaper than a chicken; here: go fuck your grandmother . . . (*She becomes conscious of becoming tearful and of being alone; then, in reaction,* *baby voice:*) Aaw, have they gone and left you on your own? Is Baby Vera lonely-wonely? A-a-a-w! (*Followed by several mock sob-sniffles, derisive of herself. Then:*) Don't be so fucking stupid. Get up! (*Rises. Shouts after* **Finbar***:*) You! If you'd stop, let me think what I should do, I would fuck off and do it! Okay? (*Sits again. 'I'm'*) Fucking crazy, nuts. But one of these days, Baby Vera, you're going to have to pull that tiny mind of yours together. (*She realises that she is seated again:*) What?! Get up! (*Starts to rise, does not manage it the first time; then:*) Get up, cunt! (*And stands defiantly, legs apart:*) See! Okay? Okay . . . (*She sees* **Finbar** *returning:*) You! –

Finbar (*is alarmed and pacificatory*)   No, I swear – solemn oath – I'm not – There's someone coming in the!

Vera *starts laughing at him. She takes up a mug or a plate or plates.*

Finbar   No, Vera – Please – at the gate – Maybe the guards again –

Vera   The money you stole from my wallet!

Finbar   Aw Jesus, I would never –

Vera   Twice!

Finbar   No, Vera – Don't!

She has gone out with mug/plates and fires them. They smash outside.

Vera   Fuck off! (*And she is returning for further missiles.*)

Finbar   Fuckin' Jesus –

Henry (*off*)   Don't shoot!

Finbar   Please – Fuckin' – Stop!

Henry (*off*)   Don't shoot! Don't shoot! Friend! A friend!

Henry *is outside. He has drink taken but he can carry it. He is wearing an old-fashioned coat (a type of black frock-coat), carries a cane and a black hat. (He produces the letter later.)*

Finbar   Who? (*To himself.*)

Henry   Finbar? Finbar? Henry Locke-Browne!

Finbar   Henry Locke-Browne. He has the suit on.

Henry   I have come unarmed and alone! Don't shoot! I come as a messenger!

Finbar   I'll have to go out to him. Will I?

Henry   Let down the bridge! I pray you in the name of the Most High!

Vera *goes out to* **Henry**, *as for a confrontation, but his style – unorthodox attire and greeting – appeals to her, privately.*

Vera   Yeh!?

Henry   Good Lord! I'd no idea you were such a handsome woman!

Vera   Yeh!?

Henry   May I come in?

She returns to the room. He follows.

How are you, Finbar!

Finbar   I'm not so bad at all, Henry, how's yourself!

Henry   Plu-perfect! For you. (*Gives the letter to* **Vera**.) It's from your brother Tom and sister Mary Jane.

Vera   And your wife?

Henry   No. At very best, Marcia's a bit-player in the plot: She's been promised the trinkets. I shouldn't bother to read it: It's a horrible composition. I steamed it. I'd ask you to put your shoes on and come out for a drink but the authorities are uncommonly active this evening about the licensing hours. Something has upset them. The sergeant himself is posted on the usually dependable Mannions of the Hollow.

Finbar   They're after promotion all right.

Henry   You don't have something in the house by any chance?

There is nothing to drink in the house.

Finbar   They become very dedicated when they're upset.

Vera (*tears the letter in two*)   Fuck this for a game of toy soldiers. I know where there's plenty of drink. Would you like a drink?

Henry   I could be persuaded.

Vera   Would you like a drink?

Finbar   I don't mind. But I've a man in the morning calling early about a lock of bentwood chairs.

During the above, **Vera** *dressing – simply, her mac over her slip – while* **Finbar** *is finding his old overcoat. She puts the pills she left on the table into her pocket, collects her bag and leads them off.*

Scene Six

Street light coming up and in, colouring rather than lighting the dark; vague shapes that will turn out to be a piano, an upholstered couch and armchairs draped in dust sheets: an upstairs room in the hotel, overlooking the square.

Off, below, a glass shattering. (A window.)

And, after a few moments, **Vera**, **Henry** *and* **Finbar** *come in.* **Vera** *has her overnight bag. (***Vera***'s silence.)*

Henry   Up here you would have us?

Finbar   I was in the back bar down there all right a couple of times . . .

Henry (*moves to the window to look down at the square, left and right*)   No. No.

Finbar   But I was never up here.

Henry   Not a soul. The enemy sleeps. This is Georgian! ('*This is great!*' *He finds a switch, tries it:*) It don't work, Inspector. (*He tries another.*)

Finbar (*sniggers*)   Maybe someone didn't pay the bill.

Henry   I know I've seen Tom and Mary Jane go in and out of here at night, I know I've seen a light.

Finbar   The mainswitch.

Henry   Where is the mainswitch? . . . Vera?

Vera   Oh. Downstairs. There's a storeroom off the kitchen we came through.

Henry   You understand such matters, Finbar.

Finbar   A switch? A child would! . . . A switch whether it's main or not is only a switch. (*But he goes out.*) I'm not a maid.

Henry   . . . Poor dumb building: The innocence of it.

Silence.

I should go perhaps and assist him?

Vera   This is where I was born.

Henry   I'm sorry?

Vera   Why didn't they ask me for it?

Henry   Ask?

Vera   Yeh. Rigmaroles about auctions.

Henry   You are not an innocent.

Vera   No, I'm not an innocent. But that's all they had to do, I think.

Henry   Surely to simply ask for something would sound suspiciously uncomplicated.

Vera   Why did my mother leave it to me?

Henry   To take a last harsh laugh to the grave?

She laughs with her breath in the dark – incidentally, a sound rather like crying.

. . . You are cross with them.

Vera   They're so *busy*. And do they get any special comfort from it? . . . I'm cross with myself. All my life the feeling of belonging has eluded me: Why should I go on thinking I'll find it? The thought of here *hasn't* kept me going: the thought of here cripples me. (*To herself:*) Yeh know?

Henry   Yeh. (*To himself.*)

Vera   . . . Why is Mary Jane supporting Tom?

Henry   Greed. It is the only sensation that moves her. She will die of it. Anything that does not add to her life will be substracted from it. Mary Jane: And what she once was. (*He reins himself in the next:*) Why, she has castrated that poor shopkeeping husband of hers and . . .

Vera   And she despises him for allowing her to do it.

Henry   *She* is the innocent. But I speak out of turn?

Vera   No, I'm getting used to it. Why are they doing this together, Tom and Mary Jane?

Henry   Team spirit. Are you really not one of them? It is a clanship between night-runners. One containing the usual, concessional understanding: when he tumbles the sheep she will get the hindquarters . . . I should not take it too personally to heart: These marauding family expeditions happen on a national scale. A member of course is sacrificed, but it is done for the greater good of the pack.

Vera   What's in it for you?

Henry   Rescue me . . . I jest. I should like to exceed the deeds of my father.

Vera   What is it worth?

Henry   Two-eighty thousand? Thereabouts . . . It doesn't bring a smile to your face?

Vera   What do I do with it?

Henry   Sell it . . . You don't want money?

Vera   I want-need-money but.

Henry   Put yourself in my hands – no fees. Withdraw it from auction – You are not bound to the auction – put a price on it and sell by private treaty. To Tom if you wish –

Vera   I don't know that I –

Henry   Dick or Harry then. That's what your brother's emotion will do with it if he gets it: He'll sell it. He'll first get large grants off the Tourist Board to do it up, then – The silk of my degrees is at your disposal.

Vera   I don't know that I want to sell.

Henry   Lease it, for an income . . . Keep it.

Vera   I don't want it. No: This, I think, is going to be my last throw in the game of family and, if that is so, I want to do something more than selling, keeping, leasing.

Henry   Those are the options.

Vera   Burn it to the ground?

Henry   By Jesus yes! The generosity of it! Now I follow! Put it to the torch, leave it in ashes and I'll purify myself in the flames with you bejesus! And we'll hike it out of here the two of us together – without baggage! – for a land I will show you where they do not make you sick discussing the cherished values that are under threat and their duties to the God they've reduced to a huckster.

A light comes on on the landing, a spill from it coming into the room.

Quick, your instructions!

Finbar (*off*)   They're on!

Vera (*switches on a light*)   I want to see them.

Henry   Do not underestimate them.

Vera   We wait. Let *them* make the next move.

Finbar (*coming in*)   They're on.

Vera (*to* **Finbar**)   Thanks.

Henry   I'll draw the drapes.

Vera   No.

Henry   No drapes?

Vera   Why? (*She switches on the other lights.*)

Henry   I like it.

Finbar   What? (*He does not know what is going on.*)

Vera   What are these? (*Rolls of architect's drawings she has picked up off a chair.*)

Henry   What did I tell you! Architect's drawings. Someone – already! – has plans for your property. Yes, our affairs are critical but first things first: What're we all having?

Vera   What would you like?

Henry   What would you like, Finbar?

Finbar   What're you having yourself, Vera?

Vera   Champagne?

Finbar   Champagne? Hydrogen!

Henry (*sharply*)   A pint is out of the question.

Finbar (*just as sharply*)   I know that, I'm not a fool.

Henry   Any kind of whiskey.

Finbar   Same.

Vera   With?

Henry   Half-and-half.

Finbar (*nods. And*)   If you please.

Vera   Okay.

She leaves.

Finbar *frowning 'What?', and suspiciously watching* **Henry** *during the following.*

*And **Henry** sets to work, putting away his hat and cane, removing dust sheets, folding them, arranging furniture to his taste, busy concentration, talking to himself. (The piano is left covered.)*

Henry   Yes I like her, yes I do – (*Winks at **Finbar**:*) We're on a good thing. To work, Henry: put away your cap and cane, we might as well be making a start. Yes I do. And she has the stuff bejesus to immortalise herself in this town, and maybe rescue you as well. Why, she is a veritable female Achilles if you want my opinion. No buying or selling or leasing for Achilles. There was only one of him and there'd never be another and he knew it.

Finbar   What?

Henry   By Jesus the skin and hair is going to fly at last.

Finbar   What?

Henry   And her deportment is remarkable – Yes I grow inordinately fond of her. And she is still in her fitness and flowering, more or less.

Finbar   What?

Henry   What more is there to say? And will she do the *other* thing? Oh-ho-ho! And what is more, she will do it without emotional imposition! Think of that.

Finbar   What?

Henry   Or inhibition.

Finbar   What?

Henry   Heroically. Yes, let them off and welcome – if that's what keeps them happy: Their ceremonials and rituals, play-acting superstitions – Stolen from the Jews bejesus! – if that's what they think is the purpose of existence.

Finbar   Shouldn't the curtains be –

Henry   What? But we know better. Yes, because the purpose, the true essence and the core of all things is the ecstasy in the act of copulation. No, there is nothing like a bit of jack.

Finbar (*frustrated; indicating the lights and the window*)   Like a fuckin' lighthouse!

Henry   How are we doing, Henry? Your assistance! (**Finbar**'s.) We're nearly there.

Finbar *assists* **Henry**, *folding the largest dust sheet.*

Henry   So, we must be brave. Unless they get her first of course. What? No. What? . . . (*Briefest glance towards the window.*) No, curtains-drapes shall not prevail against us: Out in the open, I like it. Why, man dear alive, once on a high and windy hill, a maiden, her blue knickers down around her ankles and the wind whistling through the hairs of my balls.

Finbar   Fuckin'!

Henry   And the world stood still.

Finbar (*whispering*)   Shh, she's back! (*To* **Vera**:) You're back!

Vera *entering with a tray of glasses, water, whiskey.*

Henry   Shh she's back and she wasn't too long about it at all now! Now! isn't this nice? Neat? Tidy? (*His preparation of the room.*)

Vera   Sit.

They sit. She pours the drinks. Gives a drink to **Finbar**.

Finbar   Thank you.

Vera (*giving* **Henry** *his drink*)   Hmm?

Henry   We wait for them.

Finbar   What?

Henry   Good health!

Finbar   Good!

Vera (*raises her glass*)   And, meanwhile, there's plenty more where this came from. (*She goes to the window – as to watch and wait.*)

Silence. They sip.

Finbar   What?

And, the lights fading, **Henry***, content, starts to sing quietly to himself:*

Henry   'Breeng (*Bring*) flowers of the rarest, breeng blossoms of the fairest, from garden and hillside and woodland and dell; our hearts are full swelling, their glad voices telling, the praise of the loveliest flower of the May: O Mary we crown thee with . . .'

Interval.

The lights come up and it is now near dawn. And dawn will move into morning.

The strangely attired party continues: **Vera***'s mackintosh hanging open over her slip. Her black eye.* **Finbar***, throughout, in his old raincoat;* **Henry** *in his frock-coat.*

The bottle/s and the water jug are on the floor and they lean forward out of their seats for them as required. (There is no table.) They are now animated in their individual ways and, generally, they find even their most ordinary remarks hugely entertaining. Something perverse/anarchic in how they complement one another with laughter.

Vera   This room, this room, this very room – !

Finbar   Vera! – (*Meaning: he's listening.*)

Vera   The day my father was buried –

Henry   Vera! –

Vera   I don't know where the table is gone to –

Finbar   Vera! –

Vera   But after the funeral, that day, my mother gathered us all here and the table was there and my father's things were laid out on it – you know, the things he kept about him –

Finbar   Personal effects! –

Vera   For each of us, myself, Tom, Marcia and Mary Jane, to pick something –

Henry   Vera! –

Vera   I was called first – I was *honoured*! –

Finbar   You were –

Vera   But Mother was both testing me and trying to train me –

Finbar   Aw she wouldn't do –

Vera   Judging me! Well, us all! For instance, his wallet was there, which she said was 'intact' – (*Laughter.*)

Finbar   Did *you* get that?

Vera   Mary Jane.

Henry   Ah!

Vera   Then Tom selected a sort-of small white pin, symbol of something – I think he still wears it sometimes in his lapel –

Finbar   The White Star! (*To* **Henry**:) Remember them? – The symbol of a clean tongue.

Henry   'Flaming'! –

Finbar   Fuckin'!

Henry   Every time I meet your brother I think of Joan of Arc: Flaming.

Vera   But Tom wanted something else –

Henry   The last argument of the Church will always be the stake –

Finbar   Let Vera, Henry –

Vera   He didn't stand back from the table: ('*He*') Looked at my mother like this – (*She demonstrates.*) – And my mother – (*Demonstrates her mother's expression and nod to* **Tom**.) And he

took the watch – (*Laughter.*) – And you won't like this: But
Marcia – (*She is laughing:*) Marcia's turn and, first, she took
the pioneer pin – my father never drank –

Laughter. **Henry** *raises an elegant glass –*

Vera   Then she took collar-studs, a coloured handkerchief,
the rosary beads, two fountain pens and a packet of
Rennies! You know those things for –

Finbar   Indigestion! Ah no! –

Vera   Yes! – (*Laughter.*) –

Finbar   What did you get, Vera?

Vera   I got his, I took his – (*Trying to control her laughter:*)
My father's pipe! – (*Laughing: A genuine question:*) Am I a
fool?

Finbar   That's a nice memory.

Vera   Is it?

Henry   (*'I'*) Hate Catholics.

Finbar   You're a Catholic!

Henry   Ah! But Protestant and protesting genes: my
mother's side, the Lockes. By Jesus, (*'there'*) wasn't a
member of that family – man or woman – couldn't tumble
down the finest staircase without injury to limb or loss of a
drop to their glasses! (*Laughter.*) –

Finbar (*to* **Vera**)   D'you know what a thurible is? –

Henry   That's where I get it from.

Finbar   A thurible –

Vera   A thurible, Finbar.

Finbar   Thing for burning incense that you swing? Well,
that school I was in in Connemara –

Henry   Letterfrack, the borstal?

Finbar (*touchy*)   Letterfrack, Connemara, borstal, Industrial

School – all right? Establishment.

Vera Finbar. (*She's listening.*)

Finbar There's a graveyard there with one hundred children.

Henry Thurible!

Finbar You're fuckin'! (*'distracting me'.*) But there was a coonic back there in the area anyway, a priest (*who*) used to come in to say Mass. Thurible: I'm holding it: two or three – like lozengers (*lozenges*) – burning, glowing, in the bowl. The coonic then: little silver spoons of incense in on top of the lozengers. But I'm in charge, swinging it, keeping it going for your man while he's, yeh know, *Dominus vobiscum*, his other business, until he needed it. This was on the altar. But I mustn't have been minding my business anyway, 'cause didn't I set him on fire. What? Aw Jesus! – Smoke! – His vestments! The fuckin' coonic caught fire! (*Laughter.*) – Oh but in the sacristy afterwards: 'I'm sorry, Father, I'm sorry!' – (**Finbar***'s hands covering his head: The beating he received.*) – Fuckin'! Did he give me the! (*Beating.*) 'I'm sorry, Father, I'm sorry!' (*Laughter.*)

Vera I used to watch my father. I never saw him angry.

Henry You didn't!

Vera I never saw him the other way either: You know? The idea of gaiety made him – (*She does it: 'Close his lips'.*)

Finbar 'I'm sorry, Father, I'm . . . !' –

Henry My father, the colonel: Developed taste for Bushmills whiskey and young women – women all-sorts. Died in – parlour? – of a neighbour of yours, Finbar. But you knew that of course?

Finbar *manages to nod yes and no* –

Henry Mama misinterpreted. Why wouldn't she, the creature? Sitting at home alone, contemplating, I am sure, the social masquerade about her. (*'The'*) Meaninglessness of – it all! Protestant friends fled – Forty – Sixty thousand of

them in our own lifetime?! – Father out riding, myself at
boarding school. How was she in her own country – her
own home! – to survive her – homelessness! And she comes
up with the notion – Suggests desperation. Worse: Long-
distance suicide? The aberrant notion of escaping it here by
going off to Kenya of all places to become some kind of
lay, Protestant missionary *nun*, God love her. And died
there – Kenya! – the creature, before she could lift a
blessed finger to relieve the lot of our black brethren –
(*Laughter.*) The colonel then, to be sure, renewed vigour, up
on his horse – his steed – up to your place, Finbar –

Finbar   Aw he was some – (*'man.'*)

Henry   Like an ageing Ulysses bejesus, up to the Punjab,
Nighttown, for a breath of fresh air! (*Laughter.*) The outcome
was predestined – of course it was: He would be beaten.
But, by going out, offering defiance – grinning yellow
lecherous teeth back at what *they* had on offer – he would
not be *completely* beaten – (*Laughter.*) – But d'you see what I
mean!

Finbar   Some man all right the colonel. No but, Vera,
you're given a hundred pounds by your –

Henry   *O mio babbino caro!*

Finbar   No but, Vera –

Henry   A man of mighty thews! Sorry, Finbar: I
interrupted you. *Your* family.

Finbar   Ah, I'm grand.

Henry   Who was your father?

Finbar   . . . Maybe he was the same man as yours.

Henry   Maybe he?

Vera *is laughing and, because she is, though he has taken offence at
the above,* **Finbar** *starts to laugh too.*

Vera (*now becoming sentimental, throws her arms around*

Henry)   I've always wanted – all my life! – to celebrate
something in this town: To do something – you know? –
without being judged – without caring whether I was
judged or not – D'you know what I mean?

Henry }   Yes –

Finbar }   Yes – But you're given –

Vera   Without the advice or consent of anyone, for God's
sake!

Finbar   But you're given –

Vera   I ask you! Not that I ever wished anyone or
anything dead here, but I used to think that when they did
– Lord be good to them! – so what? It's no longer going to
matter to them or embarrass them! – I'd have one right
crazy rave-up of a party.

Henry (*a toast*)   A woman of necessity, a boy for pleasure,
a goat for ecstasy!

Finbar   That's a *dis*gusting – (*'thing to say'. But the others are
laughing and he laughs too.*) No but, you're given – You're
given, Vera, you're given a hundred pounds by your wife
to go to the fair and you have to come home with a
hundred animals. Now, the animals cost five pence each for
a sheep, a pound for a cow and a fiver for a horse –

Henry   What is this?

Finbar   No! Vera. Now, you have to buy some of each
and they must add up to, add up to a hundred, and –
And! – you can't bring home change out of the hundred
pounds –

Henry   What is he talking about?

Finbar   No! How many of each kind of animal d'you
come home with?

Henry (*to himself*)   What!

Finbar   Vera.

Vera   I don't know.

Finbar   . . . You do.

Vera   I don't! –

Finbar   You do –

Vera   I'm no good at sums.

Finbar   I'll give you a clue.

Henry   What *is* this?

Finbar   Work for a start – Work for a start, Vera, in multiples of twenty.

Henry   What?! Stop this! This is oral sex, Irish style, you are engaging in.

Finbar   That's a *dis*! (*'disgusting thing to say'.*)

But **Vera** *and* **Henry** *are laughing.*

Vera   My Uncle Stephen!

Henry   Mm, Stephen! –

Finbar   The Odeon! –

Vera   The Odeon Cinema, The Wool Stores, the other things he owned. Well, he was an A-okay all right-guy – yeh? – I think. But, my father had died rather suddenly, and he nearly died without making a will, and, so, now, my mother started to work on Uncle Stephen. Reminding him that he was three years older than my father, that he was living alone – And he was a bachelor.

Finbar   I've a better one than that –

Henry   Finbar! (*'Listen.'*) –

Vera   Anyway, she frightened him, and on the fear of sudden death Uncle Stephen came to live with us here –

Henry   Vera –

Vera   And this room again! – Shortly afterwards – I don't know where the table's got to – my mother assembled us all here again, this time around our Uncle Stephen. I mean the man was sitting there! Tom got his house – I mean, the man was sitting there – *alive*! Mary Jane got the Odeon and the little shop next door to it –

Finbar   The Magnet.

Vera   Marcia?

Henry   Shamrock Ballroom – White elephant.

Vera   Shamrock. Anyway, my mother took my shoulder to pull me forward to the table – like this. Because the Wool Stores had been earmarked by her for me. Tom – he was only a youngster! – nodding, encouraging me. My mother – (*Pulling her forward to the table.*) – Like as if the Wool Stores was on top of the table! The man was upset! I didn't take them.

Finbar   No!

Vera   (*a bit lost – though laughing*)   What am I talking about? I mean, *should* I have taken them? *Am* I a fool? All my life? What's my point?

Henry   (*going out with empty jug*)   The danger to one's immortal soul of dying intestate.

Laughter. (Though **Finbar** *is now growing self-conscious, and he would like to apologise for hitting her earlier.)*

Vera   (*half to herself*)   Tom got the Wool Stores too. Wait a minute! There was an agreement – a *deal* – between my mother and Tom – maybe between her and the others as well – that when he started working he would pay *her* for getting Uncle Stephen's property and because he – maybe the others too – never came across with the money, she left this place to me. Is that my point? I have to get out of these. (*Clothes. Instead, she tops up her drink.*)

Finbar   (*nods at the window*)   The dawn.

Vera   Yes. Good. You're not going to fall asleep on me?

Finbar (*'No.'*)   I'm sorry for hitting you.

Vera   It was honest.

Finbar   What?

Vera   It was honest, Finbar. D'you know what I mean, Finbar?

Finbar (*he doesn't but he is moved, grateful to her. Something nice to tell her*)   D'you know anything about pyramids?

Henry (*returning with a jug of water*)   Well, ye're a nice pair the three of ye!

Finbar   How d'you keep a razor blade sharp? Vera.

Henry   How d'you keep a razor blade sharp? Finbar.

Finbar   A pyramid!

Henry   Come again?

Finbar   We're not fools, Henry!

Henry   Never said –

Finbar   I'm not talking a big fuckin' Egyptian thing! I shouldn't have. (*He regrets using offensive language about pyramids.*) I'm talking a small one, to scale – I've one at home I made myself: a model. It's only six inches high but if you put a razor blade into it – that's why I made it! – but with the cutting edges facing east and west, it keeps sharp. I don't know how many shaves I can get out of a blade.

Vera   I heard about them.

Finbar   Yes!

Vera   People meditate in them.

Finbar   If you make one big enough, to sit in. It depends on what you want to do with your pyramid. Or milk for instance will keep in them. They work.

Vera   How?

Finbar   Ions.

Henry   What else!

Finbar   No, Henry! – There's more. Dimensions – Energy: The 'just' dimensions, 'divine' proportions!

Vera   What did you make your one out of?

Finbar   Cardboard. The Rishis and the Devas of the Third Root Race handed down the knowledge to teachers, initiates, Vera. Modern skills, going to the moon? Child's play to them. They'd have gone there if they wanted to. They were Priest-Architects. And it was all here – not up there, the moon, *or* heaven. Here on earth. I know I'm only talking Mickey-fuckin'-Mouse about razor blades and milk. They knew *real* wonders, *real* wonders *they* worked. People out there are impressed because the tractor took over from the fuckin' horse. But the *real* knowledge is lost. Not just calculations – Wisdom! And I think it's lost because the teachers, who could have become initiates, became violent.

Henry (*impressed by* **Finbar**'*s sincerity*)   Mmmm!

Finbar (*grows self-conscious and laughs*)   Nickerdepazze!

Henry   Nickerdepazze!

Vera (*she could be talking to herself*)   Being fostered out was not an unusual thing in the past. But the reason why I was sent to live with my grandmother was – has-to-be: She had a farm. They wanted her to sign it over. Because there were rows: 'I'm not dead yet' sort of rows that I didn't understand then. And because my beloved grandmother wouldn't sign the farm over to them, to punish her they brought me home. Yeh, I think that's my point. (*Gets up, collects her overnight bag:*) Let's see what I've got in here. Or maybe there's something of my mother's (*Clothes. She goes to the window:*) People are going up to Mass.

Henry   The pious shuffle is precise, the piety is exact.

Vera (*an imperitive*)   Don't go to sleep on me, *either* of you! (*She goes out with her bag.*)

Finbar (*stands, whispers*)   What?

Henry   Yes I like her, yes I do, and if she has a single flaw other than that her shoulders are a fraction high, a trifle square, I cannot see it. One for the road for you, Finbar – What more is there to say? (*He has gone into action: The remains of a bottle into* **Finbar**'*s glass. He wants to get rid of* **Finbar**.) Now, knock this back you.

Finbar (*whispers*)   Where's she gone to?

Henry   Why are the Chinese slant-eyed? – Because when they come down in the morning they say O Jesus not rice again. No don't sit down again – Your bentwood chairs.

Finbar   What about them?

Henry   You've a man calling early about a lock of bentwood chairs.

Finbar (*dismisses the chairs*)   I'll tell *you* one –

Henry   I've business to discuss with her. On my oath: Family matters – I've become her legal representative.

Finbar   You're drunk.

Henry   I'm?

Finbar   We've been up all night: it's gone eight o'clock in the morning!

Henry   *I'm!* (*He's proud of his drinking prowess.*)

Finbar (*sits?*)   I'm not a married man.

Henry   I'm sorry? You're not a married – What're you talking about?

Finbar   Nothing! You tell *me* what I'm talking about.

Henry   'He's not a married man.'

Finbar   Oh yes, it's all right for the likes of you to talk to me but it's a different matter for the likes of me to say anything to you.

Henry   Haven't the foggiest idea what you are –

Finbar   Sex.

Henry   True as Our Lady is in heaven, Finbar!

Finbar   She's your fuckin' sister-in-law! Sex! Amn't I watching the two of you all night? And fuckin' incest! Don't-tell-me! Fathers and their daughters – Fuckin' clergy! Driving round the country, screwing young ones in their Volkswagens, then going home (*'and'*) doing their housekeepers – Sex! Christian Brothers in the schools – (*Intensely, to himself:*) Faaack! Beating the children, Henry, then buggering them: I was 'in care', Henry, them establishments, Henry? (*Pulls himself back somewhat:*) And young ones and aul' ones getting pregnant and praying to fuckin' statues about it. Country is rotten with it. (*He finds himself in the window.*) But what else was the country taught to think about?

Henry   There's worse! (*Coming to the window.*)

Finbar   I wish I was a bigger man.

Henry   Respectability!

Finbar   Don't tell me anything.

Henry   Their use of it.

Finbar   They're looking up at us – (*Retreating from window.*)

Henry   Respectability: the miserable tragedy. It can absorb anything – it is unbeatable – you cannot even insult it! (*He laughs, probably at himself:*) And I betrayed my genius to become part of it!

Finbar   (*intensity of hatred; and, as well as everything else, he resents* **Henry**'s *ability to continue in the window*)   Fuck you. And the colonel and Mama. And Herr the fuckin' German living in your Big House now. And just because you can't lord it over people any more, big words. And big and all as they are, you haven't a good word to say about anything. Fuck you: What're you talking about?

Henry (*simply*)   Precisely.

Finbar   Ooh! precisely, ex-actly. Fuck you: Who d'you think you are?

Henry (*simply*)   I wish to God I knew. And not much chance of finding out: It is, as you have said, a most distressing country.

Finbar (*containing his rage*)   I need – a *piss*. (*He is going out.*)

Henry   I'll come with you.

Finbar   What?! What?! You think you have all the answers? She's my ride. (*And a harsh laugh.*)

Henry   Then we both like her – Yes we do. And there is an abundance of her in it. And she is not going to save for one – 'tis patently clear – what one cannot possibly use up. Shh, she's back!

And **Vera** *comes in swinging a bottle/s by her side. She has changed and done herself up. The dress is makeshift but it creates the effect she wants: The marks of a whore and sexy.*

Vera   Okay, boys, show me what you've got.

Henry   Your mother's? (*The dress.*)

Vera   Yeh. D'you like it?

Henry   Mm!

Vera   My property. (*Turns to* **Finbar** *for his opinion of her body and dress.*) Hmm?

Finbar *is a mixture of fear and attraction: To stay or to go.*

Henry   We were only this minute discussing your property and reached impasse. So would you care to declare which of us you're going to have or shall we let the contest in drink continue 'til it's decided?

Vera (*assesses them in turn. Then*)   It's my birthday!

Finbar   It's not – What? – Is it? (*And, confused, goes out.*) Fuckin'!

A telephone – on the floor somewhere? – starts ringing.

Henry   The drums (*phone*) have started, they have heard we are in occupation.

Vera (*pelvic thrust – direction of phone or window*)   Font of love: Who's first?

Henry   Are you going to answer it?

Vera   No. They're going to have to arrive in person. I want to see them. *Here.* They *will* arrive, won't they?

Henry   The drums continue for three days, I believe: then they attack.

Vera   And I've bolted the door. Because when they arrive they're going to have to break it down to get in here. Just like what had to be done to my grandmother's house. Only, I won't be on the floor. Then, as regards this place (*the hotel*) I'll do – (*shrugs:*) something. But it'll be clean, final.

Henry   We are hopelessly outnumbered – And Finbar will desert: His nerve is cracking. They captured him once before and tortured him. But depend on me: I'll keep two rounds: They'll take neither of us alive.

Finbar (*making a tentative return*)   Happy birthday, Vera!

Vera *and* **Henry** *start laughing.*

Vera   Finbar, you old ponce, come to Mama!

Henry (*pouring drinks – welcoming*)   Nickerdepazze!

Finbar (*coming to join them*)   I'm not taking my clothes off in front of him.

More laughter. And the phone is ringing again.

Finbar   Nickerdepazze!

Henry   Nickerdepazze!

Vera   Let's *start* the party. (*A toast:*) Nickerdepazze!

Scene Seven

A table and four chairs (as in the bay of a window): **Tom***'s house.*

Caitriona, **Tom***'s wife, stands there (upstage) in forgotten purpose, a glass of water in her hand. She is pretty, petite. Long dress: Arab-type, perhaps, with the bodice done in coloured threads and beads. Now, a slow movement – a delayed reaction – to a noise off.* (**Tom** *letting himself in with his keys.*)

And **Tom** *comes in (leaving the door, off, open). He is upset and he starts to snivel. (No acknowledgement of* **Caitriona**.*)*

Caitriona *(upstage of him), unmoved, watching him, sidelong. A slow movement of her fist to her mouth: pills. And washing them down with water.*

The doorbell rings and **Mary Jane** *marches in (leaving the door, off, open). Briefest of greetings.*

Mary Jane   Caitriona.

Tom   I never thought I'd ... (*He is blowing his nose.*)

Mary Jane   How do we stop this?

Tom   Treasure, door please.

Caitriona *goes out, closes the door, returns in a moment.*

Mary Jane   It's a circus.

Tom   I never thought I'd ...

Mary Jane   What're we going to do?

Tom   Can we get you anything?

Mary Jane   Glass of water.

Tom   Little Treasure, glass of water for Mary Jane.

Caitriona *goes.*

Mary Jane   What action? (*'do we take?'*)

Tom   I never thought I'd live to see a day like this.

Mary Jane *(to herself)*   Wonderful. And Henry Locke-Browne: That parasite.

Tom (*to himself*)   No. No. (*He refuses to call his brother-in-law a parasite.*) But he'll peter out.

Mary Jane   I know he will *peter* out, I know his form. Are you saying that we wait until she peters out, see what *she's* going to do next? O-Toole, Ve-rah!

Tom   I left word on the way home for Father Billy.

Mary Jane   *Why!* are you bringing priests into it, what use are *they*?

Tom   It's their flaming business, Mary Jane!

Mary Jane   They've been extraordinarily quiet about it for the past six and a half days!

Tom   Father Billy Houlihan is a personal friend of the family, Mary Jane, and a personal friend of mine! I don't know *yet* what we can do: That's what we're here to find out.

Mary Jane   How do *we* stand?

Tom   Head. (*His hand to his head: He has a headache.*)

Mary Jane   The situation of the auction is now totally confused in the eyes of the public: The auction is no longer a foregone conclusion: So where does that leave our arrangement?

Tom   We have a deal.

Mary Jane   It would give me *peace* to be shut of this.

Tom   When I get the hotel, the Wool Stores are yours, to develop or expand or . . . What're you going to do with them?

Mary Jane   The Wool Stores are just sitting there.

Tom   Prime position. When I get the hotel the Wool Stores are yours for nothing.

Mary Jane   *Sell* them to me.

Tom   I never go back on a deal.

Mary Jane   I've-done-every-thing-I-can for you!

Tom   As a sister should.

Mary Jane   As a sister should and as a brother would, sell the pff-wretched – sheds – to me! –

The doorbell is ringing –

Name your price! –

Tom (*calling*)   Caitriona! –

Mary Jane   And I'll see if I can meet it!

Tom   Treasure!

Mary Jane   Is there an ashtray in the house – glass of water?

Tom   Simmer down. (*To room door to meet his guests.*)

Mary Jane (*to herself*)   Geesstupid! (*Producing cigarettes.*)

Father Billy (*off*)   Caitriona! How are you! Sure you're grand!

Tom   Father!

Father Billy (*off*)   Tom!

Tom   Come in, come in!

Mary Jane (*lighting cigarette; to herself*)   Wonderful!

Father Billy (*coming in*)   Where did you get the gorgeous dress, Caitriona?

Marcia, *pushcar and* **Norman**, **Father Billy** *and* **Caitriona** *are coming in.*
Marcia'*s face is bloated from crying. She is angry, too: She has stopped* **Norman** *from going to school.*
Father Billy *is reluctant to become involved in the O'Tooles' problem. He is big-chested and broad-shouldered. Edge of white silk scarf inside the collar of his waisted overcoat. He is a nice, uncomplicated man and celibacy causes him no problems. He is mostly*

aware of people using him but he cannot do much about it but laugh and clap his hands.

Father Billy (*announcing it*)   We arrived together – And the baby! Mary Jane!

Tom   You're very good, Father.

Father Billy   Oh now! Norman, and are you not at school?

Marcia   He's not.

Father Billy   And are you sick?

Marcia   He's not.

Tom   Come in – Welcome! – I'll take your coat – Treasure!

Father Billy   No, I can only stay a minute, Tom – And what age is she now, Marcia?

Marcia   Four months, Father.

Father Billy   Four months, Baby Carol!

Caitriona (*suddenly*)   Welcome one and all! How are you, Mary Jane!

Mary Jane   I'm fine, Caitriona – Glass of water please?

Tom   A glass of water, Treasure, for Mary Jane, and Father Billy would like?

Father Billy   No, no, no, Tom, thanks! I – Caitriona, if you're going out to . . .

Caitriona (*drifting out of the room*)   I am the doctor's daughter!

Father Billy   If she's gone out for tea or –

Tom   Would you like a drop? (*Of tea.*)

Father Billy   Oh, tea, now, stop!

Tom *laughs heartily.*

Mary Jane   We sit down? (*She sits / she is already seated.*)

Father Billy   Is she all right, like? (**Caitriona**)

Tom   Dr Kelly has her on a new course of pills.

Father Billy   And she's responding.

Tom   If these ones don't work he'll sign her in somewhere he said. (*Indicating where she should sit:*) Marcia.

Father Billy   Oh well now, please God it won't come to that.

Marcia (*turns on* **Norman**)   Run out in the garden and play! You're becoming too old-fashioned entirely! (**Norman** *goes. Bridling herself before she sits:*) No, he's *not* going to school!

Tom   Sit here, Father. (*Centre chair, a carver.*)

Father Billy   No! That seat belongs to the man of the house, this is my seat. The old nerves (**Caitriona***'s*) can be the boyos. (*Sits.*) Well now, the gang's all here.

Marcia *starts crying.*

Father Billy   Oh, sure, now, like. (*He contains a sigh. And:*) What's the latest?

Tom   It's becoming serious.

Mary Jane   It's *becoming* serious? The car is out of control!

Marcia   I only want Henry to come home.

Mary Jane   And it's been going on now for six and a half days and *people* in authority are standing idly by.

Father Billy   But what can *we* do, Mary Jane? These aren't like the old days.

Mary Jane   *Nothing* can be done? Wonderful. For inexplicable reasons our sister arrived home from America six and a half days ago: For inexplicable reasons she then went to live – In *sin*? – in the New Estate with someone everyone here knows to be of questionable, dangerous and proven disreputable character – let's not beat about any bush – who is up to every deceit, graft, double-dealing, confidence trick in the book to put it mildly. We tried, we failed, to make civilised contact with her –

Tom   She nearly took – (*The nose off him in the door.*)

Mary Jane   Shall I or shall you?

Marcia   Vera wants everything.

Mary Jane   Two and a half days ago she moved into the hotel, breaking a back window – we found out about the back window half an hour ago – to do so. (*'For'*) Two and a half days every window in the hotel has been lit up, day and night, the middle of the town, with our sister, brother-in-law and one Mr Reilly parading themselves in all manners of drunkenness, undress, unseemly behaviour in those same windows for all or any outside who cared to stand in the Square and watch. Now, are four grown people sitting here at this table – including myself – telling me that nothing can be done about it? I find this extraordinary. Are there no laws – ones of decency perhaps? – statutory, common, moral, to be enacted or observed? What other society, town, civilised country would put up with it?

Tom   I's lunacy.

Mary Jane   This morning then – Well, what were people to think when they started to assemble for more of the continuing show? The lights still on in every window but no sign or trace of life from them in there any more, no answer to the doorbell, phone, knocks on the door – what were people to think? 'Were they dead?'

Tom   Send for the guards, send for an ambulance.

Marcia   I could roast her, I could scald her! –

Tom   Marcia! –

Marcia   She wants everything! –

Father Billy   Oh sure, now sure! –

Tom   There's no point in getting angry! –

Marcia   I'd stick a knife in her, Father!

Tom   Marcia!

Father Billy   . . . Ambulance?

Tom   Ambulance.

Mary Jane   Half an hour ago –

Marcia   Henry is only trying to help.

Mary Jane   Half an hour ago we get our second call from the police –

Tom   The guards are up to here (*their necks*) with her –

Mary Jane   Our second call in less than a week: Come up to the hotel immediately, try our keys in the front door –

Tom   Can we do nothing to protect her from herself! –

Mary Jane   We tried our keys –

Tom   Ambulance waiting –

Mary Jane   But it was bolted from inside –

Tom   Locked.

Mary Jane   So – (*Gestures: What else could they do?*) We nodded to them to go ahead.

Tom   Break in the door, Father, force it.

Mary Jane   The humiliation. That's the present situation – the *latest*!

Father Billy   But they were all right?

Mary Jane   Pfff! (*Dismisses his question.*)

Father Billy   But you went in. Did you not go in?

Mary Jane   We did *not* go in!

Marcia   The guards and Dr Kelly went in.

Mary Jane   That's what Vera wanted us to do!

Father Billy (*is shocked that they did not go in*)   But they were all right?

Mary Jane   I know her!

Marcia   They'd fallen asleep, Father.

Mary Jane   She wants a bigger scene –

Marcia   They were asleep, they weren't doing anything –

Mary Jane   Well, she's not having it! And don't forget I know Henry Locke-Browne too –

Marcia   They were asleep! –

Tom   Marcia! –

Marcia   They weren't doing anything –

Mary Jane   Well, now that the police and Dr Kelly have woken them up –

Tom   Marcia! –

Marcia   How dare you, Mary Jane Mansfield, insinuate that my husband would –

Mary Jane   They're up and at it again!

Marcia   How dare you! How dare you! (*Crying again:*) How dare you.

Tom   Marcia!!!

Father Billy   Oh sure, now sure. It isn't nice to see families fighting. (*He looks at his watch.*)

Mary Jane (*looks at him*)   And that's it?

Father Billy   Well, now, please God, we'll sort something out, like. I'll go up – (*He looks at his watch.*) – Oh I will, I'll go up there later on, this afternoon maybe, and . . . (*He rises.*) But you'll have to excuse me now.

Mary Jane   (*'So much for'*) People in authority.

Tom (*a reprimand*)   There is much work remaining to protect the Catholic ethos in this country, Father Billy.

Father Billy   Oh sure, there is. And I know it's upsetting, but what'll I say to her?! D'you see my point? Not like the old days, what! And whatever I say to her, will-she-listen?! (*And he laughs and claps his hands.*) What?

Mary Jane   Nothing can be done? Fine.

Marcia (*venomously*)   I'd lock her up!

The reaction to this is: Perhaps they have found the solution.

Father Billy   Well, you understand that I have to be going.

Tom *rises and sees* **Father Billy** *to the door of the room.*

Tom   Caitriona! Father Billy is leaving! Treasure!

Father Billy (*going out*)   God bless you all now. I'll go up to them, Tom, I will, later on, and –

Tom   You're very good.

Father Billy (*off*)   Gorgeous dress, Caitriona! God bless, God bless . . .

The silence has continued at the table except for **Marcia**'s *sniffling.* **Tom** *returns to his chair.*

Tom   This needs thought. What did you say, Marcia?

Marcia (*weeping*)   I only want Henry to come home.

Tom   What did she say, Mary Jane?

Mary Jane   Insanity. Lock her up.

Tom   I's, yes, lunacy.

Mary Jane   She needs a shock.

Tom   Marcia?

Mary Jane   She needs a good fright.

Marcia (*venomously*)   Lock her up and maybe they'd keep her in there for ever! And it wouldn't be the first or the last time that that's what people have to do!

Mary Jane   Because – Who knows?! – what she is going to do next.

Tom   She needs care?

Marcia   And, no more than if it were Caitriona, you only need Dr Kelly's signature – one signature – to do it.

Mary Jane   Because she will never be content. Never.

Caitriona *comes in with a glass of water.*

Caitriona   Now. A glass of water shall we say.

Mary Jane   Thank you.

Caitriona   Smashing weather again thank God for the time of year. (*And she goes out again.*)

Mary Jane   Are we agreed? (*They are agreed.*) Now, there is one other issue. The hotel has to be withdrawn from auction: With all this confusion anyone, frankly, in the country would bid against you.

Tom's *concerned face nods,* **Marcia** *weeps,* **Mary Jane** *takes a sip from her glass of water.*

Mary Jane   Let us not be sentimental: when she comes out – as-out-she-will-come – let us be prepared for her.

Scene Eight

Late afternoon. Upstairs sitting room in the hotel. (Items of clothing strewn about.) Cushions and dust sheets provide a makeshift bed on the floor.

There is something light-headed about **Vera**, **Finbar** *and* **Henry**, *'morning-after-the-party' kind of stuff – and caused by the guards' and Dr Kelly's breaking-in earlier. Various degrees of undress.*

Finbar *is sitting up in the bed, cocky, celebratory.* **Henry** *is in/on* *the bed too; apart from a few shoulder-shaking fits of the giggles and a few gestures, he is immobilised.* **Vera** *is by the window, a dust sheet draped around her. (She is growing impatient; her situation remains unresolved.)*

Vera   Where are they?

Finbar   Do we have, Vera, any more cigarettes?

Vera   No! Where are they, do they exist, are they real?
(**Tom** *and* **Mary Jane**.)

Henry (*hoarsely, whispers, his hand held out*)   Vera? (*He dearly needs a drink.*)

Vera (*to* **Henry**)   No! Why didn't they come in when the guards and Dr Kelly broke in?

Finbar   'Hullo?' (*Rural accent of a guard.*)

Giggling-laughter.

Vera   No! No! (*To herself, to stop her own laughter.*)

Finbar   You can sue the guards for the damage to the door. Fuckin' red-necks: 'Hullo?': coming up the stairs. 'Hullo?': coming in the door. Mouth on the first fella like the top of a hot-water bottle.

Renewed giggling.

Vera   No, I'm annoyed! What do I have to do to get them here?

Finbar   But it was clear for all to see they expected to find us in a coma at the least.

Vera   Finding us asleep wasn't how it was meant to have happened.

Finbar   And Dr Kelly: 'Open your eyes. Can you hear me?'

Vera   I-want-to-see-them. Do I have to go out for them?

Finbar   Aw but Jesus, Vera waking up! Scattered them!
(**Vera***'s sitting up suddenly out of her sleep frightened the guards and*

Dr Kelly.)

Vera, *unlike the others, isn't laughing any more. She has come to a decision: 'Okay'. Into action: She finds a bundle of dresses – goes off for them? – to select one, and/or to abandon the idea in favour of simply putting on her mackintosh over whatever she is wearing. Next, she is looking around for something – an 'invitation brick', etc.*

Vera (*to herself*)   Okay. Where'd you leave the car?

Finbar   Just around the – (*Corner.*)

Vera   Car keys.

Finbar   What?

Vera   Car keys! I've a short run to do. Annoyed, annoyed, annoyed, annoyed, annoyed! (*Collects her car keys.* **Finbar** *has reached out of the bed for his trousers for the keys.*) And the money.

Finbar   What?

Vera   Look!!! Just give it to me! – No old plámás (*bullshit*) – the money you stole from my wallet. (*And while he gets the money for her, she is looking around for something:*) What am I looking for? A calling-card, an *invitation*-card.

A gesture from **Henry**, *this time to restrain/warn her from going out.*

Vera   No, something has started, I want it finished, I'm not waiting.

Finbar   Is the party over? (*Giving her the money.*)

Vera   The party isn't over yet: One more celebration to go to finish it. I'd like them to attend me here for an occasion. Maybe an invitation-*brick* through Tom's window will do the trick: Better still – bigger window! – Mary Jane's supermarket is only down there: I'll walk (*In answer to another gesture from* **Henry**:) No! If you're up, dressed, I'll unlock – the cellars! – when I get back. This'll only take a second. (*And she's gone, purposefully.*)

Finbar (*swings his legs out of the bed*)   I couldn't give a shite!

(*Finds his underpants under the sheets, puts them on:*) Do you smoke after you've had intercourse? Well, she said, I never looked. (*To the window:*) Look at her striding! Oh, 'Hullo?': the red-necks are down there, your man with the mouth. Look at them watching her. (*Dressing through the following:*) But from my knowledge – well, you're meant to be the expert – they can't touch you while you're on your own property. Or where you're a guest they can't. Unless you're dead of course. That's why they didn't lay a finger on us earlier. Though you could see they wanted to. Aw Jesus, Henry, get ready, she'll be back in a second! (*He finds* **Henry***'s shoes and dumps them at his feet:*) But you're some man for it all right, I have to hand it to you, the way you can carry it. (*A jibe at* **Henry**.)

Henry, *slow mechanical movements, dressing.*

Finbar I never had such a nice few days! (*To the window again:*) The red-necks are gone. Hmm? . . . No, I never had such a nice few days. Still, d'you ever give any thoughts to reincarnation? If I have any say in the matter I'm going to ask to be let back as a dog. A greyhound. I know it's only a toy they're after but the way that they go after it. Beautiful. Pure. (*He's dressed, ready.*) She (**Vera**) should be coming back.

The lights are fading a little. They continue to fade.

What? (*Why isn't* **Vera** *returned.*) . . . No but, we were talking there: I'll tell *you* one. And this was only last year. But I was giving a man a hand to dig a grave. An aul' one out there in Bungesh side that'd died. Grave dug, we're putting her down, a voice from the back. 'Take her up! That's *my* plot of land!' May I drop down dead here myself this minute if I tell a lie. And why did he wait till the grave was dug? We had to dig another! . . . Unless she (**Vera**) met someone? (*Still looking out the window; absently.*) Take her up, that's my plot of land. That'll tell you the lengths people from round here will go to make a point about property. What?

Henry They've got her. (*He's dressed.*)

Finbar   What?

Henry   They are unbeatable. But put yourself in my hands: You and I together shall take our custom to Mannions of the Hollow. (*He leaves.*)

Finbar (*following*)   What?

Scene Nine

Upstairs sitting room in the hotel. (It is three and a half days later.)

Vera *comes in with a pair of candlesticks and candles. She is sober and in a simple dress. The room has been arranged (by her) as for an occasion. A table has been added (the one she adverted to in Scene Six.) The dust sheet has been removed from the piano: she puts the candlesticks on it. Drinks, formally arranged, wait. Civilisation.*

Doorbell, off, downstairs. A beat. And she calls:

Vera   It's open!

And **Father Billy** *comes up and in.*

Father Billy   It's only me.

She waits for more, as from one who has been sent on a message.

They're on their way. Well, (*'they're'*) sitting in the car out there for a minute, having a chat. So . . . (*He is not at ease.*) They suggested that I be here, but if you'd prefer? (*That he should leave.*)

Vera   Open house.

Father Billy   Because you'll have business to discuss.

Vera   No, there will be no business discussed. (*Which is a surprise for* **Father Billy**.) What would you like?

Father Billy   Ah no sure.

Vera   Do.

Father Billy   Well . . . is that Tropicana?

Vera   That is Tropicana. (*She pours for him.*)

Father Billy   I love Tropicana. It's from Florida. But you're doing the right thing, asking them nicely to visit after all the, all the – Thanks, thank you, God bless! All the comuffle.

Vera   Sit down.

Father Billy   It was a mistake – They know it – having you put into that place.

Vera   Maybe not. (*Which is another surprise for* **Father Billy**.) Sit down, Father.

Father Billy   But it's a blessing that you're well again and that they let you out.

Vera   And is everything well with you?

Father Billy   Why wouldn't it! I told them you're calm. (*After a beat, impulsively:*) I *hate* trouble, Vera, I *hate* it.

Vera   There will be no trouble.

Father Billy   We'll say no more.

Vera   And did you find Henry and Finbar?

Father Billy   I did. But they're . . . (*Drunk.*) Maybe they'll come.

Vera   Thank you.

The doorbell rings.

It's open!

Father Billy   That'll be them now . . . Here they are now.

Mary Jane, **Marcia**, **Caitriona**, **Norman** *and* **Tom** *are coming in: Varying degrees of self-consciousness. (***Mary Jane***, now, seeming to treat the past events as if they were a joke;* **Marcia** *resentful but instructed to contain herself;* **Caitriona***, 'responding' to the pills but cranky;* **Norman** *has been told what to say;* **Tom** *looking both enthusiastic and fearful at the idea of meeting* **Vera** . . .)

Father Billy Look who's here!

Mary Jane How yeh!

Father Billy And Marcia!

Mary Jane How yeh? (*Coming to shake hands.*)

Father Billy Wonderful!

Vera Mary Jane.

Mary Jane We didn't have to break the door down this time!

Marcia *is shaking hands with* **Vera**.

Vera Marcia.

Mary Jane Oh boy is it a crazy world!

Caitriona How the hell are you, Vera!

Vera Caitriona.

Father Billy That's it!

Vera Norman?

Father Billy Isn't he getting big?

Norman Welcome home, Auntie Vera!

Vera Thank you.

Father Billy That's the man!

Tom Lookit! (*Hoarsely, emotional, his hand out but his feet are stuck to the floor.*)

Vera *goes to him and shakes hands with him.*

Father Billy Lovely hurling, girl!

Tom I couldn't be! (*He couldn't be happier about anything.*)

Caitriona Up on your bike! (*Strident.*)

Tom (*turns on her to reprimand her but, instead, laughs heartily, and*) Gas woman!

Vera – *a gesture – invites them to sit down.*

Mary Jane   Well, you're looking well – considering! Are you?

Vera (*'Yes'*)   Sit down.

Mary Jane   We won't stay. We got your – summons – and we are only popping in. We all do things, mistakes frankly, when we are heated. The situation got out of control, there was the medical opinion, among the other factors, and – oh boy is it one crazy world and do we all contribute to it! And we're sorry. Now, Tom has a suggestion.

Vera   You won't stay? (*She doesn't like it.*)

Tom   Tomorrow, Vera: If we could meet in the solicitor's office?

Vera   That won't be possible. I'm eager to get back to the States, clear up the rest of my act, start afresh.

Tom   But.

Mary Jane   When?

Vera   What?

Mary Jane   Might you?

Vera   Go back to the States? First thing in the morning . . . If not sooner.

Mary Jane   Well, in that case. Where would you like us to sit?

Vera   Anywhere.

Tom   Where are *you* sitting, Vera?

Vera   Anywhere.

Father Billy   Yes, do, sit and we'll have a chat.

Tom   This was Mam's chair. Not joining the circle, Treasure?

Caitriona   Here? – Here? – Where exactly would you like me to sit?

Mary Jane   I see you've resurrected the table?

Tom   The deals that were done across this table, Mary Jane!

At this point, **Vera** *is lighting a candle. What is she up to, they wonder. She lights the second candle.*

Father Billy   But d'you know who I love? Esther Williams. D'you know her, Caitriona, d'you, Marcia?

Tom   The swimmer, Father?

Father Billy   The film star sure! I switched on the telly last night and there she was. But you don't see much of her any more: I wonder why is that, like?

Tom   Wouldn't she be getting on now, Father?

Father Billy   Aw she wouldn't be that old! What? (*They are not sure what age Esther Williams might be.*) . . . But the film was called *Dangerous When Wet.* Dangerous when wet, what! I looked it up in the papers. Where Esther has to swim the Channel. She's called Annie in the film, Annie Higgins, like, I think. I think maybe she was meant to be Irish. I wonder? 'Cause I missed the beginning. I wouldn't say it was one of her best because I've seen a few of them. But there was a French lassie in it too. Denise? Denise? Denise Darcel! Oh, a bit of a lady! And says Denise to Esther: 'You sweem ze Chan-nel and you mebbe win ze med-al, but that won't kip you warm at night.' You never saw, Caitriona, *Dangerous When Wet*, Marcia?

Marcia   No, Father.

Vera   Now, what can I get everyone – Caitriona?

Caitriona   What's it like being locked up?

Vera   . . . Oh. (*She doesn't want to talk about it.*)

Father Billy   Oh but it was well done!

Caitriona   But what's it like?

Tom   She told you –

Caitriona   She didn't! They had you locked up in a mental home – what was it like?

Vera   I've put it behind me, Caitriona. Marcia?

Marcia   Port!

Caitriona   She's put it where?

Tom   Treasure –

Caitriona   But there's nothing wrong with her!

Tom   Little Treasure –

Caitriona   Is she mad? – Are you mad? –

Tom   Haven't we talked about it enough? –

Caitriona   She's been locked up for three days –

Mary Jane   Caitriona!

Caitriona   D'you mind?! I'm interested in these matters! Did they find anything wrong with you?

Vera   No.

Caitriona   Did they find anything wrong with you, find anything wrong with you, did they?

Vera   No.

Caitriona   They found nothing wrong with her!

Tom   ⎱   Caitriona!

Mary Jane   ⎰   Caitriona!

Caitriona   I rest my case.

Vera *hands port to* **Marcia**.

Father Billy   Love Esther.

Vera   What would you like, Mary Jane?

Caitriona   So why did they keep you in for three days?

Vera   Three and a half. (*To herself:*) Okay. (*She has decided to talk.*) It was awful. (*To* **Caitriona**:) I had to wait my turn for the psychiatrist. But I used the time. Well, why not: To think about this place (*the hotel*): How much it meant to you, and what did it mean to me. And how did I come to find myself in, well, a loony bin. That I've been in a bit of a state since I came home. In a bit of a state for a *long* time. Well, I mean, I've been praying for a long time now for the grace that would change me, conform me, make me worthy. I used to think I was real because I came from here.

Mary Jane   Yes, Vera, we know about – (*All that kind of stuff.*)

Vera   And all that American jazz, Mary Jane! Then the psychiatrist: We had a great talk. A test. But he gave me this. (*Producing a slip of paper:*) A little fella. He wrote it down: that I'm not a threat to myself or to anyone else, and that I'm capable of making decisions. And I've made them. (*She offers the slip of paper for their inspection. They do not 'need' to see it.*) So, I'm the only certified sane person in the room. And that the reason I came home in the first place, I told him, was to pay my respects to an old woman, my grandmother, who was the nearest in family or friend anyone could hope for: That I hadn't quite paid my respects but that when – *if* – I got out I would finalise the matter. And that's all that remains to be done.

The reason for **Vera**'s *coming home is news to* **Mary Jane** *and* **Tom**.

Mary Jane   The reason, Vera, why you weren't informed sooner about grandmother's death was because we were all upset.

Father Billy   May she rest in peace.

Vera (*acknowledges* **Father Billy***; impassive previously to* **Mary Jane**)   So what would everyone like? Tom?

Tom   Well, d'you know what I'm going to say to you? A bit of openness is all I want. You don't have to go to any solicitor's office: We'll do it across this table.

Vera   Ahmmm!

Tom   You don't understand me! I don't think you'll be disappointed in our proposition. Daddy sitting there. (*'Man dear alive'!*) What used he say? You can get nothing for nothing!

Vera   You can.

Tom *opens his mouth to speak –*

Vera   I won't discuss it across any table. I've decided what to do with the hotel.

Tom   What?

Vera   You'll have to wait and see.

Mary Jane   Relax, Tom. (*Aside to him.*)

Vera   I want to finalise, bury everything and mark the occasion with – a wake. Now, is that not possible?

Mary Jane   Open the wine, pass round the pipes, call the fiddler! Vera gets her way again! (*She starts to pour drinks.*)

Vera (*takes a Coke to* **Norman**)   We've been neglecting you.

Tom (*to* **Mary Jane**)   What?

Mary Jane   A Jemmy for Tom! – (*Jameson whiskey. To him:*) Play along with her –

Father Billy   Now, Marcia – (*Another port.*)

Mary Jane   Father Billy is all right –

Father Billy   Oh now! –

Mary Jane   With his camouflaged drink! And would you like a song, Vera?

Father Billy   Did you hear that, Marcia, a song!

Caitriona   'Summertime an' the livin' is easy . . .'

Tom   'Fish are jumpin –' Coke for Treasure!

Mary Jane (*aside to* **Tom**)   Relax. (*To herself:*) She's a fool.

Father Billy   This is more like it!

Vera   And for yourself, Mary Jane?

Mary Jane   Oh what the hell, life is short! (*She has a whiskey.*)

Tom   Well? (*Glass raised: A toast.*)

Father Billy   To God and St Patrick! (*Laughing.*) –

Tom   And to our native land! (*Laughing.*)

Vera   To the dead!

And as they drink, **Caitriona**'*s toast:*

Caitriona   Prozac! (*And singing again to herself:*) 'Summertime and the livin' is easy . . .'

Off, downstairs, the doorbell.

Tom   This's what we should have done last week –

Vera (*calls*)   Come in! –

Tom   Six months, a year ago!

Doorbell.

Caitriona   'Your daddy's rich . . .'

Henry (*off*)   Let down the bridge!

Father Billy   That'll be Henry, like –

Vera   Push!

Marcia   Let him in! (*Alarm.*)

Caitriona   'So hush little baby . . .'

Father Billy   And Finbar.

Vera (*to* **Tom** *who has been asking her would she like him to* *answer the door*)   Open house!

Tom (*going out*)   This's more like it!

Marcia   He hasn't been home in a week. And now he's sleeping up in that dirty fella's dirty house.

And, during the above, **Henry** *appears to have discovered that the door was open: He is on the stairs. (He is very drunk but he is straight-backed; he knows very well where he is; despair behind his attempted panache. And* **Finbar** *appears to be reluctant – wary at first – about joining the group.)*

Henry (*off*)   Finbar, you can make it! –

Tom (*off*)   Henry! –

Henry (*off*)   There is water beyond this rise: I am sure of it! (*He comes in.*)

Tom (*off*)   Come on up, Finbar! –

Henry (*enters*)   I have nothing to declare but my schizophrenia!

Marcia   He's killing himself.

Henry (*to* **Father Billy***, as to a barman*)   Same again!

Marcia   He's like a tramp.

Henry (*to the four women, equally*)   How are you, how are you, how are you, how are you! (*Nothing to* **Norman** *though* **Norman** *is clearly visible to him.*)

Father Billy   How are you, Henry boy!

Henry   Ah! – (*as if only now recognising who* **Father Billy** *is*) – he comes with garlic and crucifix.

Tom (*coming in with* **Finbar**)   Come in, my friend, and take off your coat!

Father Billy   How are you, Finbar boy!

Tom   And any friend of any sister of mine is good enough for me! Come over here beside Vera.

Finbar *favours/will favour a place near* **Henry**.

Henry   What did I tell you: Water! (*The drinks.*)

Father Billy   One more (*drink*) isn't going to matter at this stage. (*To* **Marcia**.)

Tom   Two gas men! Where were we, Vera?

Vera   A song!

Henry   'Breeng flowers of the rarest . . .' (*Singing; eyes shut.*)

Caitriona   'Summertime an' the livin' . . .' (*Joining in competition.*)

Father Billy (*laughing*)   One voice! –

Tom (*laughing*)   One voice! Treasure! – Henry! (*For silence.*) Lookit, I feel! (*He feels great.*) Is there anyone here has any serious objections to a decent song?!

Father Billy   Now you're talking!

Tom   Do you, Vera?

Vera   On the contrary.

Henry   Lovely!

Mary Jane   Marcia will sing.

Father Billy   Marcia! Misty!

Tom   Folks! –

Mary Jane   Now's your chance, Marcia! –

Tom   I give you –

Caitriona   Folks! – (*Bad and cranky mimicry of* **Tom**.)

Tom   I crave silence for! Mrs Henry Locke-Browne!

Mary Jane   . . . Ah come on!

Father Billy   She will.

Tom   This is a night for reconciling families.

Mary Jane   Sing!

And **Marcia** *sings. And, whatever her propensity for distress, she is a good singer, it's her song. Indeed, in what follows (and though there is an element of prostitution in what they are doing) they succumb to their own songs and show/redeem something of their innocence.*

Vera's *recurring 'Ah-haa!' is a complex of emotions: the sound of an afternoon girl in an afternoon bar pretending to be having a good time; at another level there is harshness in it as at having been betrayed, while at the same time there is a cry in it for the thing that has done the betraying; a modern olagon at a wake . . . (and it's a preparation for the floodgates that open in the next scene).*

There is ongoing pain in **Henry**'s *repeated 'Lovely!' Unlike* **Vera**, *who will escape,* **Henry** *is caught for ever. (Suicidal thoughts.)*

Finbar, *like the scavenger, dealing in the temporalities: free drink and a degree of self-congratulations about being included in and dealing with this company.*

Marcia   'Look at me, I'm as helpless as a kitten up a tree . . . I feel misty, I'm too much in love.'

Applause, together with:

Tom   Now who's the singer!

Mary Jane   Never fails.

Father Billy ⎫   Who is the singer, who is the singer!

Tom ⎭   Can she sing?!

Mary Jane ⎫   Never better.

Father Billy ⎭   My life on you, Marcia!

Tom   Who's next, Vera?

Finbar ⎫   Excellent, Mrs Locke-Browne!

Tom ⎭   Whose twist is it?

Vera   Yourself!

Tom   What would you like?

Finbar   Three-legged dog!

Henry   Lovely!

Finbar   Three-legged dog goes into this saloon yeh see and he has a look around: I'm lookin' for the man who shot my paw! Jesus!

Laughter/applause.

Mary Jane   Jeekers! What is the world coming to?

Tom   Gas, one gas man!

Henry   Lovely!

Father Billy (*of* **Henry**)   He'll be grand.

Tom (*to* **Vera**)   Song? (*What song.*)

Vera   The Lily of Killarney.

Tom   ⎫   Aw! (*Laughing.*)

Father Billy   ⎭   Aw! (*Laughing.*)

Tom   Folks! –

Caitriona   Folks! –

Father Billy   The Moon Hath Raised – (*To the piano, to play.*)

Tom   From the Lily *off* Killarney!

Henry   Lovely!

Tom   I feel like killing a flaming calf! (*And – his introduction played – he sings on cue:*) 'The moon hath raised her lamp above / To light the way to thee, my love / To light the way to thee, my love; / Her rays upon the waters play / To tell me eyes more bright than they / Are watching through the night / Are watching through the night. / I come, I come, my heart's delight / I come, I come, my heart's delight / I come, I come, my heart's delight / I come, I come, my heart's delight / I come, I come, my heart's delight.'

Father Billy (*playing and singing*)   'On hill and dale the moonbeams fall / And spread their silver light o'er all /

But those bright eyes –'

Tom/Father Billy (*duet*) 'But those eyes I soon shall see
/ Reserve their glorious light for me / Reserve their
glorious light for me / Reserve their glorious light for me;
/ Methinks that love they do invite / I come, I come, my
heart's delight.'

Tom 'I come, my heart's delight'

Father Billy 'I come, I come, my heart's delight'

Tom 'I come, my heart's delight'

Father Billy 'I come, I come, my heart's delight'

Tom/Father Billy 'I come, my heart's delight, my
heart's delight.'

Applause, together with:

Henry Lovely! –

Mary Jane Not bad! –

Vera Ah-haa!

Finbar Lovely, Father, lovely, Mr O'Toole!

Tom (*to* **Vera**) You're not going back in the morning! –
'Cause I won't let you!

Vera Ah-haa!

Father Billy Who's next?

Tom Folks! –

Caitriona Folks! –

Tom I had one good reason for getting my humble piece
out of the way first –

Finbar Father, d'you know –

Tom There's someone here I didn't want to follow –
Ciuinness (*quiet*) there a sec, Finbar – someone, who is not
only nothing short of being a brilliant musician, but
someone –

Mary Jane   We're in suspense! –

Tom   But someone who can sing a mean song: Father Billy Houlihan!

Father Billy   Oh now!

Tom   And if there's a better organist in the whole country I'd like to meet him.

Mary Jane   'Sea, oh the sea'!

Caitriona (*of her glass of Coke*)   This is piss.

Tom   Treasure! –

Caitriona   Sedimentary, my dear Watson!

Henry   The organ is a musical JCB!

Caitriona (*pouring vodka for herself*)   Does anyone here have any serious objections to my taking a decent drink?

Henry   Lovely!

Caitriona   Cheers, everybody, cheers, Norman!

Tom (*winks at* **Vera** *and is introducing* **Father Billy** *again*)   Father Billy!

Finbar (*singing*)   'When the golden sun sinks in the hill / And the toil of a long day is o'er –'

Father Billy   Man, Finbar! –

Finbar   'Though the road may be long, with the lilt of a song / I'll forget I was weary before'

Father Billy *comes in with accompaniment.*

Finbar   'Far away where the blue shadows fall / I shall come to contentment and rest / And the toils of the day will be all charmed away / In my little grey home in the west.'

Father Billy (*speaking it, wanting the singer to get the proper tempo*)   'There are hands that will welcome me in'

Finbar   'There are lips I am burning to kiss / There are two eyes that shine'

Tom ⎫ 'Just because they are mine'

Finbar ⎭ 'Just because they are mine / And a
thousand things others may miss / It's a corner of heaven
itself –'

Henry   Lovely! –

Finbar   'Yet it's only a tumble-down nest –' (*Momentary
balk.*)

Father Billy (*providing the high note*)   'But –'

Finbar   'With love brooding there / There's no place can
compare / To my little grey home in the west.'

Applause, together with:

Mary Jane   Sentimental rubbish – My little grey home in
the – Pfff! –

Caitriona   What does anybody think of our politicians –
Can we have a serious conversation? –

Mary Jane   How are you, Henry!

Caitriona   Aren't they the most – Have you ever come
across –

Henry   Lovely, Mary Jane! –

Caitriona   Such an unhandsome bunch of flutes!

Tom   Vera? (*Whose next?*)

Vera   Mary Jane.

Mary Jane   *Me?!*

Vera   Vision of Connaught.

Mary Jane (*recites*)   'I walked entranced through a land of
morn / The sun with wondrous excess of light shone down
and glanced over seas of corn / And lustrous gardens a-left
and right; / Even in the clime of resplendent Spain beams
no such sun upon such a land; / But it was the time, 'twas

in the reign of Cathal Mor of the Wine Red Hand!'

Tom (*rapt admiration*) Shh-shh-shh for Mary Jane.

Mary Jane 'Anon stood nigh by my side a man / Of princely aspect and port sublime / Him queried I, "O my Lord and Khan! What clime is this and what golden time?" When he –' (*She has grown self-conscious; dismisses it.*) Pff, rubbish!

Tom No! –

Father Billy No! –

Finbar No, Mrs Mansfield!

Father Billy Vision of Connaught –

Tom It's lovely! – (*To* **Vera**:) Isn't it? –

Finbar It is! –

Vera Ah-haa! –

Father Billy By James Clarence Mangan –

Tom Him queried I!

Henry (*takes it up: Rising slowly but violent movement of his arms/fists, eyes shut*) 'Him queried I, "O my Lord and Khan! What clime is this, and what golden time?"' – K.H.A.N., Khan, identical with the Irish, C.E.A.N.N., Ceann, head or chieftain. 'When he – The clime is a clime to praise, the clime is Erin's, the green and bland and it is the time, these be the days of Cathal Mor of the Wine Red –' Rubbish! A pen, anybody – anybody pen, piece of paper!?

*He has a pen and is given a piece of paper (***Vera***'s 'certificate'?) and he starts to write. (We shall get his composition later.)*

Marcia Then I saw thrones and circling fires!

Mary Jane 'And a dome rose near me as by a spell / Whence flowed the tones of silver lyres and many voices in wreathed swell; / And their thrilling chime fell on my ears as the heavenly hymn of an angel band – / "It is now the

time, these be the years of Cathal Mor of the Wine Red
Hand!"'

Henry (*writing*)   Lovely!

Marcia   I sought the hall!

Mary Jane   I sought the hall

Caitriona   And behold! – a change

Mary Jane   From light to darkness

Marcia   Joy to woe!

Mary Jane   Joy to woe. Kings, nobles, all

Caitriona   }   Looked aghast and strange

Marcia   }   Looked aghast and strange

Mary Jane   The minstrel group sat

Marcia   In dumbest show!

Mary Jane   Had some great crime wrought this dread
amaze, this

Caitriona   Terr-or?

Mary Jane   Terror

Marcia   None seemed to understand.

*A beat, the trio of performers smile at one another without knowing
why.*

Vera (*to herself*)   Ah-haa . . .

Marcia   I *again* walked forth –

Caitriona   But lo! –

Mary Jane   Lo! –

Marcia   Lo!

*The three of them, now – frightening themselves with the poem – are
giggling like schoolgirls, bobbing their heads together for a moment.*

Mary Jane   But lo! the sky showed fleckt with blood

Marcia   And an alien sun

Caitriona   Glared from the north

Mary Jane   And there stood on high amid his shorn beams

Marcia   } A Skel-et-on!

Caitriona } A Skel-et-on!

Tom (*whispers his enthusiasm to* **Vera**)   Great!

Mary Jane   A skeleton. (*And tosses off the rest of it:*) It was by a stream of the Castle Maine, one autumn eve in Teuton's land, that I dreamed this dream of the time and reign of . . . ?

All (*except* **Vera**)   Cathal Mor of the Wine Red Hand.

And further drinks are poured as they applaud themselves, together with:

Father Billy   There's learning for you! –

Henry (*writing*)   Lovely! –

Finbar   I hear a sudden cry of pain there is a rabbit in a snare! (*Which also means 'lovely!'*) –

Caitriona   I am the doctor's daughter! (*Also means 'lovely!' She kisses* **Mary Jane**:) Kiss-kiss!

Tom, *laughing – though his hand to his head: his recurring headache – has joined* **Vera**. **Mary Jane**, *now, to* **Vera***'s other side.* **Vera** *knows what they are up to. The three of them watching the rest of the party.*

Caitriona (*kissing people and wanting to be kissed. To* **Marcia**)   Kiss-kiss!

Finbar (*pouring a drink for himself*)   But! – as Shakespeare'd say – more of this anon!

Father Billy   No! No! I'm not allowed that, Caitriona! (*Meaning* **Caitriona***'s kiss.*)

Caitriona   Norman: Kiss-kiss! (*She kisses* **Norman** *and gets*

him another Coke.)

Mary Jane   Good idea of yours, Vera. (*The wake/the party.*)

Tom   Good idea?! Magic! Isn't this what life is all about, isn't it?

Vera (*calls*)   Another song!

Tom   Lookit! is *she* going back in the morning, Mary Jane?

Mary Jane   I don't know.

Tom (*to* **Vera**)   Are you going back in the morning?

Vera   Another song! –

Tom   Well, you're going back over my dead body, my lady! Man dear alive sure! (*'This is what life is all about!'*) And the catching up we have to do! Wait'll you see how fast I'll be getting rid of this lot in a minute and the three of us'll sit down and finish that bottle together – What d'you say, Mary Jane?

Vera   D'you have a headache, Tom?

Vera *had produced the phial of pills that we saw in Scene Five.*
Tom *dismisses his headache: He is laughing heartily and pointing at* **Caitriona** *who is joining them:*

Caitriona   Kiss-kiss!

Mary Jane   I've had mine already, Caitriona!

Vera (*offering a pill to* **Tom**)   Take one of these.

Caitriona (*kisses* **Tom**)   Kiss-kiss. (*Turns to* **Vera**, *kisses her:*) I don't care what they say about you, I envy you. (*And pops the pill.*)

Vera (*offering him another pill*)   Tom?

Tom   You're very good. (*And he swallows it.*)

Mary Jane   What are they?

Vera (*extricating, removing herself from them*)   They're very effective. Let's finish the wake – Father Billy, 'Sea, oh the sea'!

Henry   Everybody! (*He stands.*)

Father Billy   Let him off.

Tom   Another limerick, Henry?

Henry   My dearest Marcia, by the time you read this I shall be no more.

Some laughter/recognition.

How can I explain what I do not understand myself. I am being unfaithful in going to sleep with death but have no thought in your mind that I was ever – ever – unfaithful to you in life. All my love to Norman and to Baby Carol. Yours, Henry Locke-Browne. (*He goes out to the Gents.*)

Applause.

Mary Jane   That's a new version, Henry!

Finbar (*to himself*)   Fuckin'!

Caitriona   Lovely!

Father Billy (*of **Henry***)   He'll be grand now for another six months.

Tom   In quick, Father, before someone else starts.

The lights are fading. **Father Billy** *is singing and playing a jazzy version of the ballad.*

Father Billy   I'd better because I've first Mass to say in the morning. 'The sea, oh the sea, gra geal mo croi, long may it roll between England and me . . .'

The lights are down, the music stops.

The lights come up. **Vera** *is pouring a careful – deliberate drink for herself.* **Tom** *and* **Caitriona** *are all but asleep in the couch;* **Caitriona** *is feeling amorous.* **Henry** *is back in his seat, head bowed over the table;* **Marcia** *and* **Norman** *watch and wait;* **Finbar** *seated; he is extremely drunk.* **Vera** *lights a cigarette.*

Father Billy (*off*)   Good night, God bless, Mary Jane!

Mary Jane (*off*)   Good night!

Caitriona   Bita nookey for Little Treasure.

Tom *giggles.*

Mary Jane (*returns*)   I'll see you out, Finbar.

Finbar   Is the party over?

Mary Jane *looks at* **Vera**.

Vera   Yeh.

Henry (*to himself, head bowed*)   Lovely.

Finbar   Permission to go to the cassie?

Norman (*nudged by* **Marcia**)   Dad?

Finbar (*goes out to the Gents*)   I hear a sudden cry of pain!

Norman   Dad?

Finbar (*off*)   Now I hear the cry again . . .

Henry (*finds a drink left behind by someone*)   Careless shepherds leave a feast for the wolf. (*He knocks it back.*)

Marcia   Henry, I'm your wife. Are you coming home?

Henry (*to himself*)   Lovely, lovely . . . (*He is crying.*)

Tom *and* **Caitriona** *giggle in their sleep.*

Marcia *is assisting* **Henry** *to his feet. He declines her help and gets up.*

Henry   Have you once – ever! – seen me stagger? I do not permit it in myself.

He steps aside for **Marcia** *and* **Norman** *to precede him.*
Marcia*, bridling her shoulders in some private triumph she considers she is having, leaves with* **Norman**. **Henry** *bows to the room and follows.* **Vera** *blows out the candles, sits, gauging her drink as to when she wants to finish it.* **Tom** *and* **Caitriona** *are asleep.*

Vera   They'll wake up . . . What's it worth? (*The hotel.*)

Mary Jane   . . . What are you going to do?

Vera   I think you know, Mary Jane.

Mary Jane   . . . If it's what I think?

Vera   How is Declan?

Mary Jane   Holding the fort: we're open seven days a week . . . You don't have to be so generous, you know.

Vera   It isn't worth a toss. (*She finishes her drink, collects her coat and bag.*)

Mary Jane   Vera.

Vera   We have nothing more to say to each other.

She leaves. **Mary Jane***'s smile: She has got what she wants; smile beginning to question itself: Has she got what she wants? To the window to watch* **Vera** *(and to wait there for* **Vera***'s car).*

Finbar (*off and coming in*)   I have one! Yeh see, yeh see, Jesus, Mary and Joseph are going down the road and they meet the good fairy, and the good fairy – Mrs Mansfield – the good fairy says to them anyway, think he says and I'll give you a wish, I'll give you one wish each but it can be anything you like, anything at all. I'd like says Jesus – he was first – I'd like says he to be thirty-four. And St Joseph was next. I'd like says St Joseph to have a child of my own . . .

A car starting up in the night during this – **Vera***'s car. Now the lights of the car washing the hotel, washing* **Mary Jane** *and* **Finbar** *in the window.*

Finbar   And the Blessed Virgin was last. I'd like says the Blessed Virgin, I'd like says Our Lady to go back to Mayo.

He laughs, highly amused. **Mary Jane** *hits him with her fist and leaves.* **Finbar** *staggering, reeling in laughter and pain.*

The sound of **Vera***'s car continues.*

Scene Ten

An open space: A graveyard. Morning.

Mrs Conneeley, *overcoat as in Scene One, is moving about a space in the ground, a rectangle, a grave. She picks a weed. A car, off, approaching, which she does not register until it stops. She waits.*

And **Vera** *is coming in.*

Mrs Conneeley   You're on the road early!

Vera   Yeh!

Mrs Conneeley   Did you sell! (*Which is another greeting.*)

Vera (*laughs*)   No! I called to the house: Paddy said this is where you might be he thought.

Mrs Conneeley   Yes. This is where my husband is buried. It's getting crowded, Vera? (*The graveyard is.*) . . . You're on your way back?

Vera   I am. So! (*She flaps her hands to her sides.*) Your other son.

Mrs Conneeley   Francis?

Vera   Francis, solicitor. Where is he in Newcastle?

Mrs Conneeley   The Main Street. (*And, as in Scene Two, she is both surprised at and proud of* **Francis***'s success.*)

Vera (*as if in easy dismissal of a matter*)   Nah, I didn't sell. But I'm going through Newcastle and I thought I'd call in on him. Something simple. Hmm? (*The 'Hmm?' may be silent, a look, as if she wants* **Mrs Conneeley***'s support/approval of what she is going to do.*)

Mrs Conneeley   Yes?

Vera   Oh, I just want to – (*she shrugs*) simply – sign over a place to my family. Clean. Final. (*Smiles.*) And begin again in a clean elsewhere.

Mrs Conneeley (*nods. Then, the crowded graveyard again*) . . . And I remember the day it was opened. The first person buried in it. He was a Kerrigan. They say he was forty. And in the same week, she would have been only eight or nine years old, one of the O'Malleys below, Sally. And d'you know, those two held this place for a year.

Stoops to pick another weed. And **Vera** *does the same, assisting her.*

Mrs Conneeley   I never bothered to mark it. (*Dismissive:*) Ah, headstones! What is it but an aul' hole in the ground.

Vera   . . . I was thinking about what you were saying.

Mrs Conneeley   Hah? (*Can't remember.*)

Vera   Loneliness.

Mrs Conneeley   Oh! (*And she starts laughing.*)

And **Vera** *starts to laugh too. But now she is crying. Tears that she cannot stop, that she has been suppressing throughout. She begins to sob. Her sobbing continues, becoming dry and rhythmical: Grief for her grandmother, for the family that she perhaps never had, and for herself and her fear at this, her first acceptance of her isolation.*

Mrs Conneeley *puts her arms around her and holds her and lets her sob on. And* **Vera** *holds* **Mrs Conneeley**.

Vera's *tears are subsiding.* **Mrs Conneeley** *resumes the weeding.*

Mrs Conneeley   Yes . . . No, I never bothered to mark it. But it gets overgrown. And they're known to make mistakes, Vera, d'you know. Oh and there's many's the widow-woman knocking about, waiting to get in here. And what at all in the next world would I do if they put another woman down on top of him before me?

She smiles up at **Vera**. **Vera** *smiles.*

Mrs Conneeley (*straightens up*)   That's the way we are and what about it . . . Well?

Vera   Heigh-ho!

Mrs Conneeley (*her two hands on top of* **Vera**'s)   . . . You'll be all right.

Vera *leaves. The purr of the car and it drives off.* **Mrs Conneeley**'s *hand held up in a farewell. Now, her attention on the grave (downstage side of it, her back to us), like someone preparing a bed.*

The House

for johny

The House was first presented at the Abbey Theatre, Dublin, on 12 April 2000. The cast was as follows:

Mother	Geraldine Plunkett
Marie	Jane Brennan
Christy	Patrick O'Kane
Louise	Deirdre Molloy
Jimmy	Gary Lydon
Peter	Andrew Bennett
Goldfish	Don Wycherley
Bunty	John Olohan
Kerrigan	Frank McCusker
Susanne	Ali White
Tarpey	Des Cave

All the other roles were played by:

Paul Keeley	Fergal McElherron
Fiona Kelly	Geoff Minogue
Maeve Leonard	Daithi O'Suilleabdhain

Director Conall Morrison
Set Designer Francis O'Connor
Costume Designer Joan O'Clery
Lighting Designer Ben Ormerod
Stage Director Finola Eustace
Voice Coach Andrea Ainsworth
Fight Director Richard Ryan

Characters

Mother (Mrs de Burca)
Marie
Christy
Louise
Jimmy
Peter
Goldfish
Bunty
Kerrigan
Susanne
Tarpey
Extras (to play returned emigrants, sympathisers . . .)

Setting

1950s Ireland

Scene One

Mother *and* **Marie** *have had lunch at their garden table (beneath a tree). July.* **Mother** *is a TB convalescent. One shoulder is lower than the other perhaps (due to a collapsed lung).* **Marie** *is in her thirties. (She's tall, perhaps, and angular.) A hint of spinsterhood.*

Mother *sips from a glass of Guinness and grimaces, not savouring it.*

Marie   'It's good for you.' (*They share a smile.*)

Mother   . . . Glorious! (*The day.*) . . . Thank you, love, thank you. (*For the lunch.*) . . . We'll miss our tree.

Marie   Oh, I don't know. The advantages of living in the town?

Mother *nods, as to herself, in the slow, formal manner: a characteristic.*

Marie   I saw what looked like really nice ham in McCabe's window and I'll get some for this evening and we'll have it with a salad.

Mother   Thank you, love . . . Glorious!

Marie   . . . There's someone coming up the drive . . . Mum, you have a visitor.

Mother   I have? Who?

Marie   Christy Cavanagh.

Mother   Christy?! Our lovely gentle boy. 'I'd like to be this family please.'

Christy (*off*)   Lovely day!

Marie   Lovely day.

Mother   Christy! (*Rising.*)

Christy (*coming in*)   Don't get up, Mrs de Burca!

Mother   Christy, Christy, my dear, my dear!

Christy   How're you all, how are you, Mrs de Burca?

She takes his two hands, kisses him. She would kiss him again but it might embarrass him.

He's about thirty, handsome, with a touch of masculine rawness. New suit, quality of its kind, though it would appear that he's a builder's labourer. Forties–fifties film-star influence.

There's an unusual bond of affection and ease between him and **Mother***. By contrast, he is self-conscious of* **Marie** *– and she of him. She disapproves of him, he feels (wrongly; in fact, it's the contrary). And she's older than him.*

Mother   My dear! – Now! – How are you?

Christy   Terrific! (*A nod:*) Marie. (*And wonders should he shake hands/kiss her/which. And, clumsily, does neither. He offers to assist* **Mother** *back to her chair.*) Here, let me give you a . . . You're feeling well again?

Mother   Thank you, thank you. (*She's seated.*) Now! Home again for the summer!

Christy   Home again for the summer! – (*And laughs:*) As usual!

Mother   As usual!

Christy   As usual, Mrs de Burca! How're things, Marie?

Marie   Fine, thank you.

Christy   All right, yeh?

Marie   Yes.

Mother   When did you arrive?

Christy   This morning early.

Mother   On the boat.

Christy   On the boat.

Marie   Sit down?

Christy   Thank you. On the boat, Mrs de Burca, the *Princess Maud*, cattle boat, crowded, the lot of us from Holyhead. The train before that, eight hours of it, just as bad, packed from Euston Station. I hit the sack as soon as I got in and only woke up half an hour ago. (*Celebratory:*) The scenery! Isn't it a lovely day, what!

Mother   Isn't it absolutely glorious!

Christy   Glorious, Mrs de Burca, absolutely!

Marie   Would you like some tea?

Christy   No thanks, Marie.

Mother   Christy?

Christy   No thanks.

Marie   I can make some fresh.

Christy   Amn't I grand now here!

Marie *takes the tray of lunch things off to the house.*

Mother   Thank you, love. And how are things at home?

Christy   Home? (*Momentarily puzzled. Here, de Burcas' place, is 'home' to him – at least subconsciously.*)

Mother   Your father.

Christy   Oh! (*And laughs:*) Isn't the aul bastard old now so what more damage can he do anyone! (*He indicates the lawn:*) Hay must be fetching a great price this year, Mrs de Burca?

Mother *laughs.*

Christy   How long since that lawn saw a lawnmower? I was looking at it all the way up the drive.

Mother   Tommy Smith, who was doing it for us, emigrated too last spring.

Christy   Is Tommy gone too? There'll soon be no one left. Well, it never looked like that when I used to do it. But you're keeping well again?

Mother   Not too bad now. (*And on second thoughts:*) Yes!

Christy   And McGreedy, where is Mrs McGreedy?

Mother   She died.

Christy   Aw! I knew there was something, coming in the gate, when I didn't hear her bark.

Mother   And is everything all right with you, Christy?

Christy   Oh yes, oh yes!

Mother   Plenty of work?

Christy   Plenty of it!

Mother   On the buildings?

Christy   On the, on the – (*Something evasive about him on this subject. He takes out his cigarettes to fidget with them.*) Closed down now over there of course for the annual two weeks. The changes that's happening over there: there'll be building work going on in England for the next twenty years, Mrs de Burca.

Mother   But you'll stay home for the rest of the summer.

Christy   Oh I'll stay – As usual! Oh I'll stay, let the others go back after their two weeks – let them off, off with them! But I'll take my cue from the swallows.

Mother   Give me one of those.

He looks at her: should she be smoking?

Give me one of those.

Christy (*gives her a cigarette, lights it*)   And how is Susanne?

Mother *holds up a clenched fist:* **Susanne** *would appear to be a handful.*

Christy (*laughing, disagreeing*)   No! No! Still at the secretarial?

Mother   Yes. I believe so.

Christy   Still in London?

Mother   Still in London.

Christy   I haven't seen Susanne now for . . . Or, I was in a place over there one night and I'd nearly have sworn it was her I saw, but when I got the chance to look around again she was gone. And that she spotted me. But hardly: it was hardly

Susanne's kind of place, if you know what I mean.

Mother   She'll be home on Friday.

Christy   Susanne will?

Mother (*nods*)   She's fine. And Louise is . . . (*Unease. Then:*) All fine. And your brothers, Christy, where are they?

Christy   Scattered somewhere, I do believe.

Mother   And do you ever see them?

Christy (*dismisses the matter as of no consequence to him. Then, silently:*)   Oh! Something for you. (*An object from his pocket.*)

Mother   What is it?

Christy   Hang about. (*It's a pendant and, in the manner of a child playing with a toy aeroplane, he goes:*) Z-z-z-z-z-z . . . ! (*And he presents it to her.*)

They have a great laugh. It's a crucifix and chain.

Mother   Just what I needed: a crucifix!

Christy   Glorious! (*The place, the day. Then:*) Oh! (*He has something else for her: a story.*) Yeh know Robin Hood, Mrs de Burca?

Mother   I do.

Christy   Your man with the feather, bow and arrow, Sherwood Forest?

Mother   Yes.

Christy   Well, he's dying. Aw he's very bad. And he's in bed in his bedroom. And he says to his friend the friar who's with him: Friar, pull back them curtains, open that window so that I may behold my beloved Sherwood Forest for one last time. And the friar does what he's told. Now, says Robin Hood, hand me down my bow and arrow. And he gets them. Now, says he, aiming the bow – the hands are shaky on him. But, he says, wherever this arrow is to fall it's on that spot that I'm to be buried by my merry men. And he fires. And d'you know where they buried him? On top of the wardrobe.

They have another laugh, together with:

Stupid! Stupid!

Mother   Well, God bless you, Christy!

Christy (*celebratory of the place and day again*)   But this place will never change. Absolutely!

Mother   We're selling.

Christy   . . . You're?

Mother*'s characteristic nod.*

Christy   *Here?*

Mother   We're on the move too.

As best he can he is concealing his shock. He would like to ask why are they selling but **Marie** *is returning. She has her car keys and a glass of lemonade, which she puts on the table.*

Marie   Time for your rest now, Mum.

Mother   Look at the lovely present Christy brought me.

Marie   What is it?

Mother   Dakka-dakka-dakka-dakka-neeavachchah-z-z-z-z-z-z . . . (*Aeroplane starting up, taking off on a runway . . .*)

Marie *to* **Mother***'s side to assist her, if required, out of her chair.* **Mother** *takes a folded newspaper that is on the table.*

Mother   I'll manage now. Sit for a while, Marie, and talk. (*A bow:*) Christy.

Christy   Mrs de Burca.

Mother *goes off to the house.*

Christy   That – flipping – grass is annoying me. And rushes down there near the gate. When rushes get out of hand, tck! (*Looking in a new direction – a shock:*) What happened to the wall?

Marie   What?

Christy   Look! The wall! That's a *party* wall between here and your man's: a whole section of it is down.

Marie   It – fell?

Christy   To be looking out on that'd depress anyone.

Marie   D'you want a lift back to town?

Christy   What? No. The walk. I'll go back by the wood and the river. Is this for me? (*The lemonade.*)

Marie   Yes.

Christy   And the drive is gone totally gammy. I'm surprised you've a spring left in your car. Does the lawnmower work, is there oil, petrol – a mix – in the shed?

Marie   I don't know, I expect so.

Christy   I'd do it now but – (*His good suit.*) I'll give it a lash tomorrow. What? Will I?

Marie   As you please.

Christy   If you think that's all right?

Marie   Well, call.

Christy (*silently?*)   What?

Marie   Mum loves seeing you. Well. (*She prepares to go.*)

Christy   Oh! (*He has a present for her. He offers it.*) Actually.

Marie   For me?

Christy   Well! (*Meaning, if she doesn't want it.*)

Marie   No! (*She accepts the little parcel.*)

Christy   It's only a – (*He shrugs.*)

Marie   Thank you.

He shrugs.

I have to go back and reopen the shop.

Christy   Of course.

Marie   My assistant is on holidays ... Well.

She leaves, annoyed with herself (frowning at her self-consciousness of him) and without opening the present (which is a handkerchief or small silk scarf).

Her car driving away. **Christy** *with his lemonade, wondering about this new situation, the lights fading a little. (Passage of time.)*

Another car, this time arriving. It stops, the engine is left running. **Louise** *will enter in a moment. She is in her middle twenties, youthful and curvaceous in a summer dress. (There has been a relationship between them, now unsatisfactory to him.)*

Louise (*off*)   Fancy a spin? (*Coming in.*) It's only me – I heard you were back – Isn't it a lovely day! – How yeh!

Christy   How are you?

Louise   Fine, fine – *now*. How are *you*, which is more important?

Christy   Yeh know!

Louise   The suit. Isn't it a lovely day?

Christy   Terrific, terrific! Everything all right, then?

Louise   Yeh! No, I heard you were back with the rest of the returning – exodus – and since I was passing your house I called there, just in case you might be at a loose end so to speak – wanderlust – and when there was no one there I knew – of course! – this had to be your first port of call – How are you?

Christy (*gestures that he's fine. Then*)   Your mother is looking – (*Gestures 'fine'.*)

Louise   Terrific! Well, not too bad now. She's resting, I suppose?

Christy   Yeh.

Louise   I'm on my way to Newcastle: I've stuff to pick up there before the shops close, but we could take our time on the way back? Meander?

Christy   The walk.

Louise   I understand: You've been travelling. Ooh!

Lemonade. Home-made! Did Marie make this for you? (*She has a sip from his glass. Then:*) So, when shall we two meet again? Tonight.

Christy   Aw –

Louise   Stop.

Christy   I don't know –

Louise   Ah stop, stop.

Christy   Louise –

Louise   Stop.

Christy   And you shouldn't call at my place.

Louise   There was no one around to see me – I wouldn't have called if there was! Your father's truck or anyone!

Christy   No –

Louise   No, no, no! (*A quick look around, then her arms around him to kiss him:*) Oh gosh-golly it's fantastic to see you, you're looking fantastic, I cried for days when you went back last year, I nearly died. And you never wrote.

Christy   I never said I'd –

Louise   But I forgive you. Come in the back way to our place tonight before closing time – No, Christy! Scruples, that's all you're talking about: *I* don't have them! Scruples are – scruples!

Christy   Louise –

Louise   This? (*Her wedding ring. Mouths it:*) Shite! Him? (*Her husband. Mouths it:*) Shite! And you'll give in to me in the end!

He rolls his eyes/sighs/whatever. A handful of coins from his pocket to poke a finger through them to find his present for her: earrings.

What did you bring me?

Christy   Your mother is selling here.

Louise   Quick, I have to dash.

Christy   Why is she selling?

Louise (*accepting the earrings*)   Ooh!

Christy   What's the problem?

Louise (*shrugs; she isn't interested.*)   They aren't new. They're lovely, but they aren't new. *Where* do you come by these things? See you tonight? – See you tonight. You're looking fan-tastic.

And she's gone. He stands there. Her car driving away. And, after a moment, he leaves too, with a problem to be resolved.

Scene Two

Goldfish, **Peter** *and* **Jimmy** *are drinking in* **Bunty**'s *bar/back bar/snug. (At a remove from them are* **Kerrigan** *and* **Tarpey**, *discussing business.* **Tarpey**, *fifty, in police inspector's uniform. They will leave shortly.) Night.*

Goldfish *has a gold watch, a gold ring – like a knuckle-duster – and a moustache, after a film star (Cesar Romero?). He is returned from America: his dress and vocabulary tell the story. (He is short, perhaps, and disproportionately broad-shouldered.) A lot of energy – he moves like a boxer – and he is given to drumming violent rhythms on the counter. (His attitude promises the violent development of the story.)*

Peter *is forty-ish. Essentially a simple soul, an innocent. He is returned from England and he has a bastard accent and a petrol-blue mackintosh with epaulettes to prove it.*

And **Jimmy** *is in his thirties, a local who has not gone home from work. He is in a boiler suit. In drink he's a know-all. His attitude to the returned emigrants is supercilious (the way he laughs at/mimics their accents) and envious (because of his own situation and the rolls of money they flash).*

Jimmy   You're wrong!

Peter   Naw! –

Jimmy   You're wrong! –

Peter   I'm not, Jimmy –

Jimmy   You don't know the first thing you're talking about!

Peter   But, Jimmy, like, England!

Jimmy   Bull!

Peter   But all I'm saying is –

Jimmy   Yes, and you're wrong! Talk sense! Isn't there rationing all the time over there sure!

Peter   Naw! –

Jimmy   Yes!

Peter   Steak! Twice a week! If you know the runs to the right diggins.

Kerrigan *and* **Tarpey** *are leaving.*

Jimmy   Inspector Tarpey, Mr Kerrigan!

Goldfish   Now we can all relax: Long arms o' the law is leavin'.

Kerrigan *is gone.* **Tarpey** *hangs back.*

Goldfish   'Spector Dick Tracy, always gets his man – or child.

Tarpey *leaves.*

Goldfish   Yup, Pedro! (*'You were saying.'*)

Peter   You understand what I'm talking about, Goldfish.

Goldfish   Man?

Peter   Bob's your uncle!

Goldfish   Fanny's yer aunt?

Peter   That's what I'm saying! England, Jimmy, you gets a living over there, fair fucking doos like.

Jimmy   Oh now, that's Churchill talking.

Peter   Ay?

Jimmy   The big cigar on him.

Goldfish　'Down ol' Kentucky where ho'shoes is lucky.'
(*Singing it to no one. He's bored.*)

Peter　See them! (*His teeth.*) Top and bottom. (*Double dentures.*)
Wife's the same. You walk in, the other side, there's no one is
looking down their noses (as) much as to say 'Look what's
coming in the door'. It's your right like, Bob's your uncle, they
kit you out with all the teeth you want. For free. Even if y'are
who y'are. Black or white. Ay?

Goldfish　All the pearly choppers – huh? – yeh want.

Jimmy　Karl Marx!

Peter　Ay?

Jimmy　The Welfare State: sure all that's there for sure is for
the spreading of communism!

Peter　Naw!

Jimmy　The nuns they're raping every week all over the
world!

Goldfish　'See the village smithy standin' –'

Peter　I go to Mass every Sunday!

Jimmy　I couldn't disagree with you more!

Goldfish　Simon! (*Calling for service.*)

Peter　Well, take a gloak at these. (*Producing pay packets for*
Jimmy*'s inspection.*) I was working down the road there where
you're still working, Jimmy, and what was I drawing home?

Jimmy　Oh, I'm a chargehand down there now.

Peter　Fiver a week. Two pounds for the mother, three
pounds for booze and fuck-all for myself.

Goldfish　(*beats a drum roll; then, calls*)　Simon!

Jimmy　Look it! – (*Returns the pay packets.*) – A straight answer,
Peter: do you love your country?

Peter　Ay?

Jimmy   Declare your allegiance, or do you have an anchor at all, at all?

Peter (*to* **Goldfish**)   Ay?

Goldfish   Your anchor, man: Mutiny on the Bounty?

Peter   . . . I love my country! Here, mate! This land! And I do dream about it and all.

Jimmy   Listen to him.

Goldfish   And you listen to *him*. (*Speaking it rapidly and to no one in particular:*) 'See that village smithy standin' neath that thare ol' ches'nut tree' man!

Peter (*now laughing*)   I love my country above my king, Goldfish!

Goldfish (*to no one*)   These guys here is talking Peruvian!

Christy *comes in and gives a whoop.*

Christy   Whee-hee!

Jimmy   Oh-ho look in, the hard!

Goldfish   Hee-haw!

Peter   Aw Jesus Christ, Khrisht, heigh-up, mate!

Jimmy   Put it there, me aul segoasha!

Christy   Peter, Jimmy! Martin! (**Goldfish***'s proper name.*)

Goldfish   Chris! Chris! Goddammit! Man!

Peter   Good to be home, Khrisht, ay?

Christy   Yeh! –

Goldfish   Jesu Christu, kid! Put up them dukes! (*Mock pugilistics, clenching . . .*)

Jimmy   'Jesu Christu goddammit!'

Christy   Get up those steps! (*Boxing.*)

Goldfish   Git him on the downstairs!

Peter   Good to be home like!

And **Bunty** *(proper name Simon) is coming in (behind the counter). He's fifty-ish, round, busy in speech and movement.* **Peter** *signalling to him to set up another round.*

Peter   Bunty! –

Goldfish   I love yeh, Baby! –

Peter   What're y'having, mate! –

Bunty   You're welcome, Christy, son! –

Jimmy   'I love yeh, Baby!'

Christy   What's the news, Simon?

Bunty   News, Christy? – I wouldn't know where to begin! –

Peter   Same again, Bunt, and whatever Khrisht is having like!

Goldfish *(wants to buy the round)*   Nanty-up, Pedro! Your poison, kid? –

Jimmy   What's the whore-master having – I'm getting this one –

Goldfish   Stall, man –

Peter   My round –

Jimmy   'Stall, man – my round – we makes money round here too like, heigh-up, mate – oo-aw – know what I mean like!' On the slate, Simon.

Bunty   You're all right there now, Jimmy, your mother with the tea on the table waiting on you (for) the last four hours. Custom of the house, custom of the house, first drink – (*He gives a brandy to* **Christy**.) Now, Christy, son, the same as I give everyone else – first drink of the season for the emigrants is on me, and the last when ye're all off again in a few weeks' time and we're all glad to see the backs of ye. Now, am I to start filling another round or what?

Goldfish   Set 'em up, Joe!

Christy   When 'd you get in?

Goldfish   Toosday!

Jimmy   The Boston burglar!

Christy   Plane?

Goldfish   Wild blue yonder!

Peter   You get in this morning, Khrisht?

Christy   (*'Yeh'*) You, Peter?

Peter   Yesterday.

Goldfish   We gotta make some plans! –

Peter   And the missus like –

Goldfish   Gotta do few things! –

Peter   She's English.

Christy   Yeh?

Jimmy   And the 'kiddies', Peter?

Peter   Ow-aw. (*'Yes.'*)

Goldfish   Git us some action 'n' excitement!

Bunty (*filling/serving drinks*)   News, men? – No, I wouldn't know where to begin. Sylvester Keane? – Died poor fella. Did ye hear? – Yeh.

Peter   Sylvester like?

Bunty   Forty-two. Mary Devine the Old Road? This afternoon. I only heard it in there (a) while ago myself. Lord have mercy on the soul of the – And come here to me, Sylvester's little sweetshop up for sale already in the newspaper: I'll be auctioning it for his missus next week, the creature.

Christy   Did he leave her badly off, Simon?

Bunty   That's another matter. Judge Costello – Remember him? Remains taken to the church (a) few hours ago. Party of them in there now and out here (*front and back bars*) all evening coming from the funeral, including 'the man who got there', your old friend and neighbour one time, Christy, Billy Kerrigan.

Goldfish   The DA.

Bunty   Yeh, that's the way it goes.

Christy   Is Billy Kerrigan out there now?

Bunty   No, he was there, you just missed him: left while ago with Inspector Tarpey.

Goldfish   Dick Tracy.

Bunty   We're in the County Final – Did ye hear? Yeh, the Juniors. De Burcas' place down in Woodlawn – where you used to work one time, Christy? – I have the selling of that too. Here, it's all in here, local paper, the *Sentinal* – what's on in the pictures, Stephanie Roche's recipes for how to boil an egg, ads and all the details of the auctions – I'm only wasting my time talking. (*He has put the local paper on the counter.*) Now, with yere big wads of money, which one of ye is paying for that round because though I'm a poor man I'm a busy one.

Goldfish   Stall, Pedro. (*As he gets his money.*)

Bunty   But de Burcas' place'll be a nice place for someone.

Peter   And set up my round, Bunty, mate.

Bunty (*going off*)   Haven't you only one mouth on yeh, Peter?

Goldfish   Yo-o! (*His toast.*)

Jimmy   Fair play t'yeh, Goldfish!

Peter   Men!

Christy   Cheers!

They drink. **Christy** *takes up the local paper, folds it/rolls it up, possessively.*

Jimmy   Yeh married or anything, Goldfish?

Goldfish   Few times. Guess I durn't darn recall 'xactly! (*Which they find funny.*)

Christy   Give us a hand with a bit of a wall in a day or two?

Goldfish   Sure thing. You, Jem-boy, married or anything?

Jimmy   Married – Me? – Naaw! I'm like Gregory Peck here. (**Christy**.) We know where to get it for free.

Goldfish   Yeah?

Jimmy   The married ones! Up on your bike, Cavanagh!

Christy   Saturday be all right? (*To mend the wall.*)

Goldfish   Sure thing. (*To* **Jimmy**:) Yeah?

Jimmy   Married women!

Peter   Yeh like?

Jimmy   And they're broke-in for you sure – Oi, Christy? – and there's safety in them: they can't hold you responsible for nothing.

Goldfish   Ride 'em cowboy!

Jimmy   'Oo-aw!'

Bunty (*returning with change for* **Goldfish**)   Tom Egan the Dublin Road? On his way out too, they tell me, poor fella – Now, Goldfish. (*Change.*) Yeh, TB.

Peter   There's people dying now that never died before.

They laugh.

Bunty (*moving off*)   That's the way it goes.

They drink.

Christy   But how's it cuttin' anyway?

Goldfish   Yih gits a bit o' a kick outa the blacksmith blues!

Which they find very funny. And they drink again. And **Louise** *comes in, some paper money in her hand.*

Peter   Bunty! (*Calling for service for her.*)

Louise   Welcome home!

Peter   Ma'am!

Jimmy   Mrs Burgess! (*Arch.*)

Bunty (*returning*)   Louise?

Louise   D'you have change, Simon?

Bunty   Ye're busy down there? (*Taking her money.*)

Louise   Fairly. There's crowd from the funeral and the lads back from England of course.

Bunty   The latchycoes! (*Going off again.*)

Christy   How many kids, Peter? (*Self-consciously, he had turned his back on* **Louise**.)

Peter   Two, Khrisht.

Christy   Yeh?

Peter   They're above at home now with the mother, and the missus. She's English like.

Christy   Yeh, you were saying.

Jimmy   Get them off yeh! (*An undertone, sexual innuendo to do with* **Louise**.)

Christy   You're in where, Peter?

Peter   Well, I'm on the move like but Brum, Birmi'ham I go back to. Steel-fixin', with me mate like, Davy, Davy Johns, yeh know, he's a Taffy like, and we travels all over. (*He gives his pay packets to* **Christy**.) Ay?

Jimmy   Steel-fix that! (*Innuendo as before.*)

Christy   That's good money.

Peter   Fair ol' touch, ay? MacAlpine, Laing, Higgis and Hill – we works for them all. Wimpey, Gallaghers, William Moss.

Jimmy   Ay! (*As before.*)

Peter   And smashing bloke and all, Davy, me mate like, yeh know. I mean, for a Taffy like, for a Welshman.

Bunty (*returned with change*)   Now, Louise: I'm low on the two-bobs but it's near closing time and that should see you through down there.

Louise   Thanks.

Bunty   You're welcome, you're welcome. (*He's gone again.*)

Louise   Goodnight!

Peter   Goodnight, ma'am!

Jimmy   Mrs Burgess!

Louise *leaves.*

Jimmy   Bow-wow, bow-wow!

Peter   Fine thing that like.

Jimmy   A good night's lodgings there, boys – Goldfish, Christy?!

Peter (*starts to sing*)   'I is for the Irish in your –'

Jimmy   'I is for the Irish in your tiny heart, my dear' – Jesu Christu! (*'Oops!'*)

Jimmy, *on his last – 'Jesu Christu!' – moving to go out to the Gents, has staggered and a heavy drunken hand on* **Goldfish** *to steady himself. Big violence potential: for a moment it looks as if* **Goldfish** *is going to head-butt or hit* **Jimmy**, *but he contains himself. Instead:*

Goldfish   'Harriet, you are a fool!' (*A Bette Davis accent and line.*)

Jimmy   Y'have lovely teeth, Cavanagh!

Christy (*contains himself also. Smiles*)   No provoke! (*In a Spanish accent; probably a line from a film.*)

Jimmy   And! Peter! Cardinal Mindszenty! They're torturing him, aren't they? See?! In Hungary! So where's your anchor, where d'you belong? Lads, ye belong nowhere, ye belong to nobody. (*Going out:*) 'I is for the Irish in your . . .'

Momentarily sobering. But now, **Goldfish** *beats a drum roll in celebration of his hatred and the near violence, and Bette Davis again – And they laugh.*

Goldfish   'Harriet, I have never made a practice of slapping people but I am dangerously close to it now!'

Christy (*returns pay packets to* **Peter**)   Good money, Peter – I is for the Irish.

Peter (*singing*)   'In your tiny heart, my dear / R means right and when you're right you have no need to fear / E is for Eileen, your mother's name I mean / And L is for the lakes where I first met my own colleen.'

Goldfish   Hee-haw! (*And another drum roll.*)

Peter   'Then A is for the angels that are watching over you / N means never frown.'

Goldfish/Peter/Christy   'Keep smiling through.'

Goldfish   Hee-*fucking*-haw! (*Harsh laugh and drum roll.*)

Peter   'And D is for your Daddy's lesson.'

Goldfish/Peter   'And I hope 'twill be a blessin'.'

Christy   Simon!

Peter/Goldfish   'That's how I spell Ireland!'

The lights fading. **Christy** *indicating to* **Bunty**, *who is off, another round; another drum roll from* **Goldfish**, *this one silently;* **Christy** *stroking the local paper.*

Scene Three

Later. **Kerrigan**'s *house. (Kitchen.)* **Kerrigan** *is in his shirtsleeves, working on some documents. A glass of water nearby him. The doorbell rings, he's mildly surprised, he answers it.*

He's in his thirties. He's a solicitor. He has a private practice and he is also a State Solicitor. (A regional prosecutor, a type of DA.) His voice is mock-gruff. He's proud of himself. He likes a compliment. He's a likeable man.

Kerrigan   Oh?

Christy   Billy!

Kerrigan   The hero is back! (*Returning with* **Christy**:) Be the hokies has to be the thing to say! Home is the hero, the swallow, golondrina, St Christopher the traveller, come in, you're welcome, yes, at this delightful hour of the night, sit down! If we can find a chair for you that doesn't bear the marks of the children's . . . What did I tell you? (*The last on discovering a child's dirty nappy on the seat of a chair. He picks it up gingerly and dumps it.*) These things are all over the place. A drink you're looking for, I suppose, brandy you're drinking, I suppose – Good man!

Christy   Am I disturbing you?

Kerrigan   Are you disturbing me, you are disturbing me but I was nearly finished anyway. (*He's tidying away his documents.*) I had to leave the office early to go to a funeral, Judge Costello's, and I had to take a look at these for the morning.

Christy   How was it?

Kerrigan   The funeral? Dead. But I had to be there and be *seen* to be there. Oh I can perform my role too, though lately risen from the lower orders. Show my now august presence as another fierce and fearless upholder of the laws of the land like the good judge himself, and he was only a bollix – Sit down.

Christy (*sits. Perhaps he is fingering the local paper that he carries*)   A car crash I heard.

Kerrigan   Yes. He was drunk of course, but of course that couldn't come out, seeing as who he was. The state of this country: hypocrisy, discrimination, mediocrity: Disgraceful. There's no honesty or brains left in it, except my own. How's your father?

Christy   Ah yeh. How're the kids?

Kerrigan   Bundles of joy: can't you see the state of the place! (*And a few sniffs at the air, as to detect evidence of more dirty nappies.*)

Christy   And Sheila?

Kerrigan   Another bundle of joy! She's worn out, the creature, she tells me. (*Papers tidied away, he has found two glasses and a gin bottle containing some gin.*) Now, is this brandy good enough for you? And I had the mixers here already waiting for you. (*The glass of water. He sits.*)

Christy   No, the house is grand.

Kerrigan   (*pouring drinks*)   Hmm?

Christy   But if you wanted to do a bit of touching-up to the paintwork?

Kerrigan   No.

Christy   Or anything! Because I'll be a free agent now for a while.

Kerrigan   No thanks, you're very good. Well, *nunc est bibendum*!

Christy   Cheers, mate!

They drink.

But.

Kerrigan   What?

Christy   (*shrugs/shakes his head. He has a hidden agenda, but how to introduce it. Then*)   Jays, you've come a long way, Billy, you've some head on yeh.

Kerrigan   I'll have some head on me, my friend, in twenty-five years' time when the mortgage on this place is paid off. Are you making money?

Christy, *a clownish villain, expressing 'maybe I am'.*

Kerrigan   What? (*Chuckling.*)

Christy   (*same clown*)   By all means possible, Billy!

Kerrigan   And you'll blow it all in a week or two like all the other Paddies back from England. You will! It amazes me: holding up pub counters every year here, day and night. You

will! Why can't you! (*'Be wise/have sense.'* Quieter.) And get out of
Barrack Street. Like me. Show them. Like me.

Christy   Yeh, I agree. But.

Kerrigan   What?

Christy   I heard Sylvester Keane died, poor fella.

Kerrigan   He did, he did, poor Sylvester, he did. Forty-two?

Christy   And, I see in the paper here, Sylvester's little
sweetshop is up for sale already?

Kerrigan   'Tis. Was there trouble down town?

Christy   No.

Kerrigan   But there will be. Three seasons of the year it's
like a graveyard round here, summer it's the Wild West.

Christy   Tombstone! (*They laugh.*) And I see de Burcas' place
down in Woodlawn is up for sale too.

Kerrigan   'Tis. I'm handling the legal side of that sale.

Christy (*nods. He has read it in the paper*)   And are *they* in
trouble? Is that why they're selling – are they broke or what?

Kerrigan   Hmm?

Christy   What would that place go for?

Kerrigan   Which, the sweetshop?

Christy *nods.*

Kerrigan   Oh, it won't make the nine. Eight hundred,
thereabouts, would be my guess. I won't be far wrong.

Christy   And de Burcas'?

Kerrigan   Woodlawn?

Christy *nods.*

Kerrigan   Hard to say.

Christy   I mean, what's its value? I mean, if they had value
in money, would that keep them going, living there?

Kerrigan *frowning.*

Christy (*shrugs*)   Would there be a reserve price on that place?

Kerrigan   There would. And are they in trouble, are they broke or what and why are they selling is none of your business either. And while I'm on the subject of the de Burcas, Christy, leave Michael Burgess's wife alone.

Christy *agrees – clownish – that's what he would like/wants to do.*

Kerrigan   She's a married woman.

Christy   Yeh. (*Soberly.*)

Kerrigan   Why don't you put your feet on the ground? What has that family got to do with you? Why don't you settle down? Find some *ordinary* kind of woman?

Christy   Who?

Kerrigan   One that hasn't too much of anything. D'you know what I mean? I never trusted extremes.

Christy   Who?

Kerrigan   Who?! A maiden then, a virgin!

Christy   Where would a man start looking for one of them?

Kerrigan   Aren't they all over the place! If we're to believe Mother Church and believe in the efficacy of Mother Church's teachings.

They are laughing. **Kerrigan** *puts a finger to his lips: not to awaken Sheila and the children upstairs. (And he has talked himself out of his alertness of a few minutes ago.)*

And between you, me and the wall – I'm only marking your card for you – Mrs Burgess, 'Louise', is no good. Chocolate sweets and pricks. And you're not the first one there, from what *I* hear. (*He tops up the drinks, lal-lawing a line from the song 'La Golondrina':*) Lal-lal-lal-law, lal-lal-lal-lal-lal-law, lal-lal-lal-law! It's hard to say, you know, with those big old places, *difficile dictu.* They'll be all right now with two-three. (*£2,300.*)

Christy Is that exact?

Kerrigan They'd be more than happy, I'd say, with two-four, two thousand four hundred. That'd be my guess.

Christy Cheers, mate! (*And he sits back.*)

Kerrigan I know they were good to you one time, but – (*he touches his forelock*) – thank ye kindly for that now, God bless ye: Forget it. I'm sure it made them feel virtuous, as it does their kind. But they're an odd bunch. Even the so-called steady one, Marie, the chemist. Normans! Norman blood sure from way back: it never left them. D'you know what I mean? They're – different. Good luck! (*He is about to drink, he sniffs the air.*) D'you get it? New house, yes, but the smell of children's shit in here is something terrible.

Christy *laughs. And, now,* **Kerrigan** *begins to laugh at himself. The laughter getting out of control:* **Kerrigan**'s *finger to his lips – wife and children upstairs. The laughter subsiding, the lights fading.*

Scene Four

De Burcas'. Saturday.

Off, single, sharp, cracking sounds (like rifle fire): heavy stones being dropped, one on the other. A wall is being built. And celebration of the hard work.

Goldfish (*as a man lifting a heavy stone*) Whee-hee-hup! (*And dropping it on a wall:*) Down, you basta'd! Hee-haw!

While **Mother** *is arriving at the garden table to put a book on it (photograph album), to take out a handkerchief to cough, but contains it:* **Peter** *is coming in, as from a tap at the rear of the house, with two buckets of water.*

Without stopping, he nods / smiles 'Ma'am' to her. She nods, smiles. Then – his politeness, gentleness – he stops.

Peter It's a nice day?

Mother It is, a nice day.

And he's gone.

Goldfish (*off*)   Hey, Pedro, man, mosey! One hour ahead o' the posse, the buff-shams is hot on our trail – Whee-hee-hup! Down, you basta'd!

While **Mother** *coughs into her handkerchief. She stops because voices are coming from the house.* **Louise** *and* **Susanne** *are coming to join her.*

Susanne *is barefooted and in a silk-ish type of dressing gown that hangs open over something flimsy. She is in her late twenties. She has a mug of tea. She's self-centred, self-absorbed, self-conscious, vulnerable. But she puts on an act. She mainly only listens to herself, she exaggerates, she appears to want arguments/discussions both ways. There is some kind of rage in her – or is it hurt? Both! And there is a sense of futility. But she puts on an act.*

Louise   And is the car new?

Susanne   *Good* morning, *good* morning!

Mother   Good *mo*rning!

Susanne   Mother! And how are we today?

Louise   Morning? It's one o'clock in the day.

Mother   I sent Louise up to you with the tea.

Susanne   Right!

Mother   And not to miss the lovely sunshine.

Susanne   Right! Heaven! I can smell the grass.

Louise   The lady of leisure.

Susanne   I can hear the river.

Goldfish (*off*)   Whee-hee-hup!

Susanne   Who are they?

Louise   Christy Cavanagh.

Goldfish (*off*)   Down, you basta'd!

Mother   Christy and some 'mates'. (*She likes the word.*) Did you sleep well?

Susanne   So-so. Like a log! What are they doing?

Mother   Mending the wall. The rain brought it down.

Susanne   Such furious activity.

Mother   Yes.

Christy (*off*)   Peter, put a bit over here!

Mother   Such a waste! Those strong boys having to go away.

Susanne   And me. Aa sure now, I'm a poor emigrant too.

Louise   You didn't *have* to go away.

Susanne (*has sat with her tea and to pick at her toenails*)   Well, who has come to view the house?

Mother   Oh.

Susanne   How many?

Mother   Some. And there have been enquiries, I believe. I asked Marie to get us some coffee for you and we'll be having lunch shortly when she arrives.

Susanne   I couldn't eat a thing, Mum.

Mother   Just something light.

Susanne   Amn't hungry, Mum.

Mother   Love?

Susanne   Moth-er!

Louise   I can't stay to lunch.

Mother   Because we won't be eating again 'til half seven.

Susanne   Right! How much do you pay him?

Mother   Christy? He'd be offended.

Susanne   Would he? (*She knows better.*)

Mother   'I'd like to be this family please.' That's what he said to me once. His mother used to bring him down here with her, in a *basket*. Then, as a toddler. And then, when she died, he started to come down here on his own, a little soul. And he arrived one day with his *bundle*: 'I'd like to be this family please.' And I'd have taken him in, properly, to live here, had him educated, instead of half measures, but there was no way of talking to that father of his: A mule, a *mule*!

Goldfish (*off*)   Christy! Give's a hand with this Moby Dick! ... Whee-hee! – (*Two men lifting a stone.*)

Christy } Hup! ... Down, you basta'd!

Goldfish } Hup! ... Down, you basta'd! ... (*And laughter.*) Hee-haw!

Mother   They're working too hard. Boys, boys! You're working too hard! (*Going off to join them.*) Take a rest! We'll be having something to eat, shortly ...

Peter (*off*)   Not at all, ma'am ... (*Indistinguishable conversation.*)

Susanne (*to no one*)   What does he *want* of us all these years?

Louise   He's the real thing.

Susanne   Has he been sniffing around you since he came home?

Louise   What d'you mean?

Susanne (*to no one*)   Heathcliff. (*Then:*) Oh, come on – Baby! Standing there like someone in a romantic agony. You should spend a few years abroad and you'll find out! There's more than one of you in the world, you know!

Louise   I don't know what you're talking about.

Susanne   You know he's a pimp, don't you?

Louise   *What* are you talking about?

Susanne   Tea! (*She doesn't like tea.*) People try to use people. They *try*, but they do not get very far with me. People would walk on you – literally.

Louise   As a matter of fact he hasn't even looked at me since he came home.

Susanne   Why is she so soft? Mum. Has anyone come to view the place? Do you trust auctioneers? Tierney, that fat little person with the pub – Bunty – and his wife like Humpty Dumpty's mother. Well, I shall see to the matter.

Louise   *You're* daft.

They react to **Marie**'s *car, which is arriving.*

Susanne   And Marie, Miss Efficiency, Miss Intelligence: She would let the grass grow under her feet. Though I'm sure she thinks otherwise. This family is gone to the dogs. Honestly, every time I come home I get depressed.

Marie (*off*)   Afternoon!

Susanne   Afternoon! (*To* **Marie**, *who is coming in:*) Sister!

Marie   The wall is coming on. Sleep well?

Susanne   Yes!

Louise   Is that a grey hair, Susanne?

Susanne   Stop!

Louise   A cluster – a colony of them – Marie, look!

Susanne   Gedoutofit!

Marie   I didn't see your car properly in the dark last night when you arrived: is it new?

Louise   That's what I was asking.

Susanne   It's a car – A car? – A little thing – a Fiat? A car, for God's sake!

Marie (*laughing*)   Where *do* you get the money? (*To* **Mother**, *who is about to enter:*) Newspaper!

Mother   Thank you, love.

Susanne   A present then, if you must know. (*To no one.*)

Marie   And I got some ice cream.

Mother   Yippee!

Christy, **Peter** *and* **Goldfish** *are in tow.*

Marie   Afternoon.

Christy   Marie, Louise.

Mother   Did you see the wall?

They are looking off at the wall.

Peter   Nice stone. It'll be nice all right.

Mother   It *is* nice stone.

Peter   We're putting a bit of concrete in the middle: it won't show but it'll keep it together like.

Christy   It won't come down so fast again in a hurry. Susanne, welcome home!

Susanne   Hmm? (*Has he addressed her/has someone noticed her?*)

Mother (*to herself*)   You're bringing the place back to life. Now, boys, come over here.

Christy   All right, yeh? (*To* **Susanne**.)

Susanne   Yes.

Mother   Lunch will be ready in a jiffy. This is Susanne.

Peter   Ma'am!

Susanne   Gentlemen master builders! (*She vacates the table: could be she doesn't want to sit with anyone, could be she is flaunting herself in scant attire.*) It's a cavity wall then!

Christy   Ah, no. ('*That's ridiculous.*' *Politely.*)

Susanne   But would it not be more effective in concrete blocks?

Peter   Aw God, no!

Susanne   But some of those granite stones must weigh a ton.

Marie   Surely limestone.

Susanne   Still!

Peter   Bit of exercise for us like, keep down the old gut, ay?

Susanne   Or a ha-ha?

They don't know what she's talking about.

Mother (*pointed*)   Susanne, are you going to get dressed? Boys! (*Calling them to the table.*)

Peter   We're grand, ma'am.

Mother   Won't you have something to eat?!

Susanne (*to no one*)   But I expect you know best. (*About building a wall as goes off.*)

Christy   Martin? (*'Something to eat?'*)

Goldfish *shakes his head: this is not at all his scene.*

Peter   We got the nod from the gaffer here, ma'am: (to) go across the fields to the Halfway House: drop Coco-Colo to wash down the dust.

Marie   Some sandwiches, Mum, when they come back.

Peter   Twenty minutes then, Khrisht. (*To* **Goldfish**:) We can get out this way.

Peter *and* **Goldfish** *leave.*

Mother   Christy! (*Calling him to the table.*)

Marie   Are you staying to lunch?

Louise   I can't.

Marie *to the house.* **Mother** *opening photograph album.*

Mother   We were looking at these last night when Susanne arrived and there are one or two here of your mother. There she is. Isn't it? (*A photograph.*)

Christy *nods, looking at the photograph.*

Louise   A bicycle of one of our customers was stolen from the yard last week. (*She's feeling spare, left out of it.*)

Mother   What is the world coming to! (*Still looking at the* *photograph*:) She was a great help to me. And friend. (*Turning pages.*) I don't think she was very long working for us when that was taken. Cursed disease: whatever we did to deserve it.

Christy (*nods at another photograph*)   Marie. Solemn.

Mother   And she isn't like that at all! D'you know, Christy?! She's – practical – but of all of us, Marie is the one who lives in the present. She's the *easiest* of us all. D'you know, Christy?

Christy   Yeh! – (*And points at another photograph*:) There's yourself.

Mother   Yuk!

Christy (*laughing*)   No! No!

Louise   Oh! McCabe's are going to be fined for selling margarine as butter.

Mother   Oh dear! (*The photograph of herself*:) Although I was trim. This diet and these damned pills that they have me on: (*She blows out her cheeks: diet/pills are bloating her.*)

Louise   Well, see you!

Mother   See you, love!

Louise   'Bye!

Mother   Bye-bye, love!

Louise   'Bye!

Christy   Louise!

Louise   'Bye!

She's gone. (In a moment, her car driving away.) **Mother** *turning more pages, stops at another photograph.*

Christy   Mr de Burca.

Mother   Yes. Jack. (*And she contains a sigh over the photograph of her husband and whatever happened to him.*)

Christy   The flowers he had here.

Mother (*correcting him*)   *Wild* flowers. He wouldn't let a plough or a scythe touch the Wide Ridge, that two-acre field up there. We spent all night out in it once. (*And now becomes a little embarrassed/shy.*) Before the, before the children were born of course, before – *Wild* flowers. And it all (life) should be so easy, Christy! (*She smiles at him.*) D'you know? And he loved this house.

Christy   Why d'you want to sell it then? (*Impetuously. And laughing in an attempt to be tactful in offering her assistance, financial, if that is the problem.*) D'you see what I mean?! Life is short, Mrs de Burca – isn't that what you're saying! Is it? And if it's a question of! D'you know what I mean? You may think it's none of my business but all the same, easy come, easy go is what I say! And if it's a question of the shillings, well! Because money means nothing! Oh-ho, absolutely, it's stupid! And I think there's very few people about that care! Mediocrity – it's scandalous! And who, therefore, should be short of a bob in this day and age?! It's easy come by – There's all sorts of ways of getting it – Making it – That is one fact – I know that! – And I don't care either! Mrs de Burca. I've a few bob, means nothing to me – And if it's a question of? . . . So, yeh see.

Mother   No, it's –

Christy   The wall is nearly done, Monday I put a bit of stuff on the drive – and anything else – whatever – and you're secure, all sorted out! What's wrong with that, where's the problem? Terrific! And if people'd be more happier staying put, live where they should be living, where they want to live, that is firmly what they should do – Stay put! Because, I mean to say, one good turn deserves another! Isn't that what they say? . . . D'you know what I'm saying? Mrs de Burca.

Mother   I do.

Christy   I hope you don't think I'm talking out of turn.

Mother   No. Thank you . . . It's not a question of the money.

Christy   Don't understand it then!

Mother   It's too big. Now. It isn't working out. And –

Christy! – the past is the past.

Christy   Aw, I don't know so much about that!

Mother   No –

Christy   You wouldn't change your mind?

Mother   No.

Christy   You might!

Mother   No.

Christy   Aw, I don't know now!

Mother   And – Christy? No man about the place. Now, isn't it a pity that *Marie* and I are not good enough for you?

Christy   But, still, if you don't mind me saying so, you could be making a mistake.

Mother   (*smiles to herself that the import of her last is lost on him. Then*)   Well, I suppose I could.

He nods to this, to himself.

Mother   (*finds another photograph*)   Who is this now? Who is that little boy?

Christy   (*merely glances at it*)   That's me. (*He isn't interested, he now has a bigger problem to consider.*) I think there was a bit of concrete left over that Peter mixed, and in case it goes hard, I'll just . . .

He goes off (to the wall). **Marie** *is coming from the house with a tray of lunch things, her eyes following him.*

Scene Five

The church bell for Mass. (It continues ringing.) Sunday morning.

Bunty*'s is dimly lit. (The blinds have not been let up, the door is shut.)* **Bunty** *is cranky and uneasy, ushering* **Goldfish** *and* **Christy** *in the back way.* **Goldfish** *has a pellet gun.*

Bunty Jesus Christ, Jesus Christ, Sunday morning, wouldn't you think it's up to Mass ye'd be going, be saying a few prayers instead of breaking the licensing laws of God and man.

Goldfish We was at Mass, man.

Bunty I hope then ye heard Father Kilgarriff's sermon about how to behave. What d'ye want, quick?

Christy Martin?

Goldfish Bottle of Time.

Christy *nods 'the same'.*

Bunty (*going off for drinks*) What's the machine gun for, Goldfish?

Goldfish That fuckin' bell. (*He has a headache.*)

Bunty (*returning with drinks*) And if ye was at Mass, man, I hope ye heard and heeded the prayer that's read out at all Masses today.

Goldfish We heard.

Bunty (*quoting*) 'Guide all our emigrants down the right path abroad, stop them from ever straying, teach them abstinence and forbearance' – did ye hear that? 'Keep them in mind of the spiritual inheritance they took with them and the one true Church.'

Goldfish *What* did we take with us?

Bunty 'And keep them in mind of the land of their birth so that they may be fit one day to return to the bosom of thy heavenly mansions yeh, amen.' Did yeh hear that, Goldfish, did yeh, when yeh was at Mass, man?

Goldfish I did, Bunty.

Christy *gives him money for the drinks.*

Bunty (*going off*) Changing dollars for ye and whatnots.

Goldfish Fucker is making a fortune out of us. Yo-o!

They drink.

Fancy bit o' hunting? Better exercise than risking maybe balloonin' your bollix building a wall. (*Sips.*) Said I'd meet me bunch o' the guys 'bout one thirty up in the Square. Go on a shoot. Git us some prairie air, git us some wild turkey – (*sips*) – (or) one them thare buffaloes up in the hills. Git us a sheep?

Christy   Pellets.

Goldfish   Airgun, kid brother's. Still. (*Meaning, you could do damage with it.*) Take the eye out of a buff-sham?

Christy *laughs.*

Goldfish   What – Hah – Chris – Yeh?! (*Celebration of the idea.*)

The church bell stops ringing: his acknowledgement of it:

Well, I do declare! Holy Joes: they hate us. But with cunning. We is varmint, man, outcasts, white trash. (*Sips.*) And I hate them.

Christy   . . . How're yeh fixed?

Goldfish   Dust? (*Gold dust – money.*)

Christy (*nods*)   I'm going to need a bit of money.

Goldfish   Sure thing. Can drop you a ton?

Christy   Nah, it'll be all right.

The tapping of a coin on a plate-glass window from outside. And **Bunty** *is returning with change for* **Christy**. **Bunty***'s reaction to the tapping and the following exchanges in whispers:*

Bunty   Jesus Christ!

Peter (*off*)   Bunty! (*More tapping.*)

Bunty   Jesus Christ, Jesus Christ!

Jimmy (*off*)   Simon!

Bunty   Jesus Christ!

Peter (*off*)   Bunty, mate! (*More tapping.*)

Bunty   They can't wait twenty minutes for opening time.

Jimmy (*off*)   Simon! (*More tapping.*) Simon!

Bunty   They'll have the Church blackballing me. (*More tapping.*) Go round the back. (*More tapping.*) Go round the – friggin' back!

Peter (*off*)   Right, mate!

Jimmy (*off*)   Right, Simon!

Bunty (*going off*)   They'll cost me my licence.

Goldfish   And I hate farmers. Can't right figure out why. (*Sips.*) Yip, but I'm no son-o-fury if I don't come home sundown with a chicken.

Christy   . . . Still.

Goldfish   Chris?

Christy   All the same.

Goldfish   Yeh?

Christy   We come back every year.

Goldfish   That is a fact. And for what, I sure as shit don't know. Mother Macree?

Christy   Home.

Goldfish *looks at him.*

Christy   Home. (*Defensively.*)

Goldfish   Ho-ome?!

Christy   Yeh! Trees, landscape, air, fresh air.

Goldfish   Fresh air?

Christy   You said it yourself –

Goldfish   Landscape? –

Christy   Prairie air –

Goldfish   Trees?

Christy   Terrific – Yeh – They're perfect!

Goldfish Firewood.

Bunty *is returning with* **Peter** *and* **Jimmy**, *the local.* **Peter** *in his petrol-blue mackintosh (as always),* **Jimmy** *in his Sunday suit and, for the record, there's nothing offensive in his behaviour today.*

Bunty Ye're a disgrace to the country.

Goldfish Pedro, Jaime!

Jimmy Men!

Peter Goldfish, Khrisht!

Goldfish And how are we this fine day?

Bunty Keep the voices down now – What d'ye want?

Jimmy Pint please, Simon.

Bunty You'll get no pint, I'm pouring no pints till half past twelve.

Jimmy Bottle of Time please, Simon.

Peter Yeh – And a small one too like, Bunt.

Bunty And small one too like Bunt – (*His hand out to* **Peter** *for the money.* **Christy** *pays him.*) – and I'm dependent on the goodwill and permission of Church and State for my living. I'm surprised at you, Jimmy Toibin.

Jimmy I was *at* Mass.

Bunty You were at Mass, I know you were, with your mother, and now you're here! (*And he's gone.*)

Jimmy What's up with *him?*

Goldfish Bunty's eyes: The greed of the guy is (that's) already rich – Ever notice? (*Then, answering: 'What's up with him?'*) Disturbed the man in his only pleasure in life: counting again last week's takings.

They are amused. (Though the recurring references to **Bunty***'s revenue and wealth have begun to interest* **Christy** *privately. If he has to steal money, he will steal it.)*

Jimmy   As elegant as ever, Christy!

Peter   But the missus is up there now all right, in church like yeh know, with the mother and the kiddies. Saying her prayers with the best of them. She's English like, she's a convert. Oh, she converted all right and we was married in church and all, the other side. So who rightly should be watching me. Ay?

Bunty *returns with drinks and change.*

Jimmy   Thank you, Simon. (*To humour* **Bunty***:*) Big dance tonight, boys?

Bunty   Did the priest call it out at whatever Mass you were at?

Jimmy   'Shamrock Ballroom, nine 'til three.' Oh, he does you the favour all right, Simon.

Bunty   And I do the favour for him. The church has to get their cut, haven't they?

Goldfish   An' behave ourselves.

Bunty   He didn't mention the band? (*Hopeful that the priest did.*)

Jimmy   He didn't but doesn't everyone know! The Marveltones! And they don't sit down or anything! Only the drummer sits. And nearly all electric! Fancy steps forwards and back. And none of your black suits! Bright blue.

Goldfish   Get along!

Jimmy   A mighty orchestra!

Bunty   And a mighty price I have to guarantee them even if no one comes. Ye'll all be there, will ye?

Jimmy   Oh, we'll be there, spot the talent.

Goldfish   Charvering stakes'll be good with the girls, Simon?

Bunty (*admonishes him with his finger*)   With the 'tache on yeh! I provide ye with drink, dancing and the pictures and this's the thanks for the risks I take. (*And he's gone again.*)

Jimmy   Luck, men, Christy!

Peter   God bless!

Goldfish   Fucker is a millionaire. Yo-o!

They drink, ritualistically.

Peter (*smiling*)   But a strange thing: I wakes up this morning. Was it early? Was and all, mate, was and all. And I'm lying there like I'm drowning. Like it happens (at) times, the other side, but does you expect it at home – ay? But my eyes is so open, like you'd see in a man doesn't want to cry. You've a problem here, Peter. And the missus is there, asleep like. Kiddies over there. Snore from the mother (in) the next room. Well, this's a good one: What is it you have to do, Peter? Up I gets, puts on the togs. I'll go down the town for a gloak at the Square. Not much stirring, was there? Not half. And I'm stood in John P. Hogan's archway. Not much stirring. Dog across, asleep in O'Grady's doorway like. Nice bit of a setter in him. And I starts the walking. I mean I does the streets, I'm walking. And: Well, this's a quare thing: You're getting no satisfaction out of all this walking, Peter. Back to John P.'s archway. Then, whatever time it was, six, seven, bit of a stir. They're answering the bell. People like. Not that many mind, 'cause 'twas that very early Mass. But, you might as well, I says: Do the business. Up I goes, goes in and all, to the church like, and I says my own few prayers. And that's me kitted out for the week. Back to the Square. John P.'s archway. Stood there. Dog across, beginning to scratch the neck, stretch the back legs like. And I starts the walking *again* – Ay? Till I remember: What did I tell you before? You're only exerting yourself, Peter: Aren't you on your holidays? Back to – (*Thumbs it: John P. Hogan's archway.*) A good one – Ay? Till Jimmy here come along ten minutes ago ... Ay? And I do –

Goldfish (*quietly, on a sigh*)   Haaaay, Pedro man, you is talking Peruvian again.

Peter (*laughing*)   Am I, am I talking Peruvian again, Goldfish?

Goldfish   Fucker won't give us another 'til twelve thirty.

Jimmy   I'll try him in a minute.

Peter   And I do dream about it: Coming home and all.

Goldfish   Where's yo' bin? – Ah's bin in bed with mah honey, where's yo' bin? (*Really, to get* **Peter** *off the subject.*)

Bit of a laugh – **Jimmy** *and* **Peter**.

Jimmy   Ah's bin in bed with mah honey!

Bunty (*off*)   Keep the voices down!

Jimmy   . . . You're quiet, Christy.

Peter   Something must have worn him out last night . . . And the old nerves is going in the mother. Aw she's gone very bad with them. And I gives her seventy quid and all for herself. But it's coming up about the wedding photo I sent home four years ago. Me and the missus like, was stood outside St Chad's in Brum. She's questioning it. No, ma'am, I says, I don't know who'd be putting that in your head: That who'd be saying the arch around us in the photo isn't real at all, isn't the arch around the doorway of St Chad's, but was only took in a studio. You know how they can do it in a studio?

Christy makes some movement, straightens up as a man might to adjust his belt.

Peter   Ay? (*To* **Christy**.)

Jimmy *misinterprets – touches* **Christy**'s *shoulder – thinks* **Christy** *is getting out his money for the next round, and reasonably, generously:*

Jimmy   Christy, you got the last one: let me –

And it's very sudden and very violent (though not very loud): **Christy** *has* **Jimmy** *by the face, has him swept back against the wall – a stool is knocked over? – and is banging the back of* **Jimmy**'s *head against the wall.*

Bunty (*off*)   Noise!

Goldfish   'S okay, man!

Christy   Know what I mean, Jimmy?

Jimmy   Jesus, what's this –? (*'All about.'*)

Christy   Na-na-na, know what I mean? (*Banging* **Jimmy***'s head.*)

Bunty (*off*)   Noise!

Goldfish   Right, Simon, 's okay, Simon, everythin's under control!

Jimmy   For fuck's –

Christy   Na-na-na-na-na! Jimmy? Where d'*you* belong? I'd kill for here! Would you kill for here? I'd kill! Know what I mean? Know-what-I-mean?!

Jimmy   I don't! I don't, Christy!

Christy   . . . No provoke.

And he releases him. **Jimmy** *is practically in tears.* **Christy** *is trembling.* **Goldfish** *is delighted, beats a silent drum roll, and* sotte voce:

Goldfish   Hee-haw! (*Then:*) Hey, you guys, take it easy! Pedro, you were saying!

Peter   Ay?

Goldfish   Weddin' photo, man: proceed.

Peter   No, ma'am, I'm saying, to the mother like, Goldfish, that's not a studio, that's St Chad's.

Goldfish   And she's (*'saying'*) – Huh? – Registry Office. I dig, kid.

Peter   She's (*'saying'*) – D'yeh dig, Goldfish? And is the kiddies, was they even ever like baptised?

Goldfish   Well, I'll be!

Peter   Nerves is going in her.

Bunty (*returning, relaxed now, looking at his pocket watch*)   And as you did not forget St Joseph, the Blessed Virgin and the Baby Jesus on their flight into Egypt, remember now we humbly beseech thee our emigrants abroad – What was that rumpus about?

He has continued off, to let up his blinds, open his front door. Daylight coming into the bar. And the church bell is ringing again, the end of Mass.

Goldfish (*to* **Peter**)   Yup?

Peter   And was my missus, is my missus the landlady I took up with. Naaw, naaw, ma'am, I keeps saying: My missus ain't no landlady, naaw, and tell that to whoever's putting it in your head. I wouldn't marry, Goldfish – I ain't never rode a landlady the other side. She's a woman, ma'am, I keeps telling her, like everyone else, a convert. Ay?

Bunty (*returning – and continues off again*)   So that they may be fit one day to return to the bosom of thy heavenly mansions yeh, amen.

Goldfish (*calling after him*)   Two bottles Time – Simon! – drop of whiskey for Pedro –

Christy   Not for me –

Goldfish   And Jimmy-kid's pint! (*To* **Christy**:) Ay?

Christy   Have to go.

Goldfish   Don't fancy bit big-game huntin' then? *You* can have the gun.

Christy   Y'haven't something smaller – a Luger? See you in here tonight. (*Calls:*) Simon! (*And thumbs-up sign:*) See you later. (*Tap on the shoulder to* **Peter**, *another to* **Jimmy**, *and he's gone.*)

Peter   Ta-ta, Khrisht!

The church bell stops ringing.

Goldfish   Well, I do declare, that wasn't such a bad little Mass after all! You fixin' that round – Simon! – yes or what, minus one Time?

Bunty (*off*)   Yes!

Goldfish   And, with the good Lord's help, they'll be better little one to come! But what d'yeh pray for?

Peter   Ay?

Goldfish　'So up I goes an' all like,' you said – To church – 'an' I says my own few prayers.'

Peter　Like?

Goldfish　What d'yeh pray for?

Peter　For? . . . Some of God's grace like . . . So that I'd understand.

Goldfish　Understand? Understand what?

Peter　I don't know like.

Goldfish *continues to look at him, his sincerity.*

Jimmy (*to no one*)　Jesus Christ! (*Reaction to the experience he has had.*)

Goldfish (*to himself*)　Jesus Christ.

Scene Six

Dining room. De Burcas'. Six chairs around a table set for Sunday lunch. (This room is part of a double room. Note: The house is a four/five-bedroom affair, early Victorian.) **Mother** *and* **Louise** *are standing by, waiting. Sunday clothes.* **Mother** *has a glass of sherry.* **Louise** *is wearing a hat with a half-veil and she will sit to lunch in it. (She has a black eye.) And she's wearing her 'new' earrings.*

Mother　No Michael?

Louise　He had to go to – oh some GAA thing, a match.

Mother　. . . Very nice. (*Admiring the table.*)

Marie (*coming in with a tureen of soup, calling*)　Susanne!

Mother　Spoiled. (*She sits.*)

Marie　Michael isn't coming?

Louise *shakes her head and sits.*

Marie　So we won't need this one. (*She removes a chair.*) Susanne!

Susanne (*off*)   Coming!

Marie (*serving soup*)   Isn't Sheila Kerrigan looking well!

Mother   Isn't she looking well! Thank you, love, thank you. I'm spoiled ... Were you talking to Sheila, Louise?

Louise *shakes her head.*

Marie   And the new baby, did you see it?

Mother   Beautiful!

Marie   Susanne!

Susanne   Anseo! (*'Present'*)

She has made an entrance in an elegant dress (more suited to evening wear, perhaps); her hair arranged up. To **Mother***'s chair to kiss the top of* **Mother***'s head. Then:*

Now, what can I do to help?

Marie   Sit down! (*And laughs.*)

Susanne   Oh, the hat! (**Louise***'s.*)

Marie   The dress!

(*Note: The vacant fifth chair is Father's: a mark of* **Mother***'s ongoing love for her late husband.*)

Susanne   Nice Mass?

Mother   Yes!

Marie   They do go on though with their announcements. And that prayer for emigrants? (*Questioning its taste.*)

Mother (*agrees*)   I thought that. Feeling better, love, headache gone?

Susanne   Yes, thank you.

Marie   Oh! (*She has forgotten something and is up again, leaving the room hastily.*)

Susanne   'Gallop apace, you fiery-footed steed towards Phoebus' lodging!'

Marie (*off*)   'Such a waggoner as Phaeton would whip you to the west!'

Mother (*not performing/chuckling*)   'And bring in cloudy night im*med*iately! Spread thy close curtain, love-performing night.' Is it? Susanne? 'That runaway's-eyes may wink. And Romeo leap to these arms . . .' Mmmm! (*The soup.*)

Susanne   Leeep! 'To these arms untalkcd of and unseen.'

Louise   Is that a new dress?

Susanne   This old thing? – Yes. D'you like it?

Louise   Mm. Where'd you buy it?

Susanne   A present . . . Do you like it, Mother?

Mother   Absolutely – Mm soup, Marie!

Marie (*returning with a bottle of wine*)   'Come, gentle night; come, loving black-browed night, give me my Romeo; and when he shall die, take him and cut him out in little stars, and he will make the face of heaven so fine, that all the world will be in love with night and pay no worship . . . to the garish sun.' – Oh dear! (*She laughs, suddenly self-conscious, as if she had betrayed a secret. Then:*) Wine!

Mother   Why not!

Susanne   It's not as if it's exactly winter. (*They don't know what she is talking about.*) And I'm out in – the dew – in it. This dress.

Mother   Love?

Susanne   Only sensitive people with poetic minds catch TB.

Marie, *pouring wine, laughs at her sister's personality.*

Susanne   Thank you. (*For wine.*) Anyway, I don't much like it myself. (*Her dress.*)

Mother (*very informal raising of her glass*)   It's so seldom we're all together any more. (*Sips. Grins.*) Or-that-we'll-be-here much *longer*.

Marie   We'll be fine. Well, good luck everybody!

They drink.

Louise   And did you see the size of Catherine Healy?

Marie   Is she pregnant, Louise?

Louise *(remembers that she is wretched) shakes her head, she doesn't know.*

Susanne   It could be all that fresh white bread you have started to eat around here.

Marie *frowning, to work out* **Susanne**'s *remark, then she laughs.*

Mother   Though – and I don't know that it's too much to ask – why a woman like me, or a half-woman like me –

Marie   Mum! –

Mother   With three healthy – beautiful! – daughters shouldn't want a grandchild.

They laugh – or appropriate individual reactions.

What is wrong with my girls?

They laugh.

Marie   You can rent one, Mum. We'll be fine.

Susanne   . . . What happens to the table?

Mother   Love?

Susanne   This. (*Table.*) Has it been considered? The auction happens on – Tuesday? Does it?

Mother   Yes, it –

Susanne   And for instance – I know it for a fact – the sideboard is worth a hundred pounds.

Mother   As much as that, how interesting.

Susanne   Well, Louise can hardly have use for it in a run-down pub, and even if it fitted above the shop for you and Marie, I do not see how anyone, possibly, could get it up those narrow stairs. The furniture. This is what we should be discussing instead of – hiver-hovering.

Marie   Hiver?! (*And laughs.*)

Mother   And are you sure – Susanne – that that's where I should go? That I should move in over the shop with Marie.

Susanne   I am merely pointing out, Mum!

Mother   And are you sure that Marie should have an old woman move in over the shop with her?

Marie   Mum.

Mother   Should you?

Marie   Yes. We'll be fine. Now – children, children – eat up, drink your soup!

Susanne (*to herself*)   God's sake! . . . I am merely – (*She stops herself with a sigh.*) . . . But I find I am becoming very frustrated.

Mother   Oh dear. When it's sold and our obligations are met you will all get your share.

Susanne *is hurt/angered – both – by this.*

Marie   . . . Isn't the wall looking – terrific?

Mother   Those boys (*She pushes out her glass for a top-up.*) Marie? And when they leave again, as they'll be leaving, soon, and Christy, I wonder what kind of life, what kind of reception, have they to go back to.

Susanne (*to herself*)   I could tell you a few things about that.

Mother   Thank you, love. (*To* **Marie** *for the top-up.*)

Marie   Susanne? (*'More wine?'*)

Susanne   I couldn't care less about 'my share'! That is not what I am talking about, that is not the point!

Mother   And what is the point?

Susanne   Oh, this has become an absurd conversation!

Marie   Why continue with it then? More wine?

Susanne   No, thank you . . . The point is I am never consulted about anything in this family.

Mother   What did we not consult you about? Selling the table?

Susanne   Cheap! Selling the whole place, for instance.

Mother   You were consulted –

Susanne   I wasn't.

Mother   I write to you regularly –

Susanne   Oh, writing letters, yes –

Mother   But you don't appear to read what I write.

Susanne   Letters about her (**Louise**) and Michael Burgess's drinking problems – perhaps that is the real reason why the place is being sold: to rescue the run-down hole of a business she married into. And that will be more money down the drain – literally! Letters about – the dog! Letters about Marie and her problems – Everybody's problems!

Marie   What problems?

Louise   Don't address me as –

Susanne   I get depressed too, I get lonely too, I am not made of steel, I should like to be treated with respect, I am part of this family too – I *hope* – but I find I am becoming very left out.

Louise   Don't –

Marie   *What* is your problem, Susanne?

Louise   Marie, I wish you'd let me speak –

Susanne   Would this place be – sacrificed – for me if I were – distressed? Hah!

Louise   Susanne, don't address me as 'she'.

Mother   And are you?

Susanne   What?

Mother   Distressed?

Susanne   I'm not.

Marie   More soup for anyone or has everyone finished?

Mother   We are selling – I wrote to you about it – because we are under *some* financial pressure and because, now –

Susanne   You won't get me to agree, Mother!

Mother (*to* **Louise**)   D'you have a cigarette?

Louise *has no cigarettes.*

Susanne   . . . But if any one of you thinks that I'll be back again to stay in somebody's *box*room over a chemist shop or pub, you are all making a great mistake.

Marie (*to herself*)   Impossible.

Susanne   If that matters, of course.

Mother   Are you saying we *shouldn't* sell?

Susanne   I didn't say that.

Mother   Then you're saying that we should.

Susanne   I'm saying – I'm saying –

Marie   Your bowl, Susanne –

Susanne   I'm saying – I'm saying, even if I'm away, I belong here. I'd like to have some – standing! Somewhere! I'm saying, I'm saying . . . (*She has become very emotional. Perhaps she is crying.*) Standing! What else is there? . . . Mum . . . Mum . . . I'm saying . . .

Mother (*to herself, silently – a sigh?*)   Oh dear. (*Then, gently:*) I know, love.

Susanne   Had I been consulted, *properly*, I could have come up with alternatives.

Marie   And your alternatives?

Mother   Love? (*To* **Susanne**.)

Susanne   I said I *could* have, I *could* have!

Marie (*to herself, again*)   Impossible. SOUP BOWLS!

They begin to comply with their soup bowls.

Susanne   Could I have a glass of wine, please? . . . And there is little or no interest in the place as far as I can see so it is going to go for a song. To some – dolt – no doubt. And you are not concerned. Thank you. (*For the wine.*) And you think that I too should stand idly by? Well, we shall see about that, oh yes we shall. At the auction, I shall be standing here –

Marie   Oh, come along!

Susanne   And you make me laugh! (*An extremely rude snap. Rises.*) Oh, give the place away, I don't care, let it all fall down. (*To* **Louise**.) Are the earrings new?

Louise   'A present!'

Mother   Then let it! Fall down. Susanne!

Susanne *gestures that she has risen to assist with the crockery.*

Mother*'s anger is untypical. (But* **Susanne** *has the capacity to test people to the limit: a self-destructive drive that will find its final accommodation yet.)* **Mother** *is ill, she's a widow, she is worried about her three daughters and their futures, there is 'some' financial pressure on her, and coming to a decision to sell the family home has been difficult and complex. She keeps trying to contain her outburst, and failing – even to her final 'I'm sorry'.*

Mother   The strain, worry, effort it has been, to stop everything from falling down! To carry on! To keep it all standing! . . . Since your father was *taken* from me! . . . If any one of you had had an alternative plan for here, well then! We would have managed it, somehow! If that would have settled you! . . . That would have been a different matter! . . . Life disappearing – How much can one take?! . . . And though we are selling, this house is not 'a place', and I will not have it referred to as such around your father's table! It was his dream! And mine! . . . It was our home, once: Now it's not . . . I'm sorry!

All of them are upset. **Mother** *regrets her outburst, head turning to the vacant fifth chair, to sigh, or contain it, propping her jaw with her fist.* **Susanne** *feels remorse but she cannot help herself and, in a moment, she* *will walk out, the offended party, bridling herself.* **Louise** *touches her eyes under her veil.* **Marie**'s *characteristic frown; now she abandons her dishes to follow* **Susanne** *out of the room to have a word with her.*

Lights down for a passage of time. Dance-hall music, faint, wafted on a breeze from the town. Sunday night.

Marie, *frozen in time, is looking out at the gathering night and at whatever else might be out there.* **Mother**, *with a glass of port and a cigarette, is seated.* **Louise**, *head bowed, is weeping quietly, seated beside* **Mother**. *Her hat and veil are on the table. She has a black eye.*

Mother   Louise? Love? . . . Louise? Love?

Louise   What?

Mother   What you're doing is . . . foolish. (*'Foolish', a more diplomatic word than her first choice, 'childish'*) . . . Louise?

Louise   What?

Mother   I'm sorry. I shouldn't have let you marry him. I should have . . . somehow . . . stopped you . . . But you are married to him. There are rules . . . Louise? Love?

Marie (*comes out of her reverie*)   I might have something out here. (*She goes out.*)

Mother   Love? Is it sore? . . . Marie will find something to put on it . . . Love? I understand people's needs. I amn't criticising you. But . . . (*She smiles to herself; she doesn't have the words.*) It's a dream. A mystery, a nightmare. (*Decides against the last.*) A dream . . . Love, what you're doing is wrong. And it isn't doing you any good. What you're doing is only making you unhappy. Love?

Louise *shakes her head.*

Mother   You're not being fair to yourself. Or to *others* . . . You know who and what I mean . . . Love?

Louise (*a whisper*)   I hate him!

There is ambivalence in the 'him', but as she rises she pulls off her 'new' earrings.

Mother   Love?

Louise   Then the answer is, I shall go away too.

Mother (*as to a child*)   Oh!

Louise (*collects her hat*)   Mum. (*Kisses her.*)

Mother   Would you like to stay?

Louise *shakes her head.* **Marie** *has returned with some cotton wool and a bottle. She treats* **Louise**'s *eye.*

Marie   This will help a bit for now.

Louise   It's okay, I'm okay, it's fine, I'm fine – Marie!

Marie   Shhhhh! Come over to the shop to me in the morning.

Louise   Goodnight.

Mother   Goodnight, love.

Marie (*going out with* **Louise**)   I'll sell you a nice pair of sunglasses?

Mother (*alone*)   Oh dear! (*Part laugh-sigh-sob.*)

Marie (*off*)   Goodnight!

Louise's *car driving off.* **Marie** *returns to her place at the window, to look out.*

Marie (*to herself, absently*)   Oh dear! (*She remembers* **Mother**.) Hm?

Mother   'Oh dear!' (*They share a smile.*)

Marie   Is *she* going to emigrate too?

Mother   And from what we see of it, this emigration, whether from necessity or discontent, isn't doing much good for anyone.

Marie   Tired?

Mother   No. Why don't you put on that other dress and go up to that dance-thing for an hour or two. I'm fine.

Marie   No. (*She switches on the radio: Gigli singing 'I'll walk beside you' – or some instrumental piece.*)

Mother   And Oh – Dear – Susanne! (*Clenched fist; grinning.*)

Marie*'s humouring laugh.*

Mother   I don't understand her, I never did! . . . And 'hiver-hovering'?!

Marie   Yes!

Mother   Where does she learn those words? . . . She hasn't gone, she didn't take her suitcase?

Marie   No.

Mother   Will she come home tonight?

Marie (*doesn't know*)   She said, 'I am going up town for a breath of fresh air.' (*And laughs again to make things right.*)

Mother   I shouldn't have spoken out like that.

Marie   Oh, I don't know.

Mother (*to herself*)   Mistakes.

Marie   Mistakes? Everyone does the best they can. That's lovely, isn't it? (*The song/music on the radio.*)

Mother   . . . Does she have a boyfriend?

Marie   Yes, but it's a secret: *he* doesn't know it yet.

Mother   Not the actor one she brought home a few years ago?

Marie   No.

Mother   I didn't like him.

Marie   This one owns a nightclub, my dear – or several of them.

Mother   Well, God help him whoever gets her . . . And do you?

Marie   Hm?

Mother   Have a secret man.

Marie (*smiles. Then*)   I'm awaiting him.

Mother   *Did* I consult you properly about selling?

Marie   You have the lot of us on the roadside! You did. We'll be fine.

Mother   ... Marie: Louise, in what she does, is immature, and Susanne is a snob. Now, I am not a snob and neither was your father: and if there were someone – secret man – all three of us could live together in one little house. If *you* made the move.

Marie   Mmmm!

Mother   Because, in certain matters, men aren't ... so bright. D'you know?

Marie *nods solemnly.*

Mother   And, because life *is* short.

Marie   Mmmm!

Mother   Love?

Marie   Well, d'you know what I think? This may surprise you. D'you know what I'm going to tell you? I think, Mum, you've begun to hiver-hover.

Mother *starts to chuckle.*

Marie   Come on, bed, you're exhausted. (*Taking* **Mother**'s *glass, extinguishing the cigarette.*) And you have enough of these. (*To the radio, humming whatever song/tune is now playing, to switch it off.*)

Mother (*addressing herself, rising*)   You're a foolish, wicked, bad old woman.

Dance-hall music, faint, from the distance. **Marie** *escorting* **Mother** *off; they go off.* **Marie** *returns to switch off the lights. On her way out again, she stands in the window, moonlit, to look out.*

Marie   Come, gentle night.

Scene Seven

Bunty's *bar is crowded (as can be).* **Bunty** *is in and out, serving his two bars.* **Christy** *(in shirtsleeves) is playing volunteer pot-boy. People at the counter have their hands raised for drink, including* **Jimmy**.

Jimmy   Simon! Simon! –

Tarpey *is present, the police inspector. Aware that he is a figure of authority. (We saw him at the top of Scene Two.) He's waiting for someone.*

The dance hall is across the street. The music is loud. A quickstep. (Slow dances will be quiet.) One can see, but it's hard to hear what people are saying.

Bunty *(taking a drink to* **Tarpey***)*   You're all right here, Inspector, are you? Now, this is on me. You'll go across, will you, to the dance for a few minutes? Now, a pass for you. (*'A pass', a complimentary card/ticket.*)

Jimmy   Simon! –

Bunty   In a minute! *(As he goes out to his other bar.)*

Peter *and* **Goldfish** *are together.* **Goldfish** *is impatient, he wants to go to the dance, now.* **Peter** *is literally twisted with drink.*

Peter   Bunty! Mate!

Goldfish   No!

Peter   We'll have one more.

Goldfish   You've *got* the hooch! In your pocket, man! Chris!

The last, a call to say that they are leaving, to **Christy** *who is taking a crate of empties out the back.*

Christy   See you across in a while! *(And he's gone.)*

Goldfish   Mosey, Pedro, let's breeze, man!

Jimmy   *(from his place)*   A round in here, Simon!

Peter   Khrisht! *(Announcing that they're leaving, though* **Christy** *is well gone.)*

Goldfish   Go-go-go-go-go! (*He's gone.*)

Peter (*his glass drained*)   Wait for me, Goldfish! (*He's gone.*)

Susanne *has entered the scene, looking for diversion.*

Jimmy   Simon!

Bunty (*returning*)   Yes, Jimmy?

Christy *is returning with a crate of beer for* **Bunty**.

Bunty   Thanks, Christy!

There is not much in here up to **Susanne***'s mark and she is leaving again.*

Christy   Susanne! Susanne!

Susanne   Me?

Christy   Going across?

Susanne   Sorry?

Christy (*joining her*)   Are you going to the dance?

Bandleader (*off; muffled*)   Thank you, boys and girls, next dance, please.

A lull in the music.

Christy   Are you going to the dance?

Susanne   Mmmm. (*Keeping her options open.*)

Christy   Fancy something?

Susanne   I think I'll go home. G and T.

Christy   Gin and tonic, Simon!

Bunty (*calling a greeting*)   Susanne, isn't it?! (*He's busy with* **Jimmy** / *someone.*)

Susanne   I think so!

Christy   Classy dress.

Susanne   This place is fit only for troglodytes.

He laughs. (He's eager about something.)

And how are we this evening?

Christy   Top of the world!

Susanne   When do you go back to London?

Christy   Well now, that is an interesting question. I don't know that I'll be going back. (*He grins.*)

Bunty (*calling*)   Enjoying the holidays?

Susanne   Right!

Christy   The auction happens Tuesday.

Susanne   Does it? Are you working here?

Christy   Nah. Just giving him a hand.

Susanne   Hmm? (*She's checking out the place for a better prospect than* **Christy***'s company.*)

Christy   Actually, I'm glad I ran into you because there's a matter that's been bothering me. You won't believe this, but I thought that if I could see *you*. Because I wouldn't mind having a chat.

Susanne   With me?

Christy   Yeh. I can't discuss it with Mrs de Burca, not yet. That wouldn't be fair. Terrific woman, yeh know? Her kindness. Treated me like a son almost.

Susanne (*glancing about again*)   Yeh, she's like that.

Christy   I sound stupid.

Susanne   But you have lovely hands.

Christy   Them.

Susanne   Dem hands. What do you do on the building sites to have lovely things like those?

Christy   Oh! Gloves.

Susanne   Do you? They wear gloves now and everything

on the building sites? (*There's innuendo in her remarks.*)

Bunty   Now, Susanne, gin and tonic, welcome home!
Thanks, Christy son! (*Money. And is gone out to his other bar.*)
Yeh.

Christy   It's hard to talk here. Would you like to take
these (*'drinks'*) outside, or – Hmm?

Susanne   You would like to discuss in private your
intimate thoughts with me: I understand, how well I
understand! (*She is laughing knowingly.*)

Christy   No! No! (*Laughing.*)

Susanne   And you cannot have a *chat* with *Louise*?

Christy   (*'No'*) But we could always talk, you and me –
Remember?

Susanne   Or Marie?

Christy   Marie? (*'Hardly.'*) But this matter that's been
bothering me all week: well, I've come to a decision about
it.

Susanne   No, tell me first – tell me about Louise first!
What is going on between the builder's labourer and that
child?

Christy   Nothing.

Susanne   Nothing? Aaa! You can tell me – if we could
always talk.

Bandleader (*off*)   And the next dance, boys and girls,
will be a slow waltz. (*Music, muted.*)

Christy   Okay. There was – (*Shrugs – 'some little thing'.*) It's
over.

Susanne   Aaa! You can give me the details. What do you
do to her?

Christy   Okay. Louise came to me one night. Story about
your man, Burgess.

Susanne　Her husband.

Christy　I never liked him. How he was treating her. The town's great all-round athlete one time: look at him now. I had a word with him. Gave him a few slaps, didn't I? I was glad – Yeh, frankly – that she came to me. And . . . It became a bit – involved. But hands off that now. Louise is perfect – in many ways – but she's a married woman.

Susanne　I think you would possess us all.

Christy　What?

Susanne　And how far have you got with Marie?

Christy　Marie?

Susanne　The one with her head screwed on, and who is – she told me herself – three years and one month, exactly to the day, older than you: What naughty things have you been doing to our Marie?

Christy　(*smiles/whatever at the very idea of this. Then*)　Yeh, I suppose it's only natural Marie disapproves of me.

Susanne　Really?

Christy　Has always done.

Susanne　Is that a fact now?

Christy　And, at the same time, there's times . . .

Susanne　When you think what?

Christy　That maybe I'm getting it wrong.

Susanne　*winks to herself in the broad, shrewd manner.*

Christy　Because, there's times when I think, it's maybe that she's . . .

Susanne　Perfect.

Christy　Yeh, dead straight.

Susanne　And it's been killing her for years. You've turned the heads of the lot of them! Except me.

Christy But, you and me, we used to share some secrets
down that place of yours one time. D'you not remember?
'The Princess!' (*He bows to her.*) I had to tell all my secrets
to the princess. D'you not –

Susanne I do not remember. I deal in the present,
reality. The past is a pig. Anyway, Marie was the princess
– the queen! That's Marie again you're thinking about. *She*
demanded the tributes – and *got* them! Flowers, prizes,
secrets. Consultations, when they happened, were – are! –
always with her! Your vows of unending love. She took you
very seriously. Still does! The sensible one. She dressed you
up, for God's sake! In frillies! (*He's laughing.*) Ah, but do you
see, kinky stuff, what? Yeah?!

Christy Well, I've a secret for you now. This's going to
surprise you. And the reason why I tell you is: I wouldn't
like to think that anything I do'd come as such a surprise –
shock even – specially to Mrs de Burca. Eternally fond of
her, eternally grateful. Well, that place of yours down
there –

Susanne It's not 'a place'.

Christy No. Heaven on earth. I'm going to buy it.

Susanne *starts laughing at him.*

Christy It's going to surprise people all right.

Susanne (*laughing*) This is some chat-up line!

Christy I'm serious.

Susanne Don't be so fucking stupid! (*Still laughing.*) Tell
me, how far have you *got* with Mrs de Burca?

Kerrigan *comes in. When he's drunk he's loud – he shouts – and
most everything is on a laugh. He's drunk.*

Kerrigan Time, gentlemen, please! Can't ye see the Law
is here?! (**Tarpey**.) I'm late, Inspector! And what harm
itself if I am! Have ye no homes to go to?! Ah, the
peasantry! 'Have we not seen, round Britain's peopled
shore, / Our useful sons exchanged for useless ore?!' Oh be

the hokies, Miss de Burca! Sweet Auburn, loveliest village lassie of the plain! And you never got married? Look at that now, a fine-looking woman like you! And you must have had great chances! What're yeh talking to this fella for? – Come on, dance for your daddy! Law-law-law-law, lal-lal-lal-lal-lal-lal, lal-lal-lal-law . . . !

He has danced her away from **Christy**. **Susanne** *protesting the attention she is getting. He is dancing her to where* **Tarpey** *is drinking:*

Kerrigan   I'm late, Inspector, but can't you see I've better things on my hands?! Law-law law-law. . . ! Sure you know this/that handsome man here/there! (*Introducing them:*) Richard Tarpey of Ireland's finest: Miss Susan de Burca!

Susanne   Susanne!

Kerrigan   Susanne! – De Burca de (the) Hon! Innkeeper! – where is he? Bunty! Drinks in here!

Susanne   Are you going to the dance? (*To* **Tarpey**.)

Goldfish *exasperated, has come in, joined* **Christy**. *And, in a moment,* **Peter**.

Goldfish (*calls*)   Small one there!

Christy   What's doin'?

Goldfish (*sighs*)   'Jerry, please help me.' (*Bette Davis, though he is not amused.*)

Peter   Wouldn't let us in, Khrisht.

Goldfish   They wouldn't let *him* in. Then, when I got involved – Jesus!

Peter   Pack of fuckers.

Christy   'Shall ve just have a cigarette on it?' (*Paul Henreid – Now Voyager. Though* **Christy** *isn't amused either at this stage.*)

Goldfish   Small one, Simon!

Bunty (*coming in*)   I heard yeh!

Peter   Your missus in the box office wouldn't let us into the dance, Bunty.

Bunty   No more drink in here for him tonight.

Goldfish   Am *I* getting a drink?

Bunty   In a minute, wait your turn! Now, Inspector, ye want something over here?

Kerrigan   Whiskey! And another of whatever he's having! And, Miss Susanne?

Bunty   Gin and tonic.

Susanne   Oh, all right.

Kerrigan   'The bashful virgin's side-long looks of love, / The matron's glance that would those looks reprove!'

Bunty *has gone off again for* **Kerrigan***'s round.*

Peter   And look! (*A fistful of paper money.*) Look!

Goldfish   Put it away – Sit down – Sit! Can't you see lawyers, attorneys is present, an' ladies an' lawmen? *More* ladies.

'More ladies' refers to **Louise** *who has come in. (Hair arranged over her injured eye.)*

Kerrigan   Where's-your-husband?!

Louise   Where's your wife?! (*And joins the party.*)

Bunty *is returning with* **Kerrigan***'s round:*

Bunty   Last orders!

Kerrigan   'The curfew tolls the knell of parting day!'

Susanne   'The lowing herd winds slowly o'er the lea / The ploughman homeward plods his weary way / And leaves the world to darkness –'

Kerrigan   'And to dust –'

Susanne   'And to *me*'! –

Kerrigan   Dust! –

Susanne   Me! –

Bunty (*before going out again*)   Throw this out the back for me, Christy.

Christy *goes out with another crate of empties.*

Bandleader (*off*)   Thank you, boys and girls, next dance, please.

Bunty (*off*)   Last orders!

Goldfish   Small whiskey? (*Casually to nobody, and sighs.*)

Peter   Pack of fuckers! (*To himself.*)

He's a man in and out of a stupor. He has discovered the bottle of drink (mentioned at the top of the scene) in his pocket. He's really talking about the people outside. But he hardly knows where he is. He's lost, impotent, enraged. He offers a drink to **Goldfish**. **Goldfish** *shakes his head.*

Peter   The poxy pack of fuckers in this town. Watching me. Talking about me.

Goldfish   Take it easy, amigo.

Peter   Ay? Ay? Well, if anyone'd raise, raise a, raise one – (*finger*) – to my, to one of my, my children, the kiddies like, to my missus, I'd . . . Or say a, or say one – boo – to them, about them, I'd . . . I'd! Or to me, mate!

Goldfish   Easy! Can't you see quality is present, man?

Peter   Ain't?! Ain't?! That I, that I, that I ain't a Catholic, is it? Ay? That I, that my missus, my children, the kiddies, ain't? Ain't baptised?! . . . Are! Fuckin' are and all, mate!

Goldfish   Hey, man, Pedro relax, like *me*!

Peter   Well, would they like now, this minute like, like to say it to me now like? To my fuckin' face like, like this fuckin' minute like!

Tarpey   Watch your tongue over there!

Peter (*doesn't register it*)   Fuckin' human bein's, ain't we?
Are and all, Peter. Fuckin' Catholics, so we are!

Tarpey   You, watch your tongue!

Peter   Ay?

Goldfish   Pedro!

Tarpey   And you there beside him! (**Goldfish**.)

Goldfish   . . . *Fuck you!*

Bandleader (*off*)   And the next dance, boys and girls,
will be a mixed medley, starting with a quickstep. (*Music,
loud.*)

*Again, it's difficult to hear what is being said, but we can see it. And
see the melee starting.*

Tarpey *is afraid, but he wants to impress the company and is
coming to* **Goldfish**, **Kerrigan** *is intervening, restraining him.*
Goldfish *is going to* **Tarpey**, **Jimmy** *is intervening, restraining
him.* **Peter** *hardly knows what's going on. The jostling and pushing
start and* **Louise** *and* **Susanne** *are caught up in it. (As are other
people present – if we have them!)*

Tarpey *loses his hat at some point. His image, he feels, is suffering
because of this, and he would have it back.*

Christy *will return from his errand to find the scuffle in progress.
And* **Bunty** *from his other bar.*

Tarpey   What did you say? (*Coming to* **Goldfish**.)

Goldfish   Fuck You!

Tarpey   What did you say?

Goldfish   *Fuck You!*

Peter   Ay?

Kerrigan   Dick! Dick! Let it pass! Let it pass . . . (*Ad libs,
variations.*)

Tarpey   I know who you are!

Jimmy   Ary, Goldfish, let it go and there'll be no more about it! (*Ad libs.*)

Tarpey   I know *him*! (*To* **Kerrigan**.)

Peter   Ay? (*And he will retire to a corner with his bottle in a minute.*)

Kerrigan   Let's go, let's go! Let's leave! . . .

Goldfish   You know me all right! Dick! Dick!

Bunty   What's all this, what's going on here? (*Coming in.*)

Jimmy   Ary, Goldfish!

Goldfish   Fuck him, man, and all the guards in the town!

Christy *comes in, intervenes, takes charge. He has strength and authority.*

Christy   It's all over! It's all over now! Let out the ladies – Watch the girls! It's all over, Simon – No one here has any problems at all! . . . Has anyone here any problems at all? . . . See! See! (*He finds* **Tarpey***'s hat and gives it to him.*) It's all over? Everyone's going dancing!

Bunty   Finish up now! Glasses! (*Goes out to his other bar.*)

People are preparing to leave. The band across the street is now going into the second leg of the mixed medley, a slow dance.

Tarpey   They go to England and America to hone their criminal skills there.

Christy, *calming down* **Goldfish***, taking him aside, telling him a funny story.*

Kerrigan   Forget the dance, will we go up to the Club?

Bunty (*off*)   Finish up now! Glasses!

Christy (*energy, circling the room, collecting glasses*)   Whee-hee! Finish up now! Glasses!

Louise   I'm going to the dance! (*For* **Christy***'s benefit.*)

Christy   Whee-hee! (*Ignoring her.*)

Tarpey (*to **Susanne***)   A nightcap, Miss de Burca?

Kerrigan   Or two. Susanne, you will, up in the Club.

*She will. She has been watching **Christy**. (At this stage she, perhaps, would prefer his company, fancies him.)*

People are leaving. **Bunty** *has returned.*

Bunty   Thanks, thanks, thank ye all now, behave yourselves now and enjoy yourselves! Thanks, Inspector!

Tarpey (**Kerrigan** *and* **Susanne** *go out*)   The country would come to a stop if we had those bastards around all the time.

Louise   Goodnight! (**Louise** *leaves.*)

Bunty   Thanks, Louise, goodnight! Here, Christy, a pass to the dance for you: You're a very obliging young fella.

Goldfish   *He* (**Tarpey**) can come in here with his 'hat' and I can't?! (*To* **Bunty**.)

Bunty (*has the small whiskey ready for him under the counter; gives it to him*)   Now. (*And collects the money for it.*) Tell my wife in the box office I said it was all right for you to go in on your own. (*He goes out to his other bar, switching off a light.*)

Goldfish (*blows a sigh and knocks back his drink*)   See you across in a few minutes.

He adjusts himself, preparatory to leaving. A small gesture from **Peter**, *in a world of his own in a corner.*

Goldfish   Don't let's ask for the moon, Pedro, I've had enough. (*He's gone.*)

Christy   Go home, Peter, say hello to the missus.

Peter (*rises wearily, talking to himself*)   Oh Christ . . . Sweet Christ . . . grant me the grace, to find a small hut, in a lonesome place . . . and make it my abode.

He goes out, staggering.

Christy *is getting his jacket from somewhere.* **Susanne** *returns. (She deliberately left something behind a few minutes ago. She collects it.)*

Susanne   You are joking.

Christy   I'm serious.

Susanne (*she is courting danger?*)   We shall see about that. I am tied up right now, but I could see you tomorrow night.

Christy   Yeh.

Susanne   Where?

Christy   I'll call down.

Susanne   Don't call. Let us keep this a secret.

Kerrigan (*off*)   Susannaaa!

Susanne   Let's meet in, oh, some romantic private place.

Christy   The wood.

Susanne   Ah, the wood!

Christy   Bend of the river?

Susanne   Right.

Christy   That's on, then.

Susanne   That is on, then.

Christy   Eight o'clock?

Susanne   Five to. (*She leaves.*)

He stands there in the comparative dark for a moment, then he goes out to the dance.

Scene Eight

Tuesday morning, early. **Kerrigan***'s house.* **Kerrigan***, standing, looking at a file, from an impressive bundle of files, drinking a morning cup of tea perhaps. Doorbell. He answers it.*

Kerrigan   Oh?! Young Lochinvar has come out of the west! (*He has returned with* **Christy**.) You're up early, could you not sleep?

Christy   Morning!

Kerrigan   What?

Christy *grins/grimaces, foolishly.*

Kerrigan   Sit down, can't you see I'm a busy man? What can I do for you?

Christy   Don't want to bother, Billy, but!

Christy*'s 'Morning!', above, sounded down. And his grinning and grimacing – his laughing-boy image – aren't functioning that well either. And, unusual for him, he looks dishevelled, like a man who's been up all night. There's something wrong. (There's something gravely wrong.)*

Kerrigan   But what? Tuesday, my busiest day! . . . (*Mock casual:*) Enjoyed the dance last Sunday night?

Christy (*foolishly*)   Yeh. But last night, I arranged to meet someone. It went badly wrong.

Kerrigan (*begins to groan*)   Aw Jesus, not another one of you.

Christy *doesn't understand.*

Kerrigan   A favour. A favour, a favour! The town down there – the country – the whole economy is run on favours! And in return you'll give me a goose and a bag of potatoes, will you, for Christmas? What's the problem, what d'you want?

Christy   Trouble.

Kerrigan   You're in trouble – did you kill someone? – what kind of trouble?

Christy *looks at him, foolishly/whatever.*

Kerrigan   Prick trouble? I knew it. Mrs Burgess, 'Louise'? Doesn't the whole town know it! Devouring married

maidens out of season. Do you know that her mother –
whatever the extent of that old lady's liberal attitude – isn't
a well woman? Haven't you – if her daughter hasn't – any
sense of consideration? Or decency or propriety. Why don't
the two of you do it in the middle of the Square: that be a
good idea? What?

Christy The charvering stakes has nothing to do with it.

Kerrigan Oh? 'The charvering stakes'! Then what has?
Is Michael Burgess going to take a case against you at last?

Christy *shakes his head. But a new thought, a new tack – a way
out for him, a solution – has begun to form in his mind.*

Kerrigan Well, he should. You should be locked up, like
what's happening to some of your Paddy-confrères. Do you
know that Michael Burgess could have you for assault,
enticement, criminal knowledge of his wife? – he could
have you on a dozen charges.

Christy *nods.*

Kerrigan What?

Christy *nods.*

Kerrigan What?

Christy Yeh.

Kerrigan Didn't I warn you about her?

Christy You were right.

Kerrigan Oh? Good man!

Christy A very highly strung neurotic woman, Billy.

Kerrigan Now! I often wondered what was up with her.

Christy Well, the fact is I decided to pack it in.

Kerrigan A firm purpose of amendment – Yes?

Christy She won't agree.

Kerrigan Irresistible.

Christy   No.

Kerrigan   What? . . . Yes?

Christy, *in the following, becomes upset, bewildered, and ends in tears.*

Christy   We arranged to meet. 'That's on, then. That is on, then.' Keep it a secret.

Kerrigan   You met. (*Impatient.*)

Christy   To tell her what I was going to do. That I'd come to a decision about it.

Kerrigan   That you were packing it in.

Christy   D'you know what I mean, Billy? That I was serious about it. But that I wanted to be fair. She started to create a scene.

Kerrigan   Hell hath no fury – Splendid!

Christy   No. That she'd stand in my way, she said. Sex, yes, reality, she said, but couldn't – wouldn't – give me a reason why she'd stand in my way – 'No reason!' She became out of control, she became very out of control –

Kerrigan   Christy –

Christy   All over the place – crazy – she started saying terrible things –

Kerrigan   Christy –

Christy   Terrible. Then pulling up her dress – Hand on (*Her crotch.*) – There was no way of dealing with her – Or how to handle it –

Kerrigan   What're we talking about?!

Christy *has become tearful.*

Kerrigan (*to himself*)   Jesus Christ!

Christy (*tearful*)   I'm tired.

Kerrigan (*sighs heavily and gestures at his work. Then*)   And what d'you expect me to do about it?! A thousand and one things to do – Look at all that! (*Work*.) Two court cases in Newcastle later this morning, an auction this afternoon – your 'friends'' place, de Burcas' place – I have to attend that too . . . Christy?!

Christy (*mention of the auction has galvanised him, returned him to his 'new tack'*) Well . . . the fact is, I *have* come to a decision about it.

Kerrigan And *what* d'you want me to do about it?

Christy You can. She's been following me around –

Kerrigan Who has?

Christy She drives up and down outside my house –

Kerrigan Who has –

Christy All hours! – she *calls* there! – She was there this morning – She said –

Kerrigan Who said, who-are-we-talking about?

Christy . . . Louise. Mrs Burgess. You were right about her. She said she knew I was with another woman last night.

Kerrigan And you were, I suppose. Cursed with an eye for a beautiful woman. Yes, my son, who was she and how many times? Aw, Jesus, Christy, am I a solicitor – State Solicitor, public prosecutor – or a father confessor? Go on.

Christy Now she's threatening –

Kerrigan A bigger scene – Suicide? – Lovely! – Yes?

Christy I told her I was nowhere last night.

Kerrigan Where is that?

Christy Told her I was with no one last night.

Kerrigan Meaning? Is this where I come in? I'm your alibi? That you were up here with me, painting walls maybe, here, with me?

Christy   I told her I was locked up.

Kerrigan   . . . You want me to arrange . . . ?

Christy   Well, the fact is, I told her stop watching me,
following me, watching the house. That if she – or anybody
else – seen me arrive home six o'clock this morning was
because I'd spent the night in the cells, that they'd just
released me, that I was locked up. She said prove it then,
and she'd step aside. Oh I'll prove it all right I said and
she'd step aside all right then because she'd have to,
because this was the end of the line. That I'd show her the
summons when it was issued to me – (*Shrugs, 'or'.*) Go to
the station herself if she liked, look at the records and see
my name on them. But that this was it, finito.

Kerrigan   . . . Look at the cut of you. Is that the good
suit you had on last week? . . . And you were fighting too
the other night, I hear – what's the matter with you?! With
your Yankee pal. That Goldfish is an out-and-out
troublemaker, a menace. But the guards will deal with him
yet. Okay, I'll fix it: I'll have a word with Inspector
Tarpey. You were locked up all night last night: drunk and
disorderly. (*Sighs.*) I might as well get it over with. I've to
drop these down to the station anyway. (*Bundle of files.*) Wait
here! Till I come back with your summons. Prick trouble.
You're a thundering bollix. (*He leaves.*)

Christy, *alone, a man in a nightmare, but one that he is going to
see through to its conclusion.*

Scene Nine

*The drawing room half of de Burcas' double room. An occasional
table, two chairs, a table lamp.*

Mother, **Marie** *and* **Louise** *form an uncomfortable group in the
doorway from the hall. They were about to enter but a couple of*
Strangers *– a man and a woman – are inspecting the room.*

Upstage, the dining room. Blinding sunlight falling on the table – or on one end of it. **Bunty** *is there, arranging things for himself.*

The **Strangers** *have decided to inspect the hall: the de Burcas step aside to let them out the doorway.*

Louise   Oh, excuse me!

Mother *moves towards the dining room but changes her mind: there are other people in there.*

Mother   Now we know what it's like: not to belong to a place any more.

Marie   Oh I don't know.

Louise   It's still ours!

Mother *to her chair, to consider sitting in it, to decide against it. She flaps her hands. Where to go?*

Marie's *humouring laugh.* **Mother**'s *grin.*

A car arriving outside.

Mother   Is that Susanne? See, Marie. Where-is-that-girl?

Bunty (*comes from the dining room, importantly*)   We'll start now in a minute, ma'am, when Billy Kerrigan arrives.

Marie   He's here.

Bunty *returns to the dining room.*

Mother   I didn't think it'd be like this.

Louise   People traipsing through the house.

Marie   It'll be over in no time. (*To the hall door to meet* **Kerrigan**.) Billy!

Kerrigan (*with his briefcase*)   Marie! Are we all set up? Mrs de Burca! Mrs Burgess!

Bunty *returns.*

Kerrigan   Are we all set up?

Bunty   Not that many of them in there, and some of them are only gawkers.

Kerrigan   Have you set the reserve price?

Bunty (*to* **Mother**)   Two-two-double-o.

Kerrigan   Two thousand two hundred: and you're happy with that?

Mother *nods.*

The **Strangers** *return from the hall and go into the dining room.*

Bunty   Give it another minute.

Louise   The cheek of some people. (*The* **Strangers**.)

Christy *appears in the hall doorway but retreats again when he sees the de Burcas. (They don't see him.)*

Bunty (*absently*)   Ah, it'd be a nice place all right with a bit of work done on it . . . If I can get two of them bidding against each other. Yeh. (*To* **Kerrigan**.) Will we? ('*start*'.)

They are about to go into the dining room.

Mother   But do we have to be here?

Bunty   Aw it'd be better, ma'am. To be near at hand in case a deal comes up or has to be struck. (*And looks at* **Kerrigan** *for support.*)

Kerrigan (*agrees*)   It's usual. (*And goes into the dining room.*)

Bunty   Sit down there for yourself, ma'am, and you can be sure I'm going to do the very best I can for ye. (*He follows* **Kerrigan**.)

Louise   It's like Westland Row Station.

Marie   Perhaps we should have packed our bags?

Mother (*grins; sits*)   Now we know what it's like.

Bunty   All right then, yeh. I'm offering this house for sale, Woodlawn House, private residence on over three acres, and I'll pass ye over now to this gent on my left to give us the 'foresaids and thereuntos.

Kerrigan (*reads from a document*)   I act for the vendor of this property, Sabina Esther Winifred de Burca who is the legal Personal Representative of John Louis Ulick de Burca, deceased [obit. 17/6/1943], and to whom Grant of Probate of his last Will was granted forth of the Principal Probate Registry of the High Court on the thirteenth of November 1944.

Mother   We're being sentenced. (*Grins.*)

Marie   We'll be rich.

Marie *grins.* **Louise** *brushes away private tears.*

Kerrigan (*continuous*)   The closing date of this sale will be twenty-one days from the date of purchase. Should the Purchaser fail to complete the purchase price on that date, such Purchaser shall bear interest to the date of actual completion at the rate of eight per centum per annum.

Marie   We'll be rich, everybody!

Kerrigan   The Particulars and Tenure of the property are as follows:

Marie   Rich.

Kerrigan   The property is Woodlawn House in the townland of Newcastle. It stands on its own grounds which –

Bunty   Where else would it stand? (*Some laughter from the dining room.*)

Kerrigan   It stands on its own grounds which comprise an area of three acres, one rood and thirty-eight perches statute measure and is held under two titles as follows:

Mother   We're being sent into exile. (*Grins.*)

Marie   We'll be rich!

Marie *would shield her mother from what is going on behind them. She rises / moves in impotent effort. A glance into the dining room as she does so.*

Kerrigan (*continuous*)   One. The dwelling house, messuage, hereditaments and premises on one acre, one rood and thirty-eight perches statute measure is held under a Lease for Lives renewable for ever, dated 23/2/1839, subject to covenants on the part of the Lessee and conditions therein contained, at a rent of one peppercorn, if demanded.

Mother   A rent of what?

Marie   (*shrugs/grins*)   ... Christy is in there ... I didn't see him arrive, did you?

They didn't.

Kerrigan   (*continuous*)   The Lease has not been converted to a Fee Farm Grant pursuant to the provisions of the Renewable Leasehold Conversion Act, 1949, and the Purchaser shall not require the Vendor to effect such conversion.   .

Bunty   Lookit, one of ye will have the place for ever – That's all. ('*This is a waste of time.*')

Kerrigan   Two. The balance of the lands comprising two acres, known as the 'Wide Ridge', is held in fee simple and is the subject matter of Folio 9927 of the Registry of Freeholders.

Mother   *starts to rise through the above and hangs there, half risen.*

Marie   Mum?

Mother   *shakes her head, smiles, sits back in her chair. But she's up again after a moment, to stand, grin:*

Mother   And where is Susanne? Where-is-that-girl? (*Sits again.*)

Kerrigan   I will now take any questions which you wish to put to me on the Conditions or on the Title.

Bunty   There ye are now, thereunto, whereas – Any questions?

Mother   (*grins*)   This is hell.

Marie   Mum?

Bunty   No questions?

Mother   Hell. (*And grins.*)

Bunty   I've a question. Where would a man find a
peppercorn? (*Some laughter.*)

Kerrigan   Try a peppermill. (*Drily.*)

Bunty   Right then, we'll start . . . Who'll offer me two
thousand pounds, two thousand? . . . Two thousand pounds,
a modest beginning, who'll start the bidding at two
thousand pounds, who'll start me off? . . . For this attractive
property . . . Lovely dwelling, standing on its own grounds –
(*Which he finds amusing.*) – as our learned friend beside me
told us . . . Who'll start me off at nineteen hundred? . . .
Eighteen fifty? To start me off . . . Ah, come on, don't be
thinking ye're cute! This's a wonderful chance for someone,
wonderful property with scenery, a veritable, veritable little
Ireland in itself: seventeen hundred and fifty pounds,
someone! What an active man with a spade could do to it.
Or a tractor'd soon put manners on the two-acre field
growing wild up the back there. And a lick of paint to the
windows – Seventeen hundred?

Mother *half rises again during the above. She doesn't know what to
do with herself.*

Marie   Oh, there are great shenanigans going on in
government, in the Dáil.

Mother   Love?

Marie   You didn't read your paper yet today.

Bunty   Who'll start the ball rolling, who wants first blood?
Ye're wasting my time and all that lovely sunshine out
there . . .

Marie *has risen/moved again, as before.*

Marie   The funniest thing, a big debate about flour.

Mother   Oh?

Marie   Yes!

Mother   For making bread?

Marie   Flour! What a business!

Louise   I heard something about that. What was it again, Marie? (*Encouraging* **Marie**.)

Marie   Well, it seems that the millers were demanding an increase for their flour. This – of-course! – would give the government the problem of allowing the bakers to put up the price of a loaf. But then one clever bod of a politician – a minister – came up with the solution: tell the bakers to take a slice off the loaf of bread.

Mother   Make the loaf smaller?

Marie   Yes! But don't let on to the housewife! . . . I dare not think how it's all going to end.

Bunty (*continuous*)   If you're not in you can't win – seventeen hundred pounds . . . Ladies and gentlemen, it's twenty-nine minutes past two o'clock, ye heard the et ceteras and so forths and everything is clean – start me off, start me off – Start! – At seventeen hundred pounds – and this place is going to be somebody's for ever and ever and ever, yeh amen, for eternity. That's what them big words meant.

Mother *rises*.

Marie   Mum?

Mother   I'll go to my room, Marie.

Marie   Yes.

Mother   Don't you have power-of-attorney over everything, and if anything comes up –

Marie   'A deal' –

Mother   'A deal', can't you 'deal' with it? (*Both of them grinning, going off.*) And she (**Susanne**) was out 'til all hours on Sunday night.

Louise   She was up in the Club.

Mother   Wherever she's got herself to last night.

Marie (*to* **Louise**)   I'll be back in a minute.

She follows **Mother** *out of the room.*

Bunty   Well, I don't know what this shy company is thinking, but take a care ye don't let yere shyness and cleverality get the better of ye now and miss yere chance, because I have my instructions and I'll withdraw the sale entirely. So, do I have an *opening* bid? No offers? No takers? . . . Does no one want it? Before I withdraw it . . . And that'll be all right too: because I'll find a stranger for it, a foreigner. Or a Dublin man. And see how fast they'll jump at it. (*He looks at* **Kerrigan**. **Kerrigan** *shrugs.*) That's it, then: I'm withdrawing the –

Christy *interrupts. A clown: a laugh in his voice:*

Christy   Excuse me!

Bunty   Who's that? I can't see you with the sun.

Christy   Simon!

Bunty   Christy?

Christy   That's me!

Bunty   Did you want something?

Christy   Can I ask a question of you?

Bunty   What? – are you making a bid? We're holding an auction here, not a-a-a –

Christy   Isn't there a reserve price on it?

Bunty   What?

Christy   What's the reserve price exactly?

Bunty (*dismisses the question and* **Christy**)   No one wants it then? All right, I now withdraw the –

Christy   Two thousand four hundred!

Bunty   Two?

Christy Two thousand four hundred!

Bunty Two?

Christy Two thousand four hundred!

Bunty Two thousand four hundred pounds?

Christy Two – two thousand four hundred pounds – Are you deaf, Sim-on? That's what I said! Anybody else? (*He's inviting others to bid higher.*)

Bunty Excuse me! –

Christy Anybody else?!

Bunty Excuse me – Christy! – excuse me there! Are you making a bid?

Christy Are you stupid or what?! I just did! I just made a bid! Sim-on!

Bunty It's a serious business making –

Christy Oh the money will be there! Don't fret your head about that! Sim-on! Two thousand four hundred is maybe my first bid! – Anybody else here? You ask them. I thought you were meant to be running this shebang.

Bunty I'm offered two thousand four hundred pounds for Woodlawn. Is there any advance on that? . . . As the reserve price has been met, and if there's no advance on it? . . . Going once, twice . . . sold to – Sold.

Louise *leaves to bring the news to* **Mother** *and* **Marie**.

We see **Christy** *sign a document for* **Bunty** *on the dining-room table.*

Bunty, *with the document that* **Christy** *signed,* **Christy** *and* **Kerrigan** *come to the drawing room.*

Bunty We'll get Mrs de Burca's signature on this now.

Christy Mrs de Burca? Well, I've signed it. I mean, I'm not needed now, am I? Know what I mean? So I'll be off. I'd arranged, actually – Yeh know! (*He's gone – as if to keep* *an appointment.*)

Bunty (*bemused*)   This's one for the book!

Kerrigan *is puzzled too, but he's smiling, smirking.*

Bunty   Where would he get money like that?

Kerrigan   Where did you get yours?

Marie *is coming in.*

Bunty   Now: did I do well for ye?!

Marie   Has he gone?

Kerrigan   You can sign that, Marie.

Marie (*signs the document*)   I was afraid some Tom, Dick or Harry would buy it.

Scene Ten

Bunty*'s. Evening into night. A sing-song. A celebration – Revelry.*
Christy *is a hero and he's behaving like one. He is drunk, calling the tune, abandoned. He wants to become drunker. And there are extremes of mood swings. Other emigrants are present. As are* **Goldfish** *and* **Peter***, whose arm is in a sling.* **Bunty***. And* **Kerrigan***, who does not integrate with anyone.*

A ragged, laughing chorus of voices before and as the lights come up, singing: 'A-round the corner – Oo-oo! / Beneath the berry tree / A-round the footpath, behind the bush / Looking for Henry Lee.'

Christy   Martin! ('*Sing*'.)

Goldfish   'Tonight all the folks'll cut the corn –'

All   'Cut the corn!'

Goldfish   'Tonight I'll be glad that I was born –'

Christy   Same again in that, Simon! (*He has drained his glass.*) –

Goldfish   'For my Henry Lee I'll see / He'll come cuttin'' corn with me / And we'll meet neath the bitter berry tree.'

Christy A-round the corner! (*A shout.*)

All Oo-oo! 'Beneath the berry tree / A-round the footpath, behind the bush / Lookin' for Henry Lee!'

Applause, together with:

Peter A-round the corner, Khrisht!

Bunty (*drink to* **Christy**) Some man, some man!

Peter Fair ol' dos, Khrisht, all right like!

Christy Do a round for the house, Simon!

Bunty D'yeh hear that, Mr Kerrigan?

Christy Gentle when stroked, fierce when provoked!

Goldfish Hee-haw!

Peter Gentle when stroked, Khrisht!

Bunty Same again over there, is it, Mr Kerrigan?

Kerrigan *shakes his head.*

Bunty Why wouldn't yeh? The squire is treating us again!

Christy And have one yourself, Simon!

Bunty Jesus Christ, England is a great country for some! –

Goldfish Another song! Someone! –

Bunty And me now, I slaved for seven years abroad in Dagenham and I end up back here a bigger slave – a waitress – serving drink for the new gentry! (*Laughter – everything is a laugh.*)

Jimmy *has come in, excited, in his boiler suit.*

Jimmy Where is he?

Christy Jim-ee!

Jimmy Put it there, Christy – How can you buy Killarney! I only just heard it!

Christy And a pint for Jimmy!

Jimmy But I always knew it!

Christy Or a short, Jimmy?

Jimmy Pint, Christy, thanks – Pint, Simon! No better man, one of our own sure!

Bunty Some men, some men!

Peter Heigh-up, Jimmy mate!

Jimmy Heigh-up, Peter! I hear y'have it in for the buff-shams' bicycles, Goldfish?

Goldfish Frankenstein strikes back! (*Whips out a paper, a summons to appear in court.*) Says I'm to appear afore the magistrate come Toosday, twenty-eight [28th] for a-rustlin' short-horn Raleighs.

Peter I've one too like! (*Produces his summons.*)

Goldfish Yo's t'appear afore Judge Roy Bean as well?

Peter John P. Hogan's window. Staggerin' home like, and I went like this like, and fell through the . . .

Jimmy Yeh hoor yeh, Peter!

Christy I love the smell of broken glass! (*Producing his summons:*) Me too, last night.

Peter Last night, ay?

Goldfish What they get you on?

Christy Tell you again – 'A-round the corner?!'

Others 'Oo-oo'!

Bunty Squire! (*Calling* **Christy** *to hand the drinks round.*)

Christy (*collecting drinks; calls*) Peter, yourself, a song! Have another, Billy!

Kerrigan *shakes his head. (There's something not making sense.)*

Peter (*singing*)   'A mother's love's a blessing / No matter where you roam' –

Bunty   Jesus Christ, another comeallyeh! –

Peter   'Keep her while she's living / You'll miss her when she's gone' –

Christy   Your pint is on the way, Jimmy! –

Jimmy   No better man, Christy! –

Peter   'Love her as in childhood / Though feeble, old and grey' –

Bunty   Someone else! –

All   'For you'll never miss a mother's love / Till she's buried beneath the clay.'

Applause, together with:

Christy (*pint to* **Jimmy**)   Jimmy!

Jimmy   May the hand never falter! Give us one yourself, Christy – 'I think that I shall never see!'

Christy   Nah.

Bunty   Someone else quick, or he'll only start up again! –

Peter   Or yourself, Bunty! –

Goldfish   'Wanting you, every night I am wanting you' – Chris! –

Peter   Or Mr Kerrigan?! –

Jimmy   'Here in my Heart', Christy!

Peter   Mr Kerrigan, poetry like!

Christy   Billy!

Bunty   Sure people without any education at all can quote poetry without making a boast of it! (*He winks behind* **Kerrigan**'s *back.*)

Christy (*taking a drink to* **Kerrigan**)   Here, Billy, go on, have another!

Kerrigan (*'no'*)   I'm late as it is. See yeh.

Christy   When do I sign the deeds?

Kerrigan   Must wait due process, Christopher: you heard me yourself. (*Leaving; turns back.*) Where'd you get the money?

Christy, *as in Scene Three, a 'fiddling clown'. And a laugh from others.*

Kerrigan   But there's *something* not making sense.

Bunty   No poetry, then, for us tonight?

Christy   Thanks, Billy! (**Kerrigan** *is leaving.*)

Bunty   Goodnight to yeh now, Mr Kerrigan!

Kerrigan (*to* **Bunty**)   At very best, you're an ignorant little man. (*He's gone.*)

Bunty *laughs after him. Others are laughing drunkenly. And* **Christy** *breaks into sudden abandoned song.*

Christy   'Here in my heart I'm so lone and oh so lonely, / Here in my heart I just long for you only, / Here in my heart . . .'

Marie *has come in. (Gone unnoticed for a moment or two.) He sees* **Marie** *and stops his song. A vague smile – some kind of melancholy, is it, or remorse? And is there some strange connection between him and this woman? She comes to him.*

Marie   My mother was keen that I should see you. We heard you had to dash. She asked me to tell you that she's delighted, and to wish you luck. (*He nods, soberly. Then he bows to her.*) And so am I, very pleased. (*She offers her hand for a handshake.*)

Christy (*takes it. Then kisses it*)   Will you have a drink with me, Marie?

Marie   Yes, please.

Christy   A drink for Miss de Burca, Simon.

Bunty   What would you like, Marie? (*He tends her.*)

Goldfish   Here in my heart, Chris!

Jimmy   I'm so lone and so lonely, Christy!

Christy (*perhaps he takes* **Marie***'s hand? Sings*)   'When the scented night of summer covers / Field and city with her veil of blue / All the lanes are filled with straying lovers / Murmuring the words I say to you: / Just a little love, a little kiss / Just an hour that holds a world of bliss / Eyes that tremble like the stars above me / And the little words that say':

Goldfish/Christy   'You love me.'

Bunty (*going off*)   You love me, yeh.

Peter   Night will pass. (*Gently.*)

Christy   'Night will pass and day will follow after / Other griefs and joys will come with day / Yet through all the weeping and the laughter / You will ever hear the words I say: / Just a little love, a little kiss / I would give you all my life for this / As I hold you fast and bend above you / And I hear you whispering, I love you.'

Applause. Out of which a cacophony develops. As it does, **Tarpey** *comes in. He calls/beckons* **Marie** *to him and talks quietly to her. It is clear that he is imparting bad news. And they leave together.*

The cacophony grows through the above: from applause to calls for more, to a **Christy** *shout 'A-round the corner!' to 'Oo-oos!' of replies and laughter, to four singers coming in on top of each other, progressively, with four different songs: Until, eventually, and to the end of the scene, four different songs are being sung simultaneously. Uproar.*

Peter   'Oh father dear, I oft-times hear you speak of Erin's Isle . . .' (*Etc.*)

Jimmy (*comes in with his song*)   'While the mission bells were ringing, calling for thee evening prayer . . .' (*Etc.*)

Goldfish (*coming in now with his*) 'Carolina, gave me Dinah
. . . Dinah, is there anyone finah / In the State of Carolina
. . .' (*Etc. – Eddie Cantor style, vibrant.*)

And **Christy,** *who has observed – soberly –* **Marie** *leave with*
Tarpey *– now punches the air defiantly, stomps the floor and joins
the cacophony with a fourth song:*

Christy 'Here in my heart I'm alone and so lonely /
Here in . . .' (*Etc.*)

Scene Eleven

It's a few days later. Night. De Burcas'.

*In the drawing room, one lamp, the table lamp, is lit on the
occasional table. (The vacuum of the dining room is upstage.)*
Mother *in mourning clothes is seated in one chair and* **1st
Woman** *is in the other. With them, standing, is* **1st Man**.
Louise *comes from the dining room with a tray to offer small
glasses of drink.*

Susanne *has been buried today and sympathisers still call to pay
their respects, stay for a little, drink the ritual drink and leave again.
(Movement is silent, conversation hushed, sibilant: something almost
dreamlike.)*

Marie *receives visitors at the door. The occupants of a car are
arriving:*

2nd Woman   Marie, dear, so sorry, so sorry.

Marie   Mrs Hession.

2nd Man   Sorry for your trouble.

Marie   Mr Hession. (*She ushers them to* **Mother**.) Mum?
Mrs Hession. Mr Hession.

2nd Woman   Sabina, Sabina, so sorry, so sorry.

Mother   Thank you, thank you.

2nd Woman   Louise, Louise, so sorry, so sorry.

Louise *is inclined to be tearful, nods her thanks and goes off with her tray.* **1st Man** *and* **1st Woman** *vacate their places in favour of* **2nd Man** *and* **2nd Woman**.

2nd Man   Sorry for your trouble.

Mother   Thank you, thank you.

2nd Woman   When did it happen?

Mother   Last Monday night.

2nd Woman   And she was buried today.

Mother   There had to be a post-mortem. You know. So she wasn't buried until today.

2nd Woman   So young.

Mother   Yes.

*The lights of a second car (**Bunty**'s) washing the place. (A third car will arrive shortly.)*

2nd Woman   We never know the time or the place.

Louise *(returning with a drink for them)*   Mr Hession. Mrs Hession.

2nd Woman   Thank you. *(A whisper.)*

2nd Man   Thank you. *(A whisper.)*

Marie *is receiving* **Bunty** *and ushering him to her mother.*

Bunty   Sorry again for your trouble, Marie.

Marie   Thank you. Mr Tierney, Mum.

Bunty   Sorry for your trouble, ma'am.

Mother   Thank you, thank you.

Bunty   Sorry for your trouble, Louise.

Louise   Thank you. *(And goes off again to dining room.)*

Marie   Mum? *(She has fetched a footstool which she would like*
Mother   *to use.)*

Mother *smiles her thanks but declines it.* **1st Man** *and* **1st Woman** *are leaving. More handshakes.*

1st Woman   So sorry again.

Mother   Thank you, thank you.

1st Man   So sorry.

Mother   Thank you, thank you.

Marie (*ushers them out*)   Thank you for calling.

1st Woman   So sorry.

Marie (*handshakes*)   Thank you. Thank you.

They leave. As they do so, a muted 'Goodnight' to **Kerrigan** *and* **Tarpey** *who are coming in to join* **Marie**. **Tarpey** *is in uniform.*

Kerrigan   Marie. (*Simply a nod.*)

Tarpey   Miss de Burca. We got the final reports and everything is consistent with its being an accident. We thought you should know. It's been gone into and there's no other explanation.

Marie   She slipped.

Tarpey   Yes. Or tripped, falling into the shallows. And the rocks there. (*Meaning that her head hit the rocks.*) The path is uneven at that spot and close to the bank, and there are overground roots. We thought you should know. It stops the imagination.

Marie   Oh dear, I don't understand it. (*She frowns. The explanation doesn't make sense to her. She smiles:*) But I know that this is – beyond your call of duty? (*Handshake:*) You're very kind. (*Handshake:*) Billy.

Tarpey   If there's anything further, Miss de Burca, that we can do.

Marie   Thank you.

Tarpey   But you have plenty of friends.

Marie   Not that many.

'Not that many': she is smiling bravely but she nearly cracks on the line. She ushers them to **Mother**.

Mum? (*And she retires to the dining room to deal with her emotion there.*)

Tarpey   Mrs de Burca. (*Handshake.*)

Mother   Thank you, thank you.

Kerrigan   Mrs de Burca.

Mother   Thank you, thank you.

Tarpey   We got the final reports and everything is consistent with it being an accident. (*He sits beside her.*) We thought you should know.

Mother   Thank you, thank you.

2nd Man *and* **2nd Woman** *have vacated their places – marginally – in favour of* **Tarpey** *and* **Kerrigan**. *All, including* **Bunty**, *form a circle around* **Mother**. *And* **Louise** *is arriving with her tray of drinks. (As appropriate, they sympathise with* **Louise**.*)*

And **Christy** *arrives in the doorway, is rooted there, mouth open at the hushed party, unnoticed as yet. (He has been lurking outside in the grounds for some time, wondering if he dares face* **Mother**.*)*

Marie *sees him, hurries to him eagerly.*

Marie   Christy!

Christy   I'm sorry for your trouble, Marie! (*Offering a handshake.*)

But her arms are around him, indeed, she clings to him like a woman seeking and finding shelter in a brother – or a husband.

Marie   Oh Christy! Oh Christy! I thought you weren't going to call.

Christy   . . . Marie? (*He's confused at this woman whom he considered to be aloof and disapproving.*)

Marie   I've been waiting. I've been wondering where you were. (*Releases him.*) I thought you weren't going to call.

Christy   No.

Marie (*tears of gratitude. She smiles*)   Thank you. Come in, come in!

She is ushering him to **Mother**.

As she does so, **Kerrigan** *removes himself from* **Mother**'s *group. He would avoid* **Christy**. *(He's a worried man.)*

Marie   Mum? (*Presenting him.*) Christy. (*And she retires.*)

Mother *smiles, holds out her hands to him.*

Christy   Mrs de Burca. (*A tentative bow.*)

And he steps back out of the circle to remove himself from them. He finds himself beside **Kerrigan**.

Christy   Billy. (*He doesn't know where to move.*)

Louise *comes to them with her tray.*

Louise   Billy? (*'A drink.'*)

Kerrigan   No, thank you.

Louise   Christy?

Christy   Actually, in a bit of bother myself, Louise: I'm up in court next week. Yeh know?

Louise   I'm sorry for your trouble. (*Coldly. And she leaves them.*)

Christy   Yeh going for a drink or anything on the way home?

Kerrigan   Where were you last Monday night?

Christy   Where was I?

Kerrigan   The charge you were fixed up with is in the records now signed, countersigned, sent out to the District Court.

Christy   Yeh?

Kerrigan   No games: I'm the bright lad in this town – I got out of Barrack Street and I'm not going back there.

Christy   (*'I'*) Don't know what you're talking about, Billy.

Kerrigan   The answer to my question could be very simple: You were with her, Louise, after all?

Christy (*consider this, then shrugs 'I'm sorry, but'*)   Was locked up Monday night, Billy, all night, Billy.

Kerrigan *returns to* **Mother***'s group, to bow:*

Kerrigan   Mrs de Burca.

Mother   Thank you, thank you.

Tarpey   Miss de Burca. (*Shakes hands with* **Marie**.)

Marie   Thank you. (*She sees* **Tarpey** *and* **Kerrigan** *to the door.*)

Louise   I'm going home for a while, Mum.

Mother   Do, love, do. Go to bed, have a rest.

Louise *kisses* **Mother** *and joins* **Marie** *at the door for a whisper before leaving.*

Mother *sees* **Christy** *across from her, his unease, her hand out in invitation.*

Mother   Christy. (*He comes to her.*)

2nd Woman   So sorry again, Sabina, I'm so sorry.

Mother   Thank you, thank you. Sit beside me, Christy.

He sits. (Perhaps he chooses the footstool rather than the second chair.)

2nd Woman   She's at peace now.

Mother   Thank you, thank you.

2nd Man   So sorry.

Mother   Thank you, thank you.

2nd Woman *and* **2nd Man** *are being shown out by* **Marie** *and* **Marie** *goes off with them.*

Bunty   What can we say, ma'am?

Mother   Thank you, thank you.

Bunty   What can we say, yeh. (*A nod:*) Christy. (*And he leaves.*)

Mother   Give me a cigarette, Christy.

Marie (*off*)   Thank you again!

Bunty (*off*)   Goodnight, Marie!

Marie (*off*)   Goodnight!

The final two cars driving away.

During the above, **Christy** *has given* **Mother** *a cigarette. (He is in the other chair now.) She is exhausted but she sees that he is troubled and she's caring of him. He sees her as a woman of great strength and understanding. He has something to confess.*

Christy   Mrs de Burca, I've something to tell you.

Mother   Christy? . . . And of course there are things we have to talk about. Things that should have been but weren't mentioned at the auction. (*A puff of the cigarette.*) The gravity-fed water supply to the house gives trouble. D'you know? The second filter on the line gets blocked with leaves. But another day's work for us. (*Another puff.*) The lead in the valleys of the roof, I believe, is porous. We'll list those things and come to some arrangement with you about them. (*Another puff of the cigarette and she gives it to him to extinguish it for her, smiling.*) Thank you. And we'll start getting our things together, packing. And have the place nice for you. (*And she sighs the sigh she has been containing.*) Yes, she's at home now, she's at peace, it's over.

Christy (*'no': he shakes his head to himself*)   I've something to tell you. I'm sorry, I'm so sorry, I'm sorry.

Mother   Christy?

Christy   Always admired this family, but I'm afraid I let
you down. And I'd give anything to put it right with you.
And I wish now I'd come and talked to you direct. Told
you, since you were bent on selling, hook or crook, I was
going to buy it. I'd have the money. That it couldn't be
the thing at all to let some Tom, Dick or Harry in here:
they don't *know*. They'd spoil it in a month. That I wanted
it: I don't know why that should be, but I'm surer of it
now than ever. No matter what happens. But if I'd came
and talked to you direct, it might've looked like I was
trying to get round you. Everyone is trying to pull a fast
one these days. And at the same time I'm doing the wall,
jobs about the place, you thanking me and I've started
standing there, looking at you, dumb. And at the same
time I didn't want, when I bought it, it to come as a shock.
And that was my mistake. Susanne. I talked to her . . . And
they're on to it I was with her in the wood: (I'm) nearly
sure of it. But they don't know how to jump or can't. (*He
brushes away, dismisses all authority.*) In any case, they don't
matter, they don't care. Least, I don't think they do . . . So
we arranged to meet in the wood. Susanne. Told her my
plan, so that when the time came she'd explain to you that
she knew it in advance. Told her I was going to buy it,
that that way it'd always be here, for her, for you, for
everyone, that otherwise a great mistake was being made.
She said she knew things about me, how I made a living,
things I was up to over there. (*London.*) Maybe she did
know. How therefore could I even dream of here. She said
. . . Yes, maybe I've been up to things, the other side,
things I wouldn't care to mention, not to you, Mrs de
Burca: But strange as it may seem, that's all the more
reason why a person does: Dream. It's no more strange
than a child without a tosser in his pocket wanting to
possess the setting sun going down out there . . . I said it's
up for sale. She said my mother scrubbing your floors. I
said did she want it? (*Shakes his head:*) She didn't. But I'd be
the last one to have it, face reality. She . . . (*Offered him sex
but he cannot tell this to* **Mother**.) Reality? . . . She became
very out of hand in every way. She said choice things.

There was nothing I could do. She kept on, and I don't think there was anything I could do, and that's on my solemn and dying oath. And – (*His fist: how he hit her.*) And she . . . (*Fell backwards and fell into the river.*) I hit her, Mrs de Burca . . . Mrs de Burca. Don't tell.

Mother   . . . I won't tell. I won't tell anyone.

His whispered confidence/confession alarmed her at the start. Now she's shattered, finished.

He leaves. (He may be tired/whatever, but he isn't finished.)

She emits a single moan. Her heart is broken.

The lights fading. **Marie** *comes in.*

Mother   I'd like to go to bed now.

Scene Twelve

Bunty's. *Afternoon. A few days later.* **Peter** *is drinking a glass of ale, in silence. His suitcase is somewhere nearby.* **Christy** *is sitting over a half-drunk pint of Guinness. (Just sitting over it.)*

Peter   . . . Ever work with the diddicoys over there, Khrisht? . . . English tinkers like . . . They drink tea and all . . . (*He's sensitive – in his capacity – to* **Christy**'s *mood.*)

Goldfish *comes in with his suitcase. He has dropped the American vocabulary.*

Peter   Ay? (*Referring to the suitcase.*)

Goldfish   This fucking place is getting on my nerves.

Peter   I thought you had another week?

Goldfish (*calls*)   Bottle of Time there! I'll go back like everyone else today, at least as far as Dublin, see if I can do something about the date on my ticket. Get back to the US of A.

Peter   Ay like?

Goldfish   Don't know where I am in this town.

Peter   How much the judge get you for?

Goldfish   Aw fuck it.

Peter   He fine you a pound, Khrisht?

Christy   Yeh.

Goldfish   When – where! – did this drunk and disorderly caper of yours happen?

Christy   Ah yeh.

Peter   He got me for two quid, the fine like. It would've been more but I told him –

Goldfish   I don't know who I am.

Peter   And nine for John P. Hogan's window. But that was only fair.

The rolls of money are no longer in evidence. **Goldfish** *is counting coins to pay for his drink.* **Bunty** *is coming in, pouring the bottle of Time.*

Goldfish   'People from this town are decent respectable hard-working people', Simon?

Peter   Ay?

Goldfish   That's what he said to me, the judge. 'I don't know where you come from but in this town we respect private property.'

Bunty   They do in their arses.

Goldfish   'And it's my business to see that the likes of you and your kind back from England respects it too.'

Bunty   And the law and the guards are no good, they only catch what suits them. (*Takes* **Goldfish**'s *coins and goes off.*) Where's all yer big rolls of money now, where have ye them hid?

Goldfish *sighs over the judge, and drinks.*

Peter (*sympathetically*)   How much he get you for?

Goldfish (*to himself*)   Fucking cat. 'Hold your horses there, Your Honour, two points of fact. One: I'm not come from England, I come all the way back from the United States of America. Two –' 'Take your hands out of your pockets!' 'Two: I'm *from* this town –'

Peter   But you should've –

Goldfish   'You, Your Honour, sir, from my knowledge, is the one that's not.' (*'He's'*) Another buff-sham from down there Tipperary ways. Twelve pounds fine, forty – forty! – for contempt of court, or two weeks in Limerick. Tarpey – oh you can be sure – *Dick*, had a hand in it all. And thirty-six pounds ten and six for committing grievious bodily harm to four of the buff-shams' bicycles and getting the shit bet (*beaten*) out of me. And kicked to death only for him. (**Christy**.)

Peter   But you should've said you was off today. That's the best one. That's what I told him. When they do hear you're leaving they do even sometimes dismiss the case altogether. Providing you're leaving like.

Bunty (*returning with change, for* **Goldfish** *– a coin*)   And if you voice an honest word of suspicion about anything they don't want to hear, they're fast enough to ask you if you want a slap in the face of a libel suit. Or maybe accuse you of treason. (*He's gone again.*) Yeh.

Christy's *shoulders are shaking. Perhaps he found the last funny.*

Peter   No but, the missus is gone down there now ahead of me, to the station like, with the other cases and the kiddies: I can tell you she had a jolly nice time, mate.

Goldfish   Cat, mouse, pus, corruption. (*'He'*) Doesn't know where I come from. (*He flicks/pitches his coin change into a corner of the floor.*)

Peter   Well, I had three hundred and ninety pounds, saved up like for coming home, and if I've a penny of it left in my pocket when we hit Brum, Snowhill Station, six o'clock tomorrow morning, I'll be a disappointed man.

Jimmy *comes in in his boiler suit.*

Jimmy   Men!

Peter   Heigh-up, Jimmy!

Jimmy   All roads out there leading to the train. I'm on the dinner break but I couldn't let ye go without saying goodbye.

Peter   We have another few minutes. (*Looking at his watch.*)

Jimmy   Ye have a nice day for it anyway. I heard the judge cut the two legs from under you in the courthouse, Goldfish?

Goldfish   How would you like to hop around the floor on your balls? (*No challenge in it.*)

Bunty (*returning*)   Did you want something, Jimmy?

Jimmy   No, I'm grand, I'm fine.

Peter   Aw give the man a drink. Can't you see he has the lip on him. (*He produces his money: say two pounds, two notes.*) Khrisht, Goldfish?

They decline.

Jimmy   Small one, Simon. Thanks, Peter.

Bunty *goes off with one of* **Peter**'*s pounds.*

Peter   All the same, I'm looking forward to it, going back and all, and see how Davy got on, me mate like. But the only thing bothers me: he's always telling jokes and cracking smart ones, Davy, and I don't get them – Ay? But strange like, it's quare: I don't think Davy understands them either.

Bunty *returns with a whiskey for* **Jimmy** *and brandies for* **Peter** *and* **Goldfish**.

Bunty   Jimmy. (*Change to* **Peter**.) Now, Peter: I only took for Jimmy's small one out of that. This one's on the house:

first and last drink of the season.

Peter   Bunty, you're a decent man.

Bunty   Here, Goldfish, don't let it choke yeh.

Goldfish   I don't want your drink.

Bunty   Oh? (*Leaves the drink, moves off again.*) Drink up now or ye'll miss the train.

Jimmy   Ah drink it up.

Goldfish   Did *I* order that?

Jimmy   Well, luck men whatever! God bless, safe journey!

Peter   Jimmy, mate!

Goldfish (*to* **Christy**)   Hah? What's up?

Christy *gestures 'nothing'.*

Goldfish   Your pretty brown eyes is telling me lies – What's up? Some young one you've up the pole? I'll stay – I will – for a day or two if you want, (*'and'*) say I done her too.

Christy *shakes his head.*

Jimmy   Oh, did you hear, Christy, Mrs de Burca was taken to hospital?

Goldfish   What's up?

Christy*'s shoulders are shaking again. Perhaps he finds* **Goldfish***'s earnestness amusing? (He doesn't. He has heard* **Jimmy***'s news about Mrs de Burca; he has heard more than that.)*

Peter (*drink finished, it's time to go*)   Well, comrades? You won't come down to the station with us, Khrisht?

Christy   Nah.

Peter   Bunty, we're off!

Jimmy   I'll throw your case on the carrier of my bike out there, Peter, and wheel it down for you.

Peter   Sound as a bell, Jimmy.

Goldfish (*to* **Peter**)   I'll see you down there. ('*He'll follow.*')

Peter *shakes hands with* **Bunty**, *who has returned, and with*
Christy.

Peter   Finest little fuckin' town in the world this – God
bless. (*A handshake. And another.*) God bless. I wouldn't choose
a king's ransom. Thanks for everything, fair fuckin' dos, I'd
a smashin' fuckin' time and I'll see ye all again next year
please God.

He leaves, following **Jimmy** *and his suitcase.*

Bunty   Are you drinking this, Goldfish?

Goldfish   I'm not, Bunty.

Bunty   That's all right then too. (*Goes off, taking the brandy
with him.*)

Goldfish   The sweet nature of that man.

Christy   I sign the deeds of that place couple weeks' time.

Goldfish   What?

Christy   Mrs de Burca's place, that place I bought off
Mrs de Burca.

Goldfish   Fuck that place.

Christy   Nah, heaven on earth, Mrs de Burca's place.

Goldfish   There's something up with you. Fuck that aul
fuckin' house, fuck here! We're bigger than here, we're –
the energy! They're all old – even the young ones! Fuckin'
place is dyin' – Dead! Junior fuckin' footballers – Fuck
them and their prayers for emigrants. Hop on a train with
me, *now*, take ourselves away out of here, we'll spend a few
days round Dublin, work out a plan for the two of us –
Yeh! – something really interesting! Yeh? Yeh, Chris, yeh!
. . . I'd die for yeh!

Christy ('*nah*')   Mrs de Burca's place, I bought it off Mrs
de Burca: I have to sign them deeds, finalise the matter.

Goldfish (*shrugs*)   Well. (*Reverts to his American accent:*) I gotta go, man, build up these goddamn muscles. Got me a date with Jersey Joe, Madison Square Gardens, coupla weeks from now.

Christy (*silently*)   Oh! (*Slips some money to* **Goldfish**.)

Goldfish   . . . Y'all right, sham? I'm askin' yeh!

Christy (*feints – mock pugilistics – throws a few punches. And*)   See yeh.

Goldfish (*leaves with his suitcase. Off*)   Move 'em out, hee-haw!

Bunty (*returning, sipping the brandy*)   . . . You miss them all the same . . . But we won't see Goldfish again. Yeh, I've seen it before. (*He's about to go off again. Then:*) Did I hear Jimmy Toibin say Mrs de Burca was taken to hospital? It's worse than that. She's gone, the creature.

He goes out.

Christy, *alone, his back to us, head bowed, his shoulders shaking. (He's crying.)*

Scene Thirteen

*A few weeks later. Late afternoon. Garden furniture (as in Scene One). A bag or small suitcase on one of the garden chairs (***Christy***'s). 'Trees' from the house sung by Arthur Tracy. Some smoke from a fire off. There are cardboard boxes stacked somewhere (and maybe a piece of furniture):* **Louise***'s things. And a suitcase (***Marie***'s).*

Louise *comes in, as from her car, for another box.*

Christy (*calls*)   Are you sure I can't give you a hand?

Louise   You're grand! (*Going out with a box.*)

Christy *is about the place; restless. Eager and apprehensive.* **Marie** *from the house, hauling a sack (for the fire), taking the opposite direction to* **Louise**.

Marie   *More* stuff for burning!

Christy   Hah! . . . Are you sure I can't give you –

Marie   'You're grand!' (*She's returning, having slung the bag off.*)

Christy   Arthur Tracy!

Marie   Hm? (*She stops.*)

Christy   I used to think that was your father singing.

Marie   Oh! (*And laughs.*) I thought we'd have some music while we're waiting. Why not! (*Then, the afternoon:*) Glorious! (*And, en route to the house, to* **Louise***, who has returned:*) How are you managing?

Louise   *whistles – mock gaiety and a mock stagger – going out again with another load.*

Marie   *from the house with another sack:*

Marie   Heigh-ho! (*She slings it off.*) We're nearly there. (*She stops.*) You're staying here tonight, aren't you – Is that all you brought with you? (*The bag. She laughs.*) You haven't changed your mind, have you?

Christy   No.

Marie   (*moving again*)   He'll be here in a minute. (*And meets* **Louise***.*)

Louise   (*returning*)   My car is full to the gills, so it won't take much more. That was a clever thing to say. This rubbish of mine. Was ever such – stuff! I'd forgotten about most of it. How it accumulates!

Marie   And Mum's papers, and clothes. Oh dear. (*And she becomes tearful.*)

Christy   *watching them, remembering their mother. And* **Louise***, who has matured, somewhat, rescuing* **Marie***:*

Louise   Oh, wait'll I tell you – Marie, Marie: I heard this this morning. You know Mrs 'Chisley Park' who doesn't go out that much – or hardly at all any more? And Mrs

Doyle who's about the same age? Two ancients! Well, they were out yesterday, both of them – This's true! And they met on Church Street. 'Oh hello!' said Mrs Chisley Park: 'Oh hello! I thought you were dead!' 'Well, if I was,' said Mrs Doyle, 'I didn't see you at the funeral!' 'But, my dear,' said Mrs Chisley Park, 'you were dead for a month before I heard it!'

They laugh, leaning their heads together, touching each other, embracing.

(*The words of the story. Then, her belongings:*) Childhood things! Child*ish* things! What do I want this rubbish for? (*Taking most of what's left and dumping it on the fire. Then, going into the house:*) I'll take a last look in here.

Marie   These are the keys, Christy. I've labelled them for you. I wanted to give you a set weeks ago, but the Law says it can't be done until the signing's done. Billy Kerrigan said no, an emphatic 'No'. (*She puts the keys on the garden table.*) D'you want this garden stuff? I've no place for it – D'you want the gramophone? You know you paid over the odds for here? (*She laughs.*) So most of the furniture is left in there and you can have it as far as Louise and I are concerned. I know that's how Mum felt.

Christy   Marie.

Marie   My place over the shop is furnished and all but finished. I thought I'd give it – a try-out? – tonight.

Christy   You don't have to. (*She looks at him.*) If – Yeh know?

Marie   Stay? Here?

Christy   Well. (*Shrugs:*) Yeh. (*Then:*) Yeh.

A self-conscious moment between them. A car is arriving, which they register.

Marie   Here he is. (*And she goes off to meet the car.*)

Louise   The big moment has arrived. (*She is coming from the house to collect her final box.*)

Christy   All done now bar the signing.

Louise   I'm not staying for it. My big sister will look after you. She knows where everything is – located and et cetera. She's the one loves you. But you're probably too – obtuse – to know it. Are you?

He's not.

In case you're interested, I don't. Talk to her. Best of luck. (*Leaving:*) If you find anything that looks like mine, just – phh! – burn it.

Kerrigan   (*off, during the above*)   You want it done out here?

Marie   (*coming in with* **Kerrigan***; to* **Louise**)   Are you not staying for –

Louise   (*without stopping; mock gaily*)   No! (*Off.*) No!

And her car drives away during the following.

Kerrigan*'s pride has been compromised. He feels corrupted and he is bitter and angry. And impotent. So, he's talking nonsense. He refuses to look at* **Christy***.*

Kerrigan   You want the signing done out here?

Marie   Yes. And when it's done I thought we'd mark the – occasion? – with a drink under the tree.

Kerrigan   Are you sure?

She thinks he's joking.

Are you sure?

Marie   What?

Kerrigan   That you want the signing done at all?

Marie   I don't understand you.

Kerrigan   That it's the right thing to do?

Marie   Is there something the matter?

Kerrigan   Okay, you summoned me here, you want the signing done, you want it done out here – One thousand, eight hundred pounds outstanding: cheque, bank draft, cash, what?

Christy   Cash. (*A package of money – brown paper bag.*)

Kerrigan   Ah, cash! (*He starts to count the money, distastefully.*)

Christy   ... How yeh doin', Billy! (**Christy**'s *attitude is perverse. He's taunting/challenging* **Kerrigan**.) ... I was never much of a one for cheque books ... bank drafts ... (I) Keep it under the old mattress ... What?

Kerrigan   That this is what your sister would've wanted?

Marie   ... Is this necessary? (*The counting/his attitude.*)

Christy   Yeh? ... Some of it is English, Billy!

Marie   ... Won't you sit down?

Kerrigan   That this's what your mother would've wanted?

Christy   Yeh? ... All there, is it, Billy? Tell us.

Kerrigan *gives up on counting the money. He has his briefcase and the deeds to the house.*

Kerrigan   Miss de Burca: As the legal representative of your deceased mother, sign there. (**Marie** *signs.*) Thank you. (*He countersigns as witness. He points to a spot.*) Purchaser. (**Christy** *signs.* **Kerrigan** *countersigns. And is putting away the documents.*)

Marie   Oh! Lemonade. (*And she has gone off to the house.*)

Christy   Thanks, Billy!

Kerrigan (*an angry man talking to himself*)   Those documents are dirty now. There's a smell off them. This is dirty property now, bought with this (*money*): And I'm sure if I guessed I'd make a good guess about how it was come by.

Christy   Yeh?! (*Mock amazement; defiance.*)

Kerrigan   I've guesses about other things too, but what happens now? Someone else's honesty to be corrupted. Betray someone else's – trust? Hers? (**Marie**'s.) Break down and cry, tell her – *half* tell her what you did and make her feel sick for the rest of her life.

Which gives momentary pause to **Christy**'s *defiant face.* **Kerrigan** *dumping the money in his briefcase:*

Or, throw her into the river too? That what you did the night we had you 'locked up'? (*He looks at* **Christy** *for the first time:*) You *fucker*! That I should report what I believe to be true and lose my job over you, is it?

Christy Your conscience, Bill-ee!

Kerrigan You – *scruff* – back from England! Look, why don't you go and – before we do it for you – put a bullet in your head! (*Leaving.*) Good man!

Christy Cheers, mate!

In the next moment, alone, he chokes back a sob.

Kerrigan (*off*) The rest will be routinely dealt with!

Marie (*off*) Won't you stay and have a –

Kerrigan (*off*) No thank you!

His car driving away. **Marie** *has returned with lemonade and glasses on a tray. Her frown:*

Marie What was all that about?

Christy Ah yeh.

Marie I think Billy Kerrigan has a bit of a swelled head – 'on'm'. Well, shall we have a drink to mark the occasion? (*Pours drinks.*)

Christy Marie.

Marie Oh! The keys. (*She presents them to him.*)

Christy Marie.

Marie (*toast*) To the owner! (*They drink.*) May I? (*Sit.*)

Christy Marie.

The sun is reddening, going down. They are seated.

Marie   Glorious! Isn't it? (*The evening.*)

Christy   . . . I'd die for here.

Marie   This's where you belong.

She has some papers which she is putting in her bag, one of them is a photograph of **Susanne**.

I used to think everyone was in love with Susanne. Were you?

Christy   Eternally fond of you all.

Marie   She was beautiful, wasn't she?

Christy   All of you.

Marie   Oh well. (*Flattered, but she doesn't count herself among the beautiful. She puts away the photograph and papers. Then her frown.*) Though I still don't understand it. (*'How that accident happened.' And smiles at him.*) Oh dear! (*She sees that he's upset. She's caring of him.*) And-Mum-was-very-fond of *you*! She loved seeing you. 'A little soul.' She had us *bored* talking about you. July, three years ago, when you didn't come home: 'Where-is-Christy?' Your birthday – she remembered it. New Year's Eve: 'Is he celebrating, I wonder.' Bored! (*Frown again:*) And she was convalescing well, I thought, and coping with Susanne's death, but then it was as if she gave in, stopped. (*Smiles at him.*) D'you know?

He is close to tears.

Christy?

He rises, moves away to look out at the lawn.

Well, I suppose I had better start making tracks . . . Shall I?

Christy, *his back to her, nods ruefully.*

She collects her suitcase and joins him.

Christy   Look at the grass again.

Marie   . . . Well . . .

They shake hands. She leaves. Her car driving away. **Christy**
standing in the setting sun. He chokes back a sob. He deals with it.

*[Note: 'A Little Love, a Little Kiss' sung by Arthur Tracy introduces
and concludes the play. Other recordings by Arthur Tracy can be used
for bridging the scenes.]*

Alice Trilogy

In the Apiary
By the Gasworks Wall
At the Airport

for Nell, with love

Alice Trilogy was first performed at the Royal Court Theatre, London, on 10 November 2005. The cast was as follows:

Alice	Juliet Stevenson
Al/Waitress	Derbhle Crotty
Jimmy/Waiter	Stanley Townsend
Bundler/Official	Christopher Patrick Nolan
Bill	John Stahl

Director Ian Rickson
Designer Jeremy Herbert
Lighting Designer Nigel Edwards
Sound Designer Ian Dickinson
Composer Stephen Warbeck

Alice Trilogy had its Irish premiere at the Abbey Theatre, Dublin, on 6 October 2006. The cast was as follows:

Alice	Jane Brennan
Al	Mary Murray
Jimmy	Robert O'Mahoney
Bundler/Official	Enda Kilroy
Bill	Bosco Hogan
Waitress	Stella McCusker
Waiter	Des Nealon

Director Tom Murphy
Designer Johanna Connor
Lighting Designer Tina MacHugh
Sound Designers Vincent Doherty and Ivan Birthistle

In the Apiary

Characters

Alice
Al

Time

The eighties

A shaft of sunlight cuts downwards through the murk, as it might coming from a dormer window or skylight. A few objects of broken furniture – maybe just an old trunk and a piece of old carpet. We are in an attic room – or maybe it's just a roof space, accessed through a hatch.

A burst of birdsong from outside, and a second one. And, a little later, the chirruping of a solitary bird.

A door is opened and **Alice** *comes in (or she comes in on hands and knees through a hatch). She's in her twenties. She carries a cup and saucer. From down below the thump-thump, thump-thump of a washing machine engaging with the sounds of a radio.*

Alice   Hello? Yes? Anybody home? Nobody home.

Al (*like an echo*)   Hello? Yes! Anybody home? Nobody home. Good!

Alice   Good!

She shuts the door/hatch, nigh blocking out the noises from downstairs.

Now we see that there is another figure in the room, a young woman, **Al**.

Alice (*has a sip from her cup*)   So what's on the menu today, kiddo?

Al   Poetry? Song? History? Question time?

Alice   Chifff! (*She produces a small bottle of pills.*)

Al   Chifff: so it's question time!

Alice   Chiffffff!

Al   State your profession and name please.

Alice (*removes her apron – which answers the first half of the question; then*)   And my name is Alice – I think.

Al   And that is a good start to our programme today! Hockhay, Alice! (*'Hockhay, Alice': Okay, as a Spaniard might say it.*) And here is your starter for two – Start the clock! Who wrote?

Alice   ... What?!

Al   *Hamlet.*

Alice   Stupid!

Al   No-oh! I'll give you a clue. He also wrote *Romeo and* –

Alice   Jeeessstupid! (*She takes a couple of pills, and sips some coffee. And through the following she produces a bottle of whiskey from a hiding place and laces her cup.*)

Al   But let her settle herself first, nobble herself first, do whatever she's going to do with her coffee first, then any question you like, she'll give you the answer, now that she's away from that kitchen down there.

Alice   Yeh. (*Agreeing with the last clause.*)

Al   Supply the missing word to the title of this song.

Alice   Christ, yes. (*As with the agreeing of the previous speech.*)

Al   No-oh! I haven't given you the question yet –

Alice   Chiphhh –

Al   The missing word to the title of the song: 'The Green, Green' *what* 'of Home'?

Alice   Christ.

Al   'Green, Green' what 'of Home', 'Green, Green' what 'of Home' – Running out of time, Alice – what would Tom Jones like to feel, what would Tom Jones like to touch?

Alice *is shaking her head, saying 'Christ' to herself and perhaps even smiling at the persistence of inanities. And she produces cigarettes. (But perhaps she has decided – and is trying – to give up the cigarettes!)*

Al   But let her light a cigarette first – no? – Sit down and take her ease first? – No? Now that she's got?

Alice   Twenty-five minutes – (*With a glance at her watch.*) –

Al   Before collecting the children

Alice   William and Sandra and Karen-Marie

Al   From school.

Alice   Yeh. (*And sits.*)

Al   So, 'The Green, Green' what 'of Home'?

Alice   How green is your Valium. (*Sips.*) Start again.

Al   Hockhay, Alice, let me see –

Alice   Decent questions.

Al   Decent questions, start again, come again –

Alice   *Recommencer, encore une fois?*

Al   . . . Oh! I see! Very good, *very* good!

Alice   *Une fois de plus, je comprends, très bien?*

Al   So, the Loreto education *wasn't* wasted.

Alice   *blows a heavy sigh.*

Al   It's just that she's upset.

Alice   At the *moment* she's upset. (*A little testily.*)

Al   And it's just that she cannot think what it is exactly is upsetting her at the moment.

Alice   One of those days as like as not.

Al   *Another* of those days as like as not.

Alice   . . . Yeh. (*'Another' of those days worries her a bit.*)

Al   She's be fine in a little.

Alice   Will she?

Al   Stands to reason.

Alice   Will she?

Al   It *doesn't* stand to reason?

Alice   She'll be fine.

Al   Stands to reason! I mean and for instance, ask her would she be another housewife on the phone, talking to a concerned DJ over the radio and breaking down and she'll tell you?

Alice What will she tell you? (*The idea even frightens her.*)

Al I'll tell you what she'll tell you. Let Big Al, her best pal, tell you what she'll tell you. She will tell you, I'd be fucked first.

Alice (*relieved*) Yeh.

Al I mean – what?! – Radio people?! –

Alice I ask you! –

Al All of them sounding like –

Alice Like –

Al Like –

Alice Lay –

Al Fucking doctors –

Alice Talking to the terminally ill.

Al For fuck's sake! (*Then:*) Fucking –

Alice Amateurs! –

Al Exactly! –

Alice Don't be so stupid! –

Al She'd die at the thought.

Alice Die at it.

Al . . . A quiz show?

Alice Maybe.

Al Yes?

Alice Perhaps.

Al But the other thing?

Alice Don't make me laugh, chiphhh!

Al   Don't make her laugh, chiphhh! . . . What do the following have in common: John the Baptist and Marilyn Monroe?

Alice   Neither of them wore any?

Al   Correct. (*Beat.*) She smokes.

Alice   That's true.

Al   A lot?

Alice   I do.

Al   And pills?

Alice   A few.

Al   A *few* a *few*?

Alice   And! – (*Holding up her cup or the whiskey bottle to declare defiantly her drinking.*) That's true, but better than breaking down on the phone over the radio to a concerned DJ? (*And sips.*)

Al   And her drinking's becoming hardly a secret.

Alice   'Cept!

Al   Except to Big Bill.

Alice   Wonder boy.

Al   Her husband. Who works in the bank, studies four nights a week, is in line for promotion and breeds budgies out there.

They listen for a sound of the birds.

Not a peep.

Alice   But he's still at it down there.

Al   Switch him off.

Alice   Talking to the terminally ill.

Al   Break his mouth for him, get a hammer, smash the set.

Alice   And listen to the washing machine?

Al   You have a point.

Alice   Or listen to you all day?

Al   *Another* point.

Alice   I'm not very keen on you, yeh know.

Al   I couldn't agree with you more. However, we must soldier on. Who died, who died, hum-haw, 'xactly hundred years ago today?

Alice   Christ.

Al   No! Shall I repeat the question?

Alice   No. Emily Brontë, Brian Boru, Winnie-the-Pooh, Princess Di, Beatrix Potter, Winnie Mandela, Pope John the Twenty-whatever-you're-havin'-yourself and Mixtrix Quixley.

Al   Correct. Why do women have small feet?

Alice   But the person sitting here is not ill, short-term, terminally or otherwise: ask her. She is alive and she is of sound, sound mind. Ask her.

Al   I ask her.

Alice   I do not like the Pope, for instance?

Al *nods.*

Alice   And though I am prepared to believe he loses no sleep over that fact – hmm?

Al *nods.*

Alice   Though I am prepared to believe the same lump of a man is a very sound sleeper – hmm?

Al   Nevertheless?

Alice *nods.*

Al   You don't like him.

Alice   I don't like the man.

Al   Nothing now against the Poles, mind you, have you?

Alice   What could I have against the?!

Al   Nothing racist.

Alice   No. But!

Al   His Holiness?

Alice   Yeh. Penchant for skullcaps?

Al   Kissing the ground?

Alice   Yet he won't look at a woman!

Al   Or wear a condom?

Alice   (It) Begs a question of sanity!

Al   Let alone infallibility!

Alice   The Pontiff.

Al   The 'Pontiff'. (*Then laughing.*) Faaaaaaack!

The title 'Pontiff' appears to be a source of amusement to them, and not for the first time it would seem, and they are laughing. **Alice** *pulls herself back.*

Alice   No, I'm not playing.

Al   Ah yes, don't stop now – I know – Got it! Tits, speaking of tits!

Alice   No.

Al   Yes.

Alice   I'm in bad humour.

Al   Twelve nineteens?

Alice   Two hundred and twenty-eight.

Al   Speaking of tits –

Alice   No!

Al   Ah, come on –

Alice   No! No! –

Al   Speaking of tits, speaking of tits – (*She points.*) – Marko Polo, who?

Alice   No.

Al   Marko Polo who lives next door is? A queer?

Alice   Fish.

Al   Spends lot of time in his garden since he took? Early?

Alice   Confinement.

Al   She means retirement.

Alice   I mean *exactly* what I say – *always*.

Al   And lately he has started to dye his hair.

Alice   He's a queer fish alright.

Al   Those eyes.

Alice   Yeh. (*She smiles.*)

Al (*smiles*)   Well, this day last month? When she went out to hang out the washing, Marko is by their back-garden fence

Alice   Again. Ostensibly to talk to her about Bill's budgies.

Al   Well! (*Mild exclamation.*) Just for fun she stoops down –

Alice   Ostensibly to pluck a dandelion –

Al   But really to see what would happen of course –

Alice   When one of her tits pops out of its cup.

Al   Well! (*Mild.*)

Alice   Well! his fish-eyes got a fright. Well, they must have done

Al   Because he left them there

Alice   Foolishly

Al   While the rest of him got out of it

Alice   To crouch to a flower bed on his side of the fence

Al   Catching his cheek on a rose bush en route.

Alice   Iff!

Al   She met his startled eyes through a chink in the fence, tucked the tit back to where it lived and

Alice   Iff!

Al   Winced again like Humphrey Bogart at the rugby of blood on his? (*Touches her cheek.*)

Alice (*absently*)   Cheek.

She has drifted away from the 'Marko' episode – how pointless, pathetic, it is – and she's thinking of something else, of a time when she was free or whatever.

Al   And though he's not out there now, in this precious moment in time

Alice (*absently*)   . . . precious moment in time . . .

Al   He's out there a lot in his garden since.

The chirrup of a bird from outside goes unnoticed by them. **Alice** *is just looking down at her cup.*

Al   It's just that she's upset, at the moment she's upset, and she cannot think what it is exactly is – *semmmashhh* (*smash*) *something!* – is upsetting her at the moment.

On 'semmmashhh something!' **Alice**'s *face had become animated as if in the consideration of doing something violent, but she's managed to contain it and now, instead, gets the whisky bottle again and pours a measure into her cup.*

Al   *Du? Plus? Mais non, madame!* –

Alice   *Oui!* –

Al   *Non-non!* –

Alice   *S'il vous plaît?*

Al   Hockhay, Alice.

Alice   *Merci!* (*She puts the bottle away.*)

Al   Top of your class at school, weren't you, love?

Alice   *qualifies this with a gesture.*

Al   Well, damn near. And as for the Maths and English?

Alice   *thumbs up: she was the best.*

Al   So you see who you're dealing with, my friends?

Alice   *holds up a finger.*

Al   (*in response*)   For instance, that – bird-house – out there

Alice   I know that it's an aviary

Al   But ask her, go on, ask her and she'll tell you

Alice   I prefer to call it an apiary

Al   She calls things what she likes

Alice   My mind, my life –

Al   Her mind, her life – Apiary

Alice   An apiary. For budgies and canaries and – doesn't matter.

Al   She prefers to call things doesn't matter.

Alice   Yes! (*She drinks. She thinks.*)

Al   But their singing all together, early in the morning, creates a racket. (*She listens for a sound of the birds. Nothing.*) Curiously, for the rest of the day they are quiet enough in their wire-mesh and timber dwelling. Except, yes, for the occasional outburst, for reasons best known or unknown to themselves.

Alice   Curiously, they are not all that gone on sunshine. Coloured birds, yeh know?

Al   Preferring the darkness of the dorm, where, one supposes, they screw one another like rattlesnakes.

Alice   If *rattle*snakes are silent whilst screwing, that is . . .
Hmm? *Hmm?*

*Hmm?': something puzzling her: the serious manner in which they
have been speculating about how rattlesnakes might copulate: and they
start to laugh.*

Al   Faaaack! Well, that's what they're there for – What! –
Isn't it?

Alice   Yes!

Al   Breeding, isn't it?

Alice   Like us, yes!

Al   Like *you*! – What! – Three kids already! – Isn't it?
Faaaaaack! (*As elsewhere, 'Faaaaaack' is a long, deep, rasping,
sound.*)

Alice   But.

Al   But yes, you're right, I will say this –

Alice   No, but –

Al   That wire-mesh and timber dwelling's spotless clean.

Alice   Yes, it is, but.

Al   What?

Alice   What's the complaint? This is a nice area, this is a
nice house, not a bad street, neighbours, Marko Polo too –
nice, old, just-a-bit-of-a-silly, old codger – What's the
complaint? D'you see what I mean? Car!

Al   Great mortgage –

Alice   For next to nothing!

Al   'Cause Bill works in the bank.

Alice   And the children all healthy, thank God, thank
God.

Al   So, you see!

Alice   Well off, up and down, wall-to-wall –

Al   And off the wall!

Alice   What is wrong with that?!

Al   Indeed!

Alice   What's wrong with it?!

Al   Look at her!

Alice   Spoilt.

Al   Look at her: happiness!

Alice   Some little thing, yeh know, back there.

Al   Some little thing, yeh know, back there *again* today was upsetting her.

Alice   And it has passed.

Al   And it has passed, as like as not.

Alice   Yeh know? (*And drinks. And thinks.*)

Al   And as is her custom for this holy half-hour, she is sitting quiet, here upstairs, in the attic room my dear (in the roof space my dear), in the afternoon my dear, stocktaking her assets, mental and material, and not unmindful of her prospects? (**Alice** *nods or perhaps she simply does nothing.*) With the Famous Grouse whisky disguising her coffee, before collecting the children from school.

Alice   And why not? And why not a morning nip or two as well, in the future, for elevenses? Should it enter my pretty head.

Al   Why not, indeed –

Alice   Indeed, why not – It stops a person from smashing! ('*Smashing*' *something. Her sudden anger, compulsion to break something.*)

An accompanying forward thrust of **Al**'s *head in encouragement. But* **Alice** *contains herself.*

Al   Thirteen seventeens.

Alice   Two hundred and twenty-one.

Al   Correct. Why do women have small feet?

Alice   Chiff! (*Disregarding the question. She is looking up and around at the roof.*)

Al   And as attic rooms come (*or 'as roof spaces come'*), this would hardly qualify as the brightest, would it?

Alice   I like it like this.

Al   Murky.

Alice   Dusky.

Al   Dusty, actually dirty.

Alice   It's the only part of the house left untamed: where else is there to sit?

Al   And you like lying on the floor?

Alice   I do. And – Well! is anyone suggesting that downstairs with the radio is a serious alternative to up here?

Al   You have a point.

Alice (*ear cocked to the floor*)   Who's that he has singing down there now?

Al   That's what's-her-name.

Alice   She belongs up the Alps.

Al   Bit of contest going on with the washing machine.

Alice *is making sounds that are meant to be the tune of the song on the radio – kind of falsetto or high-pitched, like Indian singing – while* **Al** *in contest, is making sounds that imitate a washing machine.*

Al (*breaking off, momentarily, from the contest*)   Washing machine is winning!

Alice   What – is – her – name?

Al   Anorexia Clunt – Faaaaaack!

They are laughing. **Alice** *is about to become pensive again.*

Al   Ah no! – Forget that – I know! – Got it! DJ Good Morning: Speak to me about your husband, love.

Alice   My Bill?

Al   Your Bill.

Alice   Big Bill?

Al   Sordid Bill.

Alice   Well! He's good to the budgies? (**Al** *nods, wisely.*) *He*'s good to me? (**Al** *nods, wisely.*) Honesty is his bulletproof vest, and soon he will manage a section.

Al (*nods wisely. Then*)   Strikes me – would I be right in speculating? – he is a man who likes a well-ironed shirt.

Alice   Absolutely.

Al   Speak to me further.

Alice   He'll never look at another woman.

Al   You'll always know where he is.

Alice   My mother never said a truer word about him than on that score.

Al   He came highly recommended by your mother. Yes, love?

Alice   And you could eat the dinner off the floor in his apiary.

Al   Well, d'you know what I'm going to say to you?

Alice   No.

Al   It's hard to beat the Irish mother after all. Sure they always had the wisdom sure and the love that endures. God bless them. (But) Sorry, love, I interrupted you.

Alice   Not at all – What was I going to say?

Al *and* **Alice**   Ahmm.

Al   A bright heifer with a silver tongue will be the last to sell at market? (**Alice**: '*No.*') Your daddy looked at other women and he drank? (**Alice***: 'No*'.) It takes fourteen seconds to conceive three children, Bill's way, you reckon.

Alice   No, stop that. What was I saying?

Al   Ah! That you could eat your dinner off the floor in the – (*And she points 'out there'.*)

Alice   Yeh. Well, I kid you not, but did you hear that discussion yesterday?

Al   Who?

Alice   On the radio: DJ Good Afternoon and a panel in discussion, did you?

Al   No. What was the subject?

Alice   Shit. I kid you not. And though he didn't actually use the word shit –

Al   He *meant*! –

Alice   The word shit when he said he was told that as against the entire animal kingdom a bird will create more shit, pound for pound, ounce for ounce.

Al   And you could eat your dinner off the floor in the – (*she points*) – out there?!

Alice   Pound for pound, ounce for?! Flabbergasting?

Al   Fucking rocks!

Alice   What is the first thing you think of –

Al   He said? –

Alice   When you think of a place, coop or a yard, with a lot of chickens?

Al (*whispers*)   Shit? (**Alice** *nods.*) None of the panellists beat you to the answer to that one?

Alice   Chicken shit.

Al Yes, love?

Alice Curiously, after the birds the fish is next.

Al Pound for pound, ounce, ounce? – Wow!

Alice That's why fish farms, densely populated dontcha know, are causing sea-lice on salmon.

Al Never!

Alice Wasn't I listening! The most heated discussion about anything in a long time.

Al Speak to me more about fish shit, love.

Alice And I wouldn't have minded but Bill would've settled the matter, cleared all the shit up for them in a jiffy.

Al Banker Bill?

Alice Solid Bill.

Al Wow-ee!

Alice (*simultaneously, silently*). Wow-ee!

Alice *looks at her watch.*

Al Plenty of time, you won't be late.

Alice I'll go in a mo – Will I have another?

She gets the bottle again but now she just sits there, toying with it, lost, or looking at it blankly.

. . . (*Absently.*) He's very selfish.

Al (*quietly*) And though Wow-ee Big Bill is doing well . . .

Alice *nods.*

Al A degree course at night . . .

Alice *nods.*

Al Breeding budgies and babies and suchlike, to boot . . .

Alice *nods.*

Al And though he is the father of all three children, your considered opinion, unbiased objective?

Alice   He's not the sharpest knife in the drawer.

Al (*rising* **Alice**)   But: he's a good man. ('*For instance*') His honesty.

Alice   Oh, *his*, *his* honesty, uprightness! His *blindness*, his *mental deafness*! His – Yeh know? His. His attributes may be matters of wonder to his mother – as indeed they are to my mother, that one-time *procurer* – but I come in here somewhere too, do I not? . . . D'you know how boring it is, this, this, this drinking is? D'you know how boring it is? . . . Boring . . . His *schoolbooks*!

Al   Fuck!

Alice   His schoolbooks with the children's on the kitchen table! . . . His – his –

Al   Fucking –

Alice   Moustache! The time he spends looking at it, trimming it, sculpting it! . . . His – his –

Al   Fucking –

Alice   Fountain pens! Pencils! His –

Al   Fucking – !

Alice   Pink striped shirt! – his –

Al   Fucking –

Alice   Houndstooth jacket! – Matching –

Al   Fucking –

Alice   Coloured –

Al   Fucking –

Alice   Ties and fucking breast-pocket handkerchiefs! Yeh know?

Al   Well, he's a man!

Alice   No. No, this is serious. Or am I being selfish?

Spoilt? I practically wipe his arse for him. My name is Alice – age twenty-five – Who's Alice?

Al   Leave him.

Alice   Hah! Not feasible. (*She's dependent.*)

Al   Shoot yourself.

Alice   Yeh. I think about it. Drowning . . . We get into the car, drive the ten miles to the docks, and over the edge.

Al   With the children?

Alice   Oh I couldn't leave them behind . . . my beautiful children . . . Sandra, Karen-Marie, William. My fondlings . . . Aged six, five and – four'n'half! (*And she laughs, the laugh moving into the low-pitched rasp of:*) Faaaaack!

Al   Faaaaaaak!

Alice   Faaaaaaacck!

Al   Faaaaaaaaack!

Alice *and* **Al**   Faaaaaaaaaaack . . . !

Which ends in tears, **Alice***'s. Well, perhaps, she's half laughing, half crying through the following. She puts away the bottle, this time without having poured anything from it.*

Al   And she used to be – very, they said – intelligent.

Alice   What am I to do?

Al   Look at her now, the creature.

Alice   (I've) No one to talk to.

Al   It's slob time. Your daddy, love.

Alice   If my daddy were alive.

Al   And he used our private part of the house too.

Alice   He used the spare room as a workshop.

Al   All kinds of things in there.

Alice   Tools. Steel vice, hacksaw. What's that?

Al   That is a caulking tool, Alice.

Alice   And that?

Al   Dividers, calipers, micrometer.

Alice   And that –

Al   A magic magnet.

Alice   And that –

Al   A bottle of whiskey under the bench.

Alice   My mother drove him to it. My mother treated him like a dog.

Al   And you wished him dead.

Alice   No, *in*correct.

Al   Because he looked at other women and he drank –

Alice   Well, at least he looked!

Al   And you wished him dead.

Alice   Well, I don't wish it now, okay?! Actually, I've started looking at other men. Actually, I'm going to have an affair.

Al   I wish you would – I'm bored to death – do *some*thing.

Alice   Well, if I had the time I would!

Al   Pathetic, pitiable and you know it. Thirty-nine eighteens?! Oh?!

'Oh?!' in reaction to **Alice***'s sudden movement, getting the bottle again, to then pour a generous measure into her cup.*

Alice   *'En voulez-vous encore, Madame?'* *'Oui, un peu'* –

Al   *Mais non!*

Alice   *Oui – oui!* –

Al   *Mais non!*

Alice   *Oui – oui! –*

Al   *Mon Dieu! –*

Alice   '*A mon grand regret, je me vois force de!*'

Al (*simultaneously*)   *Excrément! Merde! Calice!*

Alice   Soupçon. (*Toasting the air with her cup. Then:*) Thirty-nine eighteens, seven hundred and two, what is the difference between a duck, one of its legs is both the same, why does a mouse when he spins? (*And she drinks.*)

Al   Because the higher the fewer.

Alice   Correct – What band or group does Mick Jagger front for?

Al *and* **Alice**   Horselips.

Al   Correct –

Alice   Correct –

Al   In what city is the London Marathon run?

Alice   Pass.

Al   What's long and thin and smells of ginger?

Alice   Fred Astaire's cock.

Al   Correct. Why do women have small feet?

Alice   So that they can stand close to the sink.

Al   And time's up!

Alice (*a half-glance at her watch*)   I'll be off now in a mo. (*She's mellow, she's smiling.*) . . . No but, really, d'you know what I think, do you? D'you know what I think? Law. Law is the only thing to do, is the only thing to take up, to study. Yeh know? I'd love to do Law. That's what I'd love. That's what I'm going to do. It's, yeh know, my dearest wish. (*She drinks.*)

A chirrup from outside.

Al   A budgie sings solo, Marko Polo chirps back a reply from his garden, the Dow Jones has plunged eighty-five points in panic trading. (*She retires a little.*)

Alice (*as before, smiling, relaxed throughout*)   I tell a lie. It isn't. Sandra will do Law. The stage, *definitely, definitely*, for Karen-Marie. And William? (*She smiles, fondly, at William's character; then:*) My sweet, sweet William. But, for me, it's ... What I want has to be ... 'O' (*She's unaware that she has not found the word, or words, but she is smiling, inhaling an 'O', slowly sucking in the air; and again:*) 'O' ... (*Her free hand describing a wide gesture. She wants to breathe; she wants the freedom to develop/discover/explore her mind and spirit.*) Yeh know? Find out. Because there's a strange, savage, beautiful and mysterious country inside me. Otherwise, give me ... a bucking bronco to deal with then. Because this is slow death. Otherwise ... *lobotomy.* (*Dreamily.*) Yeh know? (*Drinks, looks at her watch, and:*) Christ, the children! (*And she's up and doing.*) Yes? Put away the bottle. Yes? Where's my apron? – Here's my apron. Cup and saucer? (*They are in her hand.*) Cup and saucer. Car keys (on) the hall table, peppermints (in) the glove compartment. Anything else? No. (*About to leave.*) Big Al, am I heading for trouble?

Al   Why are you asking the question? (*Which is the answer.*)

Alice   (Okay.) Am I going crazy?

Al   Bit of air getting in up there alright, I'd say.

Alice   Would I ever do anything silly?

Al   I don't know.

Alice   I wouldn't. I wouldn't ever even harm a fly.

From outside, the twittering of birds.

I cannot think what it was was upsetting me, but it's gone. So! *Alles ist in ordnung.*

And she's gone. (Some downstairs noises – radio – between her opening and closing the door/hatch.)

Outside, the twittering of the birds is now grown loud and agitated, and it comes in waves. **Al** *has continued there.*

Al   And outside, listen . . . for reasons best known or unknown to themselves, the budgies are singing all together like a hacksaw cutting through wire.

By the Gasworks Wall

Characters

Alice
Jimmy
Bundler

Time

The nineties

A lane. Dusk – almost night. It looks deserted. But is it? Because it's shadowy, badly lit.

Sounds, off, of a town and, not clearly defined, those of a cattle mart in session, working late. (Words that have been spoken into a microphone and come to us distorted, bent on the air, over a distance.)

The rasp of a cough, off. Then, a shapeless kind of man of indeterminate age, in a motley of old clothes – he looks like a scavenger – comes along and, though he does not stop, as he disappears down the lane he does a full turn to look back and into the shadows as if suspicious of a pesence there.

A moment or two later, off, the rasp of his voice again, this time as in meeting someone:

Bundler   Goodnight, how are yeh! Some match that, last Sunday!

And, a moment later, a woman comes along, casually, carelessly dressed, topcoat hanging open, hands dug into the pockets and, she is, say, late thirties. She continues up the lane. As she disappears, a voice in a whisper from the shadows:

Voice   Alice!

She's disappeared from view. The whisper is louder, more insistent this time

Alice!

Alice (*off*)   Yes? . . . Yes?

Voice   It's me!

Alice   What? (*She is returning nervously.*) . . . Who?

Voice   Me! Jimmy!

Alice   . . . Jimmy?

Jimmy, *the 'Voice', has materialised, slowly, as if nervous, unsure. Fully materialised, he is in his forties. The cut/length/style of his topcoat suggest expense/fashion/a bit of glamour. Headgear and spectacles, perhaps both as for a disguise. He has a rich voice, like that of a singer, and when he laughs it, too, is rich.*

Jimmy James Godwin. Jimmy.

Alice ... No.

Jimmy Yeh.

Alice ... No

Jimmy Yes.

Alice I don't believe this.

Jimmy You can.

Alice I don't believe it, I do not believe it! Oh my God, God, it is you! I don't believe it. (*Then:*) You look different.

Jimmy Well! (*Removes his spectacles, removes his hat, turns down the collar of his coat.*) And, no make-up.

Alice This is the absolutely most incredible thing that has happened to me in I-don't-know-how-long! Ever!

Jimmy *You* haven't changed.

Alice Well, this is a surprise!

Jimmy You wrote.

Alice I know I did but I never for a second thought you'd! (show up here)

Jimmy Here I am!

Alice So what do I do with you now? (*And she laughs.*)

Jimmy Why are you laughing?

Alice I mean, James Godwin, James Godwin!

Jimmy Jimmy, you always called me Jimmy. Actually, that was the only – dare one call it cautious? – note in your otherwise very warm, I considered, very affectionate letter, I considered, your addressing me as James. Purpose in it?

Alice But everyone now knows you as James.

Jimmy So the formality of address was not a reserve of

distance on your part? Good!

Which she finds very funny, and he laughs too.

Alice A lot of water under the bridge, Jimmy. It must be nearly twenty years since –

Jimmy It's more. I was working it out on my way down. You were doing your Leaving Cert that year, you were all of seventeen – I came here to work end of '72, spring '73 we had our first date, which means –

Alice We don't have to be *too* specific about the years.

Jimmy It's twenty-one years ago. And twenty-one years since we last saw each other.

Alice In the flesh.

Jimmy What d'you mean?

Alice I see you often enough on the box.

Jimmy Yes, a long time. Indeed. Yes.

Alice And I haven't changed. (*Her dry humour.*)

Jimmy You haven't.

Alice When I think of how I was back then!

Jimmy Yes.

Alice No, tongue-tied!

Jimmy No! –

Alice Yes! And I was a prude and I was stupid –

Jimmy You were not! You were –

Alice I was, I was! –

Jimmy Quiet, maybe, reserved –

Alice How did you put up with it?

Jimmy Unassuming, certainly –

Alice Oh boy!

Jimmy　Not how I remember it, Alice.

Alice　Honestly! When things from my past come back to me now I feel so ashamed – yeh know? – I find myself talking out loud to myself – 'one, two, three, four' – to stop the embarrassment.

Jimmy　You were modest, Alice, you were shy, and you were right. You communicated inner beauty.

Alice　Well, okay – in certain matters. But compared with what the young ones are said to be up to today.

Jimmy　Actually, I was the one wasn't very communicative.

Alice　Oh you were! –

Jimmy　Indeed, to a degree, I'm still like that. Because, I mean to say, communicating, I believe, has an element of hesitation about it? is imbued with a fear? that in the process of communicating, one can be rejected? Would you agree with that observation?

Alice　Still the intellectual.

Jimmy　But-but-but, then can follow self-questioning, doubt, loss of self-esteem? You don't agree.

Alice　Oh my God! (*And her lips are pressed together.*)

Jimmy　What, what? (*Slight alarm.*)

Alice　One, two, three, four. The idea of a French kiss (back then). And how long were we going out together? Six, seven months?

Jimmy　A long time for a romance to last between young people – you see?!

Alice　(*a beat, and*)　*What* are we talking about?!

They laugh.

Jimmy　You were perfect.

Alice　Thank you. Yeh know, I sometimes think I was.

I'm very flattered by all this, Jimmy ... The last time I saw you was at the railway station.

Jimmy   I still don't drive a car. People find that strange. Do you?

Alice   No. I don't drive any more. I haven't driven for, oh, over ten years. But that's another story. How did you get here?

Jimmy   Taxi.

Alice   A *taxi?*

Jimmy   I told him to wait.

Alice   I'm *doubly* very flattered ... I-don't-know-what-to-say-to-you!

Jimmy   You're doing fine!

They are laughing.

Alice   I don't believe this yet!

Jimmy   Nor I, nor I! Why did you write to me?

Alice   Well!

Jimmy   But your timing?

Alice   I don't know. I don't know that we always know why we do things.

Jimmy   How true! That's very true.

Alice   Yeh know? (*She's flattered.*)

Jimmy   Interesting. (*He's hanging on her words.*) Yes?

Alice   I don't know that we always know. Write and ask him for a photograph, signed –

Jimmy   Yes? –

Alice   Or is that childish? –

Jimmy   Yes? –

Alice   Then, a bit of a dream? –

Jimmy   Or inspiration, or intuition?

Alice   Or courage? Wouldn't it be grand to meet him?

Jimmy   I understand.

Alice   Yeh know? Maybe simply to explain why I was such an idiot at seventeen.

Jimmy   You were never that, Alice.

Alice   I remember! Or do I? When I was writing, I thought what, if instead of this waffle, what if I said something else: (*She gestures 'maybe, for instance':*) 'Dear James, it is high time we saw each other again to compare notes.' Yeh know?

Jimmy   Indeed. And you said as much.

Alice   I said as much?

Jimmy   'I imagine, that like myself, you have been through a great deal.' Yes? ('Remember?')

Alice   Yes?

Jimmy   'And not all of it just success.'

Alice   Well!

Jimmy   'And it would be interesting to discover, first hand, where you're at now.'

Alice   And I suggested we meet here?

Jimmy   You knew I'd know here: 'I'll be free to meet you in the Lane, any Tuesday, this October, seven o'clock!'

Alice   Well! I could have written: 'I'll be free to meet you – if you are free to do so, if you wish – any Tuesday, this October, in the hotel.' Because it isn't as if by choosing here we are about to get up to anything, is it, are we? We go for a coffee?

Jimmy   No. Your choice of venue appealed to me. We always came this way when we were making for the river. Sometimes we stopped here – (*he goes to it*) there.

Alice   For mad passionate love.

Jimmy   All that would have happened at it's proper time. Youngsters today are missing out. It's a pity. Innocence has an energy, indeed excitement, unique to itself: it has so much going for it: exhilaration in the very balance of its own waiting.

Alice   Anticipation?

Jimmy (*fixed on her*)   Alice. Quite, quite wonderful. Your letter came at a very important moment for me.

Alice   Well, yeh know?

Jimmy   It was very timely.

Alice   Put it in an envelope, care of GTV, 'Please forward if necessary', I suppose, into the postbox, quickly, I'm sure, before I could change my mind.

Jimmy   Very insightful.

Alice   Well! I get these flashes of inspiration – Well, people have told me that I do. Not often, of course, every couple of years.

Jimmy   Yes? – Interesting – Like?

Alice   Oh, I suppose, like . . . There's this book of poetry.

Jimmy   Yes?

Alice   My father gave it to me – Nice, yeh know? – *Flowers From Many Gardens* – and if I was a bit down I used to dip into it one time and I'd find it uplifting – despite my determind self to be otherwise.

Jimmy   Yes?

Alice   Well, in this class, course, that I'm doing up town, there's this woman friend – acquaintance, really, because she is one high-maintenance type – Know what I mean, Jimmy? And I thought, is that book of poetry still in the house somewhere? Found it, gave it to her, 'Read this,' I said, 'and it will repay you a thousandfold.'

Jimmy I've gone back to Spenser – Sorry – Yes?

Alice I'm not saying that it wrought a complete change in her, but she is now a *comparatively* disasters-free area.

Jimmy Yes. Yes?

Alice Yeh know?

Jimmy Yes?

Alice Well, another kind of – flash – I might get might be, might be, oh . . . Well, getting in touch again with an old friend – an old *beau*? – 'high time', to discover where *you're* at, 'first hand', and sensing that, that getting in touch again might be somehow very important.

Jimmy (Yes.) Were you here last Tuesday?

Alice (I) Passed here, same time. And I'd've been here next Tuesday, and Tuesday week, DV, seven o'clock.

Jimmy I considered coming down last Tuesday . . .

Alice Well, you're busy.

Jimmy No. Well, yes. I thought about it, but . . .

Alice It's quite a trip to make.

Jimmy You have children?

Alice I have three.

Jimmy I have three.

Alice Nearly *touché* there! I didn't know if it was two or three you had. Though you do the news and host those special things, you don't give much away about yourself?

Jimmy You think that a bad thing?

Alice Chiphhh! (No) I can't wait to get rid of my three. Well, the two girls. I'm not particularly cut out to continue as their bondsmaid. Whereas my William now. You cannot imagine what a gallant escort a little boy can be. And still is. Still, to have time to myself, to read, or to – D'you know what I'd like to take up? Philosophy. I'd like to make sense of – well, myself for a start. Oh boy! Because ... I'm talking too much.

Jimmy Everything you say has a resonance (for me). You were perfect. I shouldn't be harping on about it?

Alice Harp away.

Jimmy (*laughs; then, joking*) So, Tuesday is your evening off, then?

Alice Tuesday evening is for my creative writing class.

Jimmy Oh!?

Alice Thursday morning every fortnight: book club.

Jimmy Yes?

Alice More opium for the housewife.

Jimmy Music – There was a choir in the town?

Alice Not particularly cut out to be a chorus girl.

Jimmy But surely – come along! – this writing class?

Alice If I hear another woman reading out her piece about remembering watching Daddy shaving when she was a little girl, I'll shoot myself – with a razor.

Jimmy (*laughs; then*) I remember your father. A few times, walking in that direction, to the wood, he'd cycle past us, no acknowledgement: hmm?

Alice My mother's doing. 'Up on your bike, Gerard, and let them know I know where they are and if they're up to anything.'

Jimmy Aaah!

Alice He died fourteenth of July, 1978.

Jimmy A young enough man then.

Alice Fifty-seven. She's still alive. He had a problem. (*A drink problem.*) Which, in family tradition, I upheld for a while, until I was brought to my senses with a bump.

Jimmy   Oh?

Alice   Car crash.

Jimmy   A bad one?

Alice   Ahmmm! We came out of it alive. My mother was keen on you.

Jimmy   She was?

Alice   Keen on you for *me*. She put a lot of store in anyone who worked in the bank. Look, neither of us, I think, are looking for kisses or that kind of thing – are we? – (*she has taken his hand*) but, just this, just for a minute.

They stand there holding hands, looking ahead at nothing, in their own thoughts, the night around them.

(*Smiles.*) Which one of us is dreaming this? . . . So how're things? Alright? . . . Are yeh well? . . . Fed up?

Jimmy   (*smiling at the above, shakes his head to the last. Then*)   Will you be my man?

Alice   (*remembers, smiles: it's a game they used to play; then*)   Yes.

Jimmy   Will you carry the can?

Alice   Yes.

Jimmy   Will you fight the fairy?

Alice   Yes – Will you be afraid? –

Jimmy   No –

Alice   No –

Jimmy *and* **Alice**   Phuh, phuh, phuh, phuh!

'Phuh, phuh, phuh, phuh!' blows away/out the fairy. The laughter over:

Alice   I suppose we wouldn't be here if things were alright . . . (*Suddenly.*) You aren't researching something?

Jimmy   Researching? No. Why d'you ask?

Alice   No why, I just – (*She finishes it with a shrug: she 'just wondered'.*) . . . I walk a lot. The river occasionally, the wood, what's left of it. To get away. And away from what? Because if anything, there's increasingly nothing to get away from. D'you know that word 'estranged'? Well, why wouldn't you, you know words. So, I'm walking and really I feel I'm only marking time. And for what? Things are getting emptier. So, then I'd say, 'What if I was that person?' Her. (Or) Her? No good. Okay. Well, 'What would it be like to *meet* that person? Her, him, film star, you – a ghost? . . . It's pathetic, isn't it?

Jimmy   No . . . Your husband.

Alice   Bill. He's fine, he's okay. Very good. He is good. We don't talk much. He would like me to have all sorts of things. A full-time housekeeper. (*She shakes her head, she won't have one.*) Take up golf. No. I know why he offers those things. He arrived in town not long after you'd left and, like you, to work in the National Bank. Respectable position. Studious disposition. And it has stood him in good stead, as they say.

Jimmy   He's done well for himself.

Alice   He's done well for himself. Big house, in the Grove my dear – it has 'a drive'. Though, a funny streak has appeared (in him).

Jimmy   Yes?

Alice   Yeh know, for someone who never went out much, yeh know, socialised, who didn't take his first drink until he was thirty-one: well, in the last nearly two years he's begun to knock it back.

Jimmy   Does he become?

Alice   No.

Jimmy   I mean violent.

Alice   No, but I've noticed something frankly ugly happening to the shape of his mouth. Yeh know? And I look at my own, in the mirror to check on it. And Murphy's pub – down near the railway. Well, it's – what-would-you-call-it? – the *roughest* pub in town. I've never been in it but I know the kind that goes in there and as clientele? Subhuman. I mean, he's area manager for half the banks in the country, for God's sake, so what is he doing, what is the matter with him?!

Jimmy   Colleagues.

Alice   What?

Jimmy   Colleagues getting at him. Jealousy.

Alice (*silently?*)   What?

Jimmy   Oh-ho-ho!

Alice   *What* am I saying? This is not what I want to be talking to you about. Or remembering, when you're gone.

Jimmy (*to himself*)   Oh-ho-ho!

Alice   It's not that I'm – yeh know? (unhappy)

Jimmy   Nor, indeed, I.

Alice   Unhappy: I'm not saying that.

Jimmy   No.

Alice   Three children each.

He nods.

. . . By the same woman?

Jimmy   Yes.

Alice   What's she like?

Jimmy   She's very intelligent. She's no fool.

Alice   Like me . . . But there's something wrong, isn't there?

Jimmy   There is something missing.

Alice   I've never earned my living.

Jimmy   Something has been lost.

Alice   Yeh.

Jimmy   Yeh.

Alice   ... D'you remember an evening, actually it was night because I remember there was a moon, and we got to the river and you saw ... Company.

'Company': someone is approaching. They move draw back into the deeper shadows; **Jimmy** *now facing* **Alice** *as if shielding or concealing her.*

Bundler *returns. He knows they are there – though he pretends otherwise. He stops to tie a shoelace, unnecessarily. That done, as he leaves up the lane:*

Bundler   Some hurlers them Cork boyos! Goodnight to ye!

Jimmy   Goodnight!

Alice   He knows very well it's me here.

Jimmy   Who is he?

Alice   Nobody! Somebody should have him as a pet. (*She's a good mimic of the rasping voice.*) 'Goodnight to ye!' He's a known newsmonger, though. (*Mimicry again.*) 'Jesus, d'ye know who I seen just now down the Lane in the dark with a stranger?'

Jimmy   Will he?

Alice   Who cares?!

Jimmy   Do you want us to move?

Alice   No! (*She's animated, angry, the frustrations of her innerworld making her move about and pitch the next mimicry at the town, as in defiance.*) 'Goodnight to ye! – How are ye! – 'Some fuckin' hurlers them Cork boyos'! (*To* **Jimmy**.) No, I don't want us to move! (*To the town.*) 'Some fuckin' place this town, to live!' (*To herself.*) I'll dine on our meeting here for a long time.

Jimmy (*doesn't understand this burst of behaviour*)   What?

Alice (*animated again*)   'Shake hands, brother / You're a rogue and I'm another / You'll be hung in Ballinrobe and I'll be hung in Ballintubber!'

They laugh/whatever.

Jimmy   You were going to say: 'An evening, night, the moon was out, we got to the river and I . . . !'

Alice   . . . Must have been a lie: can't remember. But I remember laughing.

Jimmy   Oh? Yes?

Alice   And at *what*? (*She's laughing.*)

Jimmy   Yes? Yes! (*He's laughing.*)

Alice   Your imagination.

Jimmy   My? – Yes? – Did I? –

Alice   Oh yes! Just letting your imagination rip –

Jimmy   My? – Did I? – Did I? –

Alice   The things you came out with! –

Jimmy   Gobbledygook? – Yes? –

Alice   Oh yes! –

Jimmy   Yes? – Yes? –

Alice   I can't remember what they were but, oh yes!

Jimmy   Yes!

Alice   *Hearing* myself laughing – you know? Can this be me making this sound? You know?

Jimmy   Considering your normal reserved nature!

Alice (*laughing – she would laugh at anything in this moment*)   What? – No! – Yes! – I don't know!

Jimmy   Wonderful! Spontaneity of the thing! Purity of the thing. Oh, yes, innocence.

A beat or two and **Alice** *laughs out again, to herself.*

Jimmy You don't agree?

Alice I do, oh, I do!

Jimmy (*to himself*) Oh yes. And we'll set out together to rediscover that state.

Alice We'll what?

She is realising now that all is not well with him; and how is she to deal with the situation? Her question above appears to go past him; he becomes philosophical.

Jimmy Hmm? Oh yes, innocence – modesty. Yes, the phenomenon of the shy person – the 'reserved nature' that we were all talking about – is an interesting one. Artists now for instance have it – and actors. I've a number of actor friends and, you know, they are invariably shy. (*Laughs:*) The good ones, this is, we're not talking cravats here. Though, indeed, mind you, I went around wearing one myself one time. (*And he's deadly serious again.*) But-but-but, the shyness factor, modesty, humility, is to be found only in the consummate artist, the one who, paradoxically, in his work reveals and exposes his deepest inner self. You agree? For all the shyness, humility! You don't agree?

Alice I do.

Jimmy You agree?

Alice Yeh.

Jimmy Oh yes . . . You were perfect, you know.

Alice Well . . .

Jimmy Hmm?

Alice Maybe.

Jimmy And I was so . . . (*Probably 'stupid'. He shakes his head.*) I've made a lot of mistakes in my time, Alice. Life is a game of bad shots. What?

Alice Par for the course. What did you mean back there when you said . . . ?

Jimmy   When I?

Alice   Can't remember.

Jimmy   Sorry?

Alice   Galloping Alzheimer's.

Jimmy   What? Oh yes! (*And laughs.*) Same as myself! But, mistakes, mistakes. Sometimes I think I'm going crazy – What?! What?

Alice *does not know what to say to him. She feels that she must keep talking at all costs, while inviting him to laugh. But he doesn't laugh.*

Alice   I don't think I'm *going* crazy, I think I *am* crazy! (*Inviting him to laugh.*) Well, a little stocktaking of how things are up here (*in her head*) and all the evidence is there to prove it: *I'm crazy.* But then, *confusion*: I'm walking up town, I meet a woman I have known for years and regarded as sensible, only to discover that her total obsession in this short life of ours would appear to be a passion for stuffing a mushroom – for crying out loud, for crying out loud! – my neighbours' determination to get the daisies, kill every last poor daisy on their lawns – for crying out loud! – and, after all that's happened – scandals, scandals! – they're still running up to the church – do you know what I'm saying, Jimmy? – up and down to the church, saying prayers by the ton. D'you know what I mean, Jimmy? I'm *confused.* They, not me, are meant to be the *normal* people? Unless sanity after all – well, (it) makes me wonder – if sanity after all is only another form of insanity. D'you know what I'm saying, Jimmy?

Jimmy   Yes. Suicide.

Alice   How d'you mean?

Jimmy   As a matter for consideration.

Alice   Oh, I see.

Jimmy   Do you?

Alice   How many times have I thought of it, how many times!

Jimmy   I've been thinking of it a good deal lately.

Alice   How many times have I thought of it, I ask you!

Jimmy   That, or make a new start.

Alice   How d'you mean?

Jimmy   You know, to start again. You know? I think I know your husband without ever having met him. You know? I think I know him. He's done very well for himself? So have I. Money? Extraordinary! He's a very senior figure. He has to see that standards are maintained, he has to remind others that codes of behaviour have to be upheld. So what happens? Jealous and resentful colleagues – both genders. Subtle harassment. Vicious and malicious whisperers. He's become a difficult man. Why wouldn't he?! He's become violent – No! You denied it too quickly when I asked you earlier. Oh-ho-ho! He's a violent man. And the shape of his mouth. I know him. I wouldn't mind finding a rough pub, if I could find the right one – to, to relieve the – if I considered that it would help – to, to relieve the, relieve the pressure – if I could find the right one, if I was fit enough for the right one, if I considered that it would be the answer.

Alice   Hold on –

Jimmy   Please. (Please: allow me to finish.) You know, something to send one wonderfully, drunkenly, reeling home, you know, instead of – phhhhh! – pressure.

Alice   Hold on a sec.

Jimmy   Or something, yes, right, correct, Alice, to sober one up to consider the alternative: to start again.

Alice   But that isn't possible.

Jimmy   It isn't possible for you to be seventeen again, for me to be twenty-three, but it's possible – it *is* possible – to backtrack to see if those emotions that were authentic then can be rediscovered. I've already started. Otherwise, what? Suicide? That's too much. But how much is it to continue to live out one's life accepting a world that is shallow, cynical, a painted thing? Should one not stop oneself subscribing to – evil? You mentioned the word shame earlier. I couldn't agree more. You know what I've been thinking? I have been thinking that everything I've done was a mistake. I ask myself how has this come about, this me, this talking sin, this walking lie. No authenticity. The purity of what we shared back then by comparison, the cleanness of this interlude – short as it is – here this evening.

Alice   I don't know that (I agree) –

Jimmy   You, you were going to – Alice! – You were going to say back there: a clear sky, a night sky, moonlight, you and I together by the river and that I saw something. Well, you're right. I think I did: see something. I'm not talking apparitions or any of that nonsense here. I *sensed* it, I *felt* it. (*To himself.*) You know.

Alice   Jimmy –

Jimmy   Please. Please. (Allow me to finish.) One simply cannot continue going through these periods of shame and guilt.

Alice   I don't feel –

Jimmy   Please. Please. Allow me to finish. These periods of shame and guilt. Recriminations – rows with oneself, with others – all in one's own mind. Anger: discovering that one's friends are false, fair-weather friends, who – in my case – express admiration for me and my work, to my face, but who really hold me cheap and want to see my humiliation.

Alice   Your family.

Jimmy   (*a simply brush of his hand deals with that subject*)   Colleagues, preening themselves in the idea of celebrity. Vanity – from the tea boy up – rampant. And

I'm concerned with objectivity, with standards. In the newsroom for instance, I have spoken out: 'Are you reading the news or do you consider that you are making it?' I want nothing more to do with that world I've been working in. I've already started – I told you – in a new direction, a path of inner exploration that will – hopefully! hopefully! – take me back to the authenticity that is you and that you allowed me to share. Please. (*Allow him to finish.*) You said you thought that contacting me might be important. Well – Please. You said – exact words – you 'sensed that getting in touch again might be somehow *very* important'. Need it be said how very important it is to me too? Perfect.

Alice   Where's the taxi, Jimmy?

Jimmy   The Square. I told the driver to have a meal in the hotel.

Alice   I'll come up with you to the taxi.

Jimmy   No. We'll keep this to ourselves. I'll go back, but I'll meet you here again – tomorrow night – same time? – Would that be alright – and we'll take it from there, right?

Alice   Stay the night.

Jimmy   Stay?

Alice   In the hotel. I'd like you to meet a friend of mine. (*She means a doctor.*)

Jimmy   No. Keep this perfectly secret until we go further into the plan. Yeh, I'll go back – it'll be midnight by the time I get there – all sorts of things to begin seeing to and wrap up. Yeh.

Alice   Jimmy.

Jimmy   (*again, to himself*)   Yeh.

Alice   Jimmy.

Jimmy   Alice.

Alice   I'm out there with you on – a number of things, but what I am, a lot of the time, is doing the ironing, and

I'm bored. What I do, a lot of the time, is wonder was I seriously incapable of doing no more than producing three children. Maybe the reason I've continued dreaming in my near dotage is to stop me thinking of how much time I've wasted.

Jimmy (You are) Perfection.

Alice No, I'm not perfect or authentic. Never was, nobody ever was. I don't believe I'm saying this, but I think it's time I said it – *to myself* – and got my head down from up there and accepted my – limitations. Jimmy, Jimmy, listen to me! How do I put this? I'm a stupid housewife, growing stupider by the day by three stupid children, and I have an extremely stupid husband. Is any of this getting through to you?

Jimmy (You're) Not stupid.

Alice Jimmy! Jimmy! You aren't well.

Jimmy No.

Alice Meat factory, cattle mart, old gasworks behind that wall, Blackberry Lane. No blackberries but this Lane that we are standing on is a sort of short cut from where I live to the town and vice versa, obviously, and, obviously, I use it quite a bit to go to the town to where I live, to and fro, to and fro, nothing very exciting, and I was on my way twenty-whatever minutes ago to a poxy Tuesday night dynamic creative writing class – 'Pack your every word with TNT'. I think the same poxy creative writing may have contributed to my writing that letter: homework is encouraged. Other than what you told me it contained, I really can't remember what I wrote, how dynamically I phrased it, but I'm sure I never thought you'd get to read it: some secretary or other (would). Let alone your showing up here! We walk up to the Square? (*He doesn't move.*) *Alice*, I'm *Alice*: 'Let's pretend we're kings and queens' is the scatty, stupid, silly side of me. I've wondered, for a long time, will this fantasising ever end, or, will a fantasy ever come true? *Both* have happened tonight. All I am looking for from here on in – I promise – is reality. We go?

Jimmy   You promise.

Alice   Yes. Shall we (go)?

Jimmy   That's excellent.

Alice   Hmm?

Jimmy   You have finished playing games with yourself then. And with me?

Alice   No.

Jimmy   That's how you regard me?

Alice   Let's go.

Jimmy   May I ask you a question? . . . 'May I ask you a question' is too much to ask after I have gone to all this trouble to come down here and see you?

Alice   No!

Jimmy   Are you enjoying your triumph?

Alice   What tri –

Jimmy   Would you like the pictures?

Alice   I don't follow.

Jimmy   Photographic evidence. How much, to what degree, do you enjoy belittling me?

Alice   Not at all. I would never think of –

Jimmy   'Not at all I would never.' And I am to tamely accept humiliation?

Alice   Let's go, Jimmy.

Jimmy   Without retaliation?

Alice   I'm sorry if I've hurt you.

Jimmy   *If?* Do you realise, because of your 'fantasising', that I could hurt you now? I could? (*He wants her to repeat the word.*) I could?

Alice   You could.

Jimmy   And I would like to. Would that suit your from-here-on-in search for reality? Fear of consequences is not stopping me. I could kill you right now? I could? I could?

Alice   You could, Jimmy, but you won't.

After a moment he walks off. She is shaken. She inhales silently, deeply, and holds it. She reacts to someone approaching.

The cavalry.

She retires to the deeper shadows – it's just a step – to take another deep breath, to compose herself. **Bundler** *arrives with a man. (The man can be* **Alice***'s husband without making any issue whatsoever of it.) Their eyes are a little 'ungoverned' searching the place.* **Alice** *emerges from the shadows. She regards them, coolly. Then she winks broadly to herself and, as she walks off, in rasping imitation of* **Bundler***:*

Jesus, some game that! Goodnight to ye!

At the Airport

Characters

Alice
Bill
Waitress
Waiter
Official

Time

2005

In the darkness and as the lights come up, a voice-over, **Alice**'s:

Alice (*voice-over*)   Where am I? Did something happen? Why am I here? What am I doing here, what kind of place is here?

A **waitress** *is putting two plates of food on a table. That done, she will go to her station, to wait there, poised, tray clapped under her arm, for anyone's bidding. She's elderly.*

A **waiter** *is ushering a sober-looking couple to the table. He seems a jolly sort – and would become jollier given the chance. He's elderly and perhaps old world. A dicky bow.*

Waiter   Down here alright, sir, madam? Alright? Alright?

Alice (*voice-over, more or less continuous*)   What is that hissing noise? (Sibilance. Like burning grass.)

The sober-looking couple are **Bill** *and* **Alice**. **Bill** *is mid-fifties, thereabouts;* **Alice** *is somewhat younger. They do not indulge the* **Waiter**, *they nod in acknowledgement of him without looking at him.*

Waiter   Madam? (*Drawing back a chair for her.*) Alright?

Alice (*voice-over*)   And is that meant to be music? (*She laughs four hollow, humourless syllables.*)

Waiter   Sir? (*Seating* **Bill**.)

Alice (*voice-over*)   Piped music. And pop songs, love songs and arias to encourage the nonsense of it all.

Waiter   Alright, alright, everything alright?

Alice (*voice-over*)   What's happening? Has something happened?

Bill   And two glasses of water.

Waiter   And two glasses of.

The above is a kind of prelude to the play proper. (It can be altered, or, indeed, dropped.)

As **Waiter** *moves away – leisurely movement of feet throughout – a* *backward jerk of his thumb at the table and the accompanying mime of the other hand drinking from a glass: an order to* **Waitress***. And he goes off (to deal with other diners).*

And **Waitress** *has gone into action, at once, going off to fulfil the order. Rather fast movement of feet throughout.*

A buzz of sound, a sibilance (like that of burning grass) hangs over the place, mingling with what would seem to be faint, nondescript music. And perhaps, perhaps, there is some kind of an unreal lighting affect. (Could be, maybe, a revolving light, coming from outside, washing the interior light.)

In any case it's a bit strange. And we see only one table. The strangeness (stylisation) can be put down to the idea that we are encountering this place through **Alice***'s odd mental state.*

Bill *is eating and continues, almost throughout, with his head down, movements of the cutlery precise. There are a couple of occasions when he glances at her, when he considers she will be unnoticing of it. She, now, is like someone suspended in a forgotten purpose (of, for example, unwrapping her knife and fork from the coloured, paper napkin).*

Alice   Looking at it rationally the worst has happened. The worst? Has it? And it is conceivable that her heart is breaking. Is it? Because if it is, it is bearable. More's the pity. More's the pity that it is not what is believed to be the standard reaction to a breaking heart. Preferable that it should get on with it, break, conclude its business, that there should be some kind of crack, perhaps, then the rush of chill air in through the crack, perhaps, that would bring numbness. Yes. Or that some kind of cloud, darkness, should descend to take care of everything. But that is unlikely, that is nonsense, this is the way it is, this is how it goes, goes, continues, goes, dully aching, no cure for it, slow, tedious, grey and, of course, bearable.

Waitress *arrives, tray clapped under her arm, to put two glasses of water on the table, to make a little bow as she backs away, and returns, silently, rather swiftly, to her station to await next orders. Neither* **Alice** *nor* **Bill** *look at her, though each nods, in an automatic way, an acknowledgement of the service.*

Alice Looking at it rationally the worst has happened, has it, and really, what is there to say about it? Not much. That woman over there looks familiar. Didn't she used to one time have a shop in? Not at all, that's crazy. The woman that used to one time own the paper shop in Shop Street would, if she were still alive, be a hundred years old now. (*Sudden, very minor agitation, like a half-swoon:*) What's happening, where am I?

Bill (*eager to be of assistance*) Alice?

Alice (*still in her train of thought*) Why am I here, what am I doing here?

Bill Alice?

Alice (*to him*) No. (*Meaning 'Everything's okay'.*)

Bill I'm sorry?

Alice No! Fine! (*And she busies herself for a moment or two unravelling the cutlery from the red paper napkin.*) Coloured tables, coloured chairs, coloured tiles on the floor, what kind of place is this? Why not balloons too? So many colours, yet colourless, elevated out of the ground floor on steel columns, accessed by an escalator. And that buzz of voices that hangs there, ascended from below, hanging in the air, strangely even, like dust caught in a haze of light, and pitiable music. A pall in sound, stopping only for (*buzz of sound has stopped*) . . . as if mankind down there holds its breath for – good news?

An announcement for the delay of an airline flight over a tannoy system. (The sound is recognisable rather than the message being distinguishable.)

Good news, no, so mankind down there observes another moment's silence, this time out of pity for itself (*buzz of sound resumes*) before remembering to start up again, the same as before, a daze in the head. What kind of place? A place as from a nightmare that is pretending to be a dream, where a party, or indeed a wake, will never really begin.

She has a sip of water, dabs her lips with the napkin and watches her husband eat.

She looks across the table at her husband who is eating a. Who looks across the table? She looks across the table. Who? She-she-her-she, this woman, me, looks across the table at that man, her husband, who is eating a meal of fish and chips in the manner of someone performing a duty and who is he, she wonders. She knows that he's very rich, and so is she, by association. So much money they don't know what to do. She knows that his name is Bill. She knows too that he does not want or need food right now, but a thing once started will be completed, becomes a duty, a must that has to reach done. Possibly admirable, who knows, who cares? But that is how that man her husband is. And as he will finish that meal in front of him, he will, in that occupational way of his of finishing things, go on finishing other things. Well, good luck to him if that's how he keeps the world at bay, or keeps it happy, or tries, which possibly makes it admirable too, enviable too, who knows, who cares, possibly yes. But he sees himself as some kind of stoic. Men, a lot of them, are like that. Whereas, emotionality, they believe, would you believe in this post-post feminist day and age, emotionality is women's territory. Women weep – yes, and they sometimes wail, howl, moan, shriek, squawk, screech! – when a thing falls out, goes wrong, and thereby somehow in the process, men believe, women cure themselves. No such luck for men. It would make a person smile, almost. It would nearly make a person cry.

During the above, **Waitress** *has again launched herself into motion in response to somebody requiring her services. She has now returned and awaits the next call.*

Alice   Really, there is no point in pushing an oblong of fish around a plate in pretence at an agreement of cutlery in action on both sides of the table, or indeed in trying to conceal from anyone that untouched food. He notices, of course, and he dislikes waste, but, this evening, he will have to put up with it. And he will put up with it, in view of what has just happened ... and because he is not a bad man of course.

She is looking in a new direction.

Party of young men. In transit from somewhere. What ages are they? Yes. And the youngest? Yes. So pale. Young men coming from a weekend-long spree, now feeling the exhaustion of it, wanting to be home.

Waiter *appears, briefly – before ambling off again in another direction – to gesture, with backward pointing thumb, to* **Waitress** *to attend a table (the party of young men). And she is into motion, tray clapped under her arm, order pad at the ready, pencil (on a string), off to take an order.*

Alice Little more than boys. They look sluggish, their dress awry. They must be baking in those heavy jackets in here. The only item awry in the formal black and white (or 'the formal dress') of the waitress are the brown stockings. An immigrant? No.

Waitress *enters and exits to make good an order.* **Waiter** *enters, as from somebody else's table, grinning, his jaw askew. He is doing his rounds.*

Alice He ambles because he is in charge. The dicky bow must prove something. 'Alright, alright, everything alright?' Every diner's friend, and becomes (over)familiar, if allowed. Everything's alright.

Waiter *is at the table.*

Waiter Alright, alright, everything alright?

Alice *laughs her dry, humourless, hollow, four syllables.* **Bill** *lifts his head but he does not look at* **Waiter**.

Waiter Sir?

Bill Yes. (*And, just as abruptly, has resumed eating.*)

Waiter Alright? Madam?

Alice Thank you.

Another suspension in the buzz of sound for another announcement over the tannoy system, while **Waiter** *moves off, continuing his rounds; while* **Waitress** *comes in to deliver a tray of food to the young men's table, off. (She will return in some moments, tray clapped under arm, to go off for supplements.) While* **Alice** *has been continuing.*

Alice   He has been very good to her over the past nearly two days, in a formal manner, of course. Not that being informally good to her would have been better, would it? No, not really. On the contrary, not at all. He had supported her arm, well, touched her elbow, getting in and out of taxis, and again, though really it was unnecessary, at the hospital mortuary. The looks they had exchanged were few, accidents, they would hardly qualify as glances: as if he feared that she, she, this woman, would swamp him if he gave her the opportunity, was it? (*She laughs her hollow laugh.*) Tears? No. Twenty years ago, maybe – twenty-five, maybe, but not now, not any more, and a good thing too. Life now is grooved. Life is inescapably harsh, cruel, self-centred, ugly, sordid, mean. It is tediously suffocating and stubbornly bearable. And humankind is vile. Well, think of it, people killing seals with – nails?

She is looking in the young men's direction again. **Waitress** *is taking a tray of things – supplements – to the young men. She will return in a little while to stand at her station, to leave again in a little while at someone's request.*

They have come awake, just about. Hunger. Young people (*A sip of water.*) And there was a time when she used to think of life as serene. Or is she dreaming things now? (And there was a time) When her life was seventh heaven, 'soul-uplifting', things like that, capable of moments of self-forgetting bliss, things like that, rapture. Moments when it all made sense. A time, twenty-five, no, thirty years ago when everything seemed possible. And *was* possible? . . . Dreaming. She was a great dreamer. Back then she was a fool to any kind of suggestion: suggestion did not take no for an answer. 'It's no use trying,' said Alice, 'one cannot believe in impossible things.' 'You haven't been practising,' said the White Queen. (*Laughs. Then her husband again.*)

He cares for her, in a civilised way. There was an ugly
period about ten years ago but he is more civilised now,
and maybe so is she. To him, their relationship is a duty.
Or is she and has she been getting it wrong? To her, it is
a what? At the moment a not very good habit. For quite
some time a silence has been growing between them, a
distance, oh, (for) one thing and another, this reason and
that. She likes him. She never disliked him. And she
concedes that she has contributed to the state of affairs. She
can no more change her personality than he can his. And
she has come to admire him. He didn't make excuses. He
didn't let anything get in his way. And how many times
has she felt it was unfair that he had not been dealt a
hand, so to speak, better than hers? But she does not
concede, agree to, accept the charge of her second
daughter, the knowing, the learned. Karen-Marie, barrister-
at-law – 'Don't dump your failure on us, Mum' – that she,
the mother, has driven them all demented – 'bonkers' – to
the extent that Sandra, the eldest, had to get out and has
now disappeared-off with New Age travellers to spread shit,
'literally shit', all over the world – fine legalese – because
that's all New Age travellers are good for. That she, Karen-
Marie, barrister-at-law and neurotic, never wants to see or
speak to her mother again, that the youngest, William –
'your darling, your pet' – will soon, if he does not already
do so, feel the same way about her and be off to join the
circus to get away from her. 'And!' before resting her case
and taking it up again, before leaving and slamming the
front door behind her, 'You-are-treating-my-father like a
dog.' (*Her dry, hollow laugh. Then:*) The defendant begs to
differ. Children are not meant to lie nesting for ever, and
late, in the family home. Whate'er befalls them when they
do leave is not at issue here. And with reference to dogs
and their treatment – thereof, if anybody wishes – may it
further please the court to know, as testament to the
defendant's good character in the matter, that it was she
who took in the strays, and that it was she and she alone
who looked after them, and that the succession – by name
of Snout, Snap and Marilyn – was regarded by all who

knew them as a canine line that had well and truly fallen on its paws. (*The young men's direction again.*) They have broken something: fair-headed, littlest one has: a glass, knocked it over and broken it while trying to remove his anorak without standing up. The others hardly notice.

Bill Would you like something else?

Alice (*simultaneously*) The dicky bow has. He (*Bill*) has said something. (*To him.*) Hmm?

Bill Would you like something else?

Alice Ahmm.

Bill We don't know how much longer we'll be here.

Alice Yes.

Bill A glass of wine?

Alice Yes! What did he say?

Bill Waiter!

Alice Glass of wine, yes of course, glass of wine, yes: the thought was a practical one, something to be doing, occupying, under the circumstances and, true, they do not know how much longer they shall have to wait. He is a very private man. Well, he isn't able to be anything else, is he? He knows it. But his guard occasionally slips. He's bad in company. That morning, New Year's morning party at their neighbours, astonishing to hear him – you could hear him all over the room – declare, in challenging tones, that his greatest distaste in life was for lame people. Lame people. What did he mean? That they were an affront to his own firm step. He must have read it somewhere. And, likely as not, misinterpreted it. Then went on to exceed himself – he couldn't stop himself – declaring, in challenging tones his other great distastes for the human imperfections in others. Shyness and self-consciousness in company drove him to that kind of thing, but that he believed in his offensive remarks was true also.

Waiter (*arriving*) Alright, alright, everything alright?! (*He is*

*grinning, jaw askew, and he's holding out his hands, which contain
the shards of a broken glass.*)

Bill   Two glasses of red wine.

Waiter (*holding out the shards of glass again*)   What?! What?!
They're still rearing them, what?!

Bill   Your house wine will be fine. (*And he's already resumed
eating or sipping from his glass of water.*)

Waiter (*to himself*)   Still rearing them.

Alice   He's offended.

Waiter   Stella!

Alice   I think he has drink taken.

Waitress, *from somewhere, to his side to take the broken glass from
him, the order 'Two glasses of red', the signal to her feet – a nod of
her head – and she's gone again.* **Waiter** *continues there, absently,
for a moment, wondering which is the best way to go for company.
The usual break in the buzz of sound for another announcement.*

Waiter (*moving off*)   Still rearing them.

Alice   'Still rearing them.' (*And her hollow, dry laugh.*) The
last time she and her husband had a glass of wine together
was the night before their son left home. William. She had
made a fish pie because it was the dish her son liked best.
Not quite a party: still – and considering the usual
quietness of the house and the usual very private nature of
the father – his remarks about Polonius were nice, pleasant
– and considering the undemonstrative type that the mother
had become – it was an occasion. An occasion. Three
people had made an effort, and they had been successful in
that effort. And she hopes this minute, if it's happening this
minute, that they are handling the coffin gently off the
plane. If that matters, of course. Does it matter? Perhaps it
does. Perhaps not, really. No.

Waitress *is arriving, two glasses of wine in her hands, tray
clapped under her arm; she has to bend her knees to put the wine on
the table; in the bent-kneed position, for a brief moment she holds a*

look on **Alice***; then she bows as she backs away and returns to stand and wait at her station.*

Alice (*as* **Waitress** *arrives*)   Why have a tray if one is to carry glasses in one's hands? (*She nods her acknowledgement of the service, as does* **Bill**.) That look: a woman frightened of her own timidity, is it, concern for an untouched plate of fish and chips, is it? A creature that would prefer to run rather than walk, is it? Look, look, look, who's interested? So, William is dead. And so, too, her mother, last January. And she was sad at her mother's 'passing' and sad, too, that her mother was not the clever woman that she thought she was. Her espousing causes was ridiculous, contradictions of herself. Feminism? She was a man's woman, she fawned on them, with, of course, the exception of her own husband. He died fourteenth of July, 1978, twenty-seven years earlier. At least he had a sense of humour. 'Classical music and your mother, Alice? Putting on airs.' 'Feminists? The lash across their backs for them and the harem.' But in drink, without saying a word, he could fix you with his eyes as if he were pinning an insect to a board, as if you were the hated enemy. There was a moment, though, when they were about to place the lid on the coffin and she had this urge, panic? to rush to them, stay them for a moment, to look at him for a last time and say – something. Goodbye? I'm sorry? She did no such thing of course. She often wished him dead. (*She has a sip of wine and:*) Tepid, dull, cheap-dry, the life taken out of it and, of course, drinkable, bearable. They talk about the unnatural event of a child predeceasing the parents, but what about the crops of children, crops of young men sent off to war and never come back? Millions. Millions of them going off, *smiling*. That begins to put things in perspective now, doesn't it? He slipped, simple as that. Leaning up against a wall, eating a bag of chips, his feet slipped out in front of him from under him, his head hit the footpath. She does not – really and truly – want further details. It wasn't as if he had been – kicked? Simple accident, plenty of witnesses, including that young girl who was with him at the time. She has the medical report in her handbag, which she can look at, sometime, if she wishes to. There is the police report too, delivered into their hands by a policeman, its contents explained in considered – and considerate, she could see – language. 'Just in case,' the policeman said. Just in case of what? They wanted to sue the footpath? A priest attended because they were Irish, to offer comfort, and he did his best. It was God's will. God chose your William. Now, to the woman sitting here, if God is anything at all he is Godlike. He, She, It cannot be explained in terms of being choosy. God is the name given to the unknown. The unknown is possibly – and probably – nothing. It's not a great line in theology to say that God, the unknown, wills, picks, chooses this or that, no more than it is sensible to suggest that he can spend his time counting the hairs on your head, unless, that is, of course, he is otherwise engaged in being an all-seeing disgusting Peeping Tom. Unless, of course, he *does* will, pick and choose his targets, from William to earthquakes to the cat crossing the road, tsunamis and car crashes, in which case he is the Almighty Terrorist. There is no explanation for what cannot be explained, no comfort for what cannot be comforted. Useless to the dead and makes not the slightest difference to the bearable ache of the living. But she accepted the explanations and the religious platitudes for the sake of the people who offered them. Perhaps she should have asked the girl who was with him at the time for a few details, for the girl's sake – had they been to the cinema? – token elaboration, just to help the girl because she was young and the fright of the accident was still in her eyes. Oh, well!

Bill   Alice? (*He's smiling.*)

Alice   But, really, what she wanted to say to them all was –

Bill (*wants to engage her, divert her / divert himself*)   I was looking, at *The Times* on our flight home and things in the US are very much on the up and up – Alice?

Alice (*to him*)   Yes.

Bill   So how is that for you under a Republican

Administration and your most favourite president ever?

Alice (*to him*)   Hmm! (*Then:*) What did she want to say to them all?

Bill   And bully for Bush! And it would seem that the recovery is durable, self-enforcing and job creation is increasing – Hmm?

Alice   Yes.

Bill   There was that slowdown in the labour market from May onwards, last year –

Alice *nods.*

Bill   But that now has changed, and as a sign of all this –

Alice   Yes –

Bill   The Fed has decided that it no longer needs to maintain interest rates at the abnormally low level they were at until recently.

Alice   – *Oh*, yes –

Bill   Dollar continues to fall – let it fall –

Alice   What she wanted to tell them all was –

Bill   That's how they like it –

Alice   Things occur, not because a divine power wills them.

Bill (*gives up*)   Theirs is a closed economy.

Alice   Or because any principle ordains them, but simply because that is the way things occur, they just happen. Things, accidents, happen for no particular reason, for no purpose: Why go on with the rigmarolling? If people want to fill in their time by saying that there are conditions, causes, superstitions reasons for what happens to human beings, then let them have the courtesy to apply the selfsame conditions, causes and superstitions for what befalls plants, animals and – why not? – stones. This continual emphasis that is put on the great importance of human life above all else is a nonsense, it's pathetic. The sun – the sun! – Galileo! That thing – book – about him in the library. The sun does not shine for humankind no more than it revolves round the earth like they wanted it to one time. Pitiful! If humankind is special it's because no other species on earth can rival human viciousness.

Waitress, *who has been standing at her station for some time, is off again to supply service to some quarter.* **Alice** *is taking a sip of wine and is now looking in the direction of young men's table.*

Alice   They are no pale. And wasn't there a time . . . well, as far as one can remember these things . . . when she felt that inside her there was something mysterious that she thought of as herself. As far as she could make out there was something special about her. Felt it, not thought it. And though it gave her a sense of isolation, also, she trusted it. All would come well. She too, would you believe, was the world. What she was giving herself to had a purpose – it could, would, overcome anything that opposed it – an end that, when it came about, she would – understand? No. Recognise. Recognise as the mysterious, beautiful and, yes, savage reality of being alive, sharing humanity . . . Well! (*And she laughs her hollow laugh and:*) It is conceivable that the worst has happened and the reality of it leaves a lot to be desired.

Bill   Should I check on things downstairs?

She continues to laugh.

(*He is toying with the wine glass.*) Alice? Alice?

Alice   Oh! (*And raises her glass.*)   Cheers!

Bill   Ah, no.

Alice   Hmm?

Bill   I'll check with Information downstairs and see how matters are progressing.

Alice   Oh, yes.

He goes off.

He's checking on what-did-he-say? Did she say 'Cheers!'?
She couldn't have said 'Cheers', could she? Why would she
say that? (Look) Does it matter? Perhaps it was that she'd
been feeling the stem of the glass like this and – Does-it-
matter? – It doesn't matter. He said he was going
downstairs to check on matters downstairs.

Waiter (*arriving*)   Alright, alright, everything alright?
Finished, finished, we clear away, madam?

Alice   Thank you. Leave the wine.

Waiter   Stella!

The last to **Waitress** *as he moves off, backward jerk of his thumb
and suitable gesture/mime with the other hand for* **Waitress** *to
clear the table.* **Waitress**, *at that moment, is en route to deliver a
tray of things to some party, registers the* **Waiter**'s *order with a nod,
and continues off.*

Alice   The young girl with the frightened eyes was nice.
No beauty, mind you, but very nice. A young woman. She
took them back to their son's flat and packed his things. All
done in silence, more or less. No, in silence. They sat
there. Well, what was there to say? 'Has the earth stopped
turning?' 'Day turned into night?' Sensible flat shoes,
glimpses of her midriff, reaching for things. She knew
where everything was, she was familiar with the place.
Nineteen, twenty? Even woman to woman, these days it is
difficult to tell. She should have asked her would she like to
keep something, the books, a gesture to the young woman.
Oh well, never mind, she has her name and address, too,
in her bag, if she, if she . . . (*She loses the thought.*) Whatever.

Waitress (*has arrived to clear the table, tray clapped under her
arm.*

Waitress (*whispers*)   Missus?

Alice (*absently*)   Thank you. Leave the wine. (*She is looking
in the direction of the young men's table.*)

Waitress *loads plates/things on top of each other.*

Alice   They've gone. That didn't take them long.

Waitress (*another whisper*)   Missus? (*She has slid into* **Bill***'s chair; she is perhaps still holding her tray; she is leaning forward, in a familiar way, and smiling gently.*)   I have to tell someone. My daughter-in-law, a lovely woman, had a baby fourteen months ago. She rejected the baby, a lovely woman, she couldn't help it. So my husband and myself took the baby and kept him for over a year. I wouldn't ever run down anybody's child but that baby was the best, we loved him as much if not more than any of our own. More than words can say. We gave him back last Thursday. She killed him two days ago. I had to tell someone.

And she has risen, two clean movements and she has loaded the tray; smiles, bows, as usual, and is gone.

Another break in the buzz of sound for another announcement. **Alice** *just sits there.*

Bill *is returning accompanied by an* **Official** *in an airport/airline uniform.* **Official** *is giving a document to* **Bill***, which* **Bill** *will sign at some point and return it to* **Official***.*

Bill   The, the hearse and limousine are ready on the, the . . .

Official   Tarmac.

Bill   So, so, everything is in order.

Official (*to* **Alice**)   Deepest sympathy.

Alice*'s mind is elsewhere.*

Official   You could have, of course, waited in the VIP lounge.

Alice   No.

Official   Had you wanted to, of course.

Bill   Thank you.

Official   Thank you. I'll be at my desk downstairs to escort you on to the tarmac whenever you're ready. (*He goes.*)

Bill Well, we're ready, aren't we?

He picks up the bill, which is on the table and produces his wallet. He is about to summon **Waitress**, *who has returned to her station.*

Alice No, pay him.

She means the **Waiter**, *who is about somewhere or who is about to enter. And* **Bill** *joins* **Waiter** *and leaves with him, as to settle the bill.*

Alice *inhales a long silent 'O'. Perhaps it is not silent. And perhaps it is the first satisfactory breath she has taken in a long, long time.*

Alice And the woman does not know what further to say, but she is crying. She hopes that her beloved son and the nice young woman with the frightened eyes slept together, that they'd been warm. She loves that young woman. She loves her husband dearly. And she loves the waitress, Stella, and clings to her for a moment in sympathy and in gratitude for releasing this power within her.

She goes to **Waitress**. *They take each other's hand, then embrace for a couple of moments. And as* **Alice** *leaves,* **Waitress**, *too, is leaving to attend someone requiring her.*